An independent, creative force in the astrological community for a quarter of a century, Frank Clifford has built an eclectic career in astrology, palmistry and publishing:

- As the writer of a dozen books, including a modern classic on hand analysis
- As a columnist and biographer
- As a Sun sign astrologer for numerous magazines
- As a consultant for clients and businesses
- As a publisher of over 30 books and booklets
- As a researcher and compiler of birth data (including a compendium for Solar Fire)
- As a media astrologer/palmist profiled and interviewed on radio, TV and in print
- As an international lecturer and the Principal of the London School of Astrology where, for the past ten years, he has been instrumental in bringing a younger generation to astrology.

In September 2012, at the annual Astrological Association Conference, Frank became the thirteenth (and youngest) winner of The Charles Harvey Award for Exceptional Service to Astrology. Previous winners include Liz Greene, Robert Hand, Dennis Elwell, Melanie Reinhart and Deborah Houlding.

Forthcoming booklets by Frank Clifford

Understanding Signs in Combination
Astro*Carto*Graphy Tips and Techniques
Understanding Your T-square
The Midheaven: Spotlight on Success
Humour in the Horoscope: The Astrology of Comedy
The Astrology of Love, Sex and Attraction (with Fiona Graham)

By the same author

2012   *Getting to The Heart of Your Chart: Playing Astrological Detective*
2012   *Astrology The New Generation* (various contributors)
2011   *Solar Arc Directions* (booklet)
2009   *Palmistry 4 Today* (revised and expanded)
2009   *The Astrologer's Book of Charts*
2004   *Palm Reading: Discover the Secrets Hidden in Your Hand*
2003   *British Entertainers: The Astrological Profiles* (revised, expanded)
2002   *Palmistry 4 Today*
2000   *The Clifford Data Compendium* (revised)
2000   *Venus: Your Key to Love* (booklet)
2000   *Mars: Your Burning Desires* (booklet)
1999   *The Essentials of Hand Analysis* (booklet)
1997   *British Entertainers: The Astrological Profiles*
1997   *The Clifford Data Compendium* (Solar Fire program)

HOROSCOPE SNAPSHOTS

ESSAYS IN MODERN ASTROLOGY

FRANK C. CLIFFORD

The London School of Astrology

To Jane Struthers, with love and thanks

With thanks to Nan Geary, Tem Tarriktar and John Green,
who commissioned or edited many of the essays in this volume

First edition published 2014 by Flare Publications
and the London School of Astrology,
BCM Planets, London WC1N 3XX, England, UK
Tel: 0700 2 33 44 55
www.flareuk.com and www.londonschoolofastrology.co.uk
email: info@flareuk.com

A CIP catalogue record for this book is available from the British Library
ISBN: 978-1-903353-22-6

Charts calculated using Solar Fire software
Cover Designer: John Green
Proof-readers: Jane Struthers, Nan Geary
Data Editor: Sy Scholfield
Layout: Frank C. Clifford

CONTENTS

Chapter 1

EXPLORING THE DEEPER, HIDDEN SIDES OF YOUR SUN SIGN

In an astrological chart, the Sun reveals our main life purpose, the core reasons behind why we've been born and what we're in the process of becoming. When we express our Sun sign, we are acknowledging our birthright: the opportunity to manifest our individual life path and potential. In the horoscope, the Sun is linked to the concept of vocation – a true and personal 'calling', rather than simply a job or career.

The Sun shows how we picture (and pursue) our individual role in life's drama and the ways in which we ascribe meaning to life. In short, the Sun (and its aspects) shows *what's important to us*. When we live out and personify the message of our Sun sign, we shine and feel alive. To experience our Sun sign is to engage in activities that allow our heart to sing. But unlike our Moon position, which reveals our knee-jerk reactions and our emotional temperament, we must strive to become our Sun sign – it can be a lifelong process of discovery.

In Chapter 2, I take a deeper look into the meaning of the Sun and I link it astrologically to the development of character process. I write, 'Character is an *accumulation* of traits, responses and behavioural patterns that becomes the *central direction, focus and set of beliefs* in a person's life. The embracing of character (the Sun) leads to healthy self-esteem and a path of integrity and wholeness (again, concepts linked to the Sun's placement, through which we are encouraged to "follow our bliss").'

Another point to consider is that we spend much time cautioning Aries to 'slow down' or pushing Taurus to 'get moving', without recognizing that we get the very *best* out of the signs when we play to their strengths and allow them to work in accordance with their own natures. There is also much wisdom in the theory that we attract the people and situations that enable us *to become more of who we were born to be*. Gemini encounters misunderstandings and people it cannot relate to in order for it to become the communicator and interpreter it is destined to be. Taurus gets pushed around early on (or has to fight to keep hold of what belongs to it) in order to help it develop a stubborn resistance to others' influence and to form strong principles to which it can attach itself. Libra finds itself surrounded by conflict in order to sharpen its skills in diplomacy. And from an early age Libra is often forced to make agonizing decisions, so the process of making the *right* choice becomes all the more important. And so on.

If we don't attempt to actively live out the meaning of our Sun sign, we risk languishing in the negative traits of its opposite sign. I tell my students: '*Follow your Sun – or wallow in the worst of its polar opposite.*'

Here is a quick guide to some of the 'purposes' of each Sun sign and what lies beneath when we fail to express the sign's true message.

> *Accentuate the positive,*
> *Eliminate the negative ...*
> *And don't mess with Mister In-between.*
> – Johnny Mercer, songwriter

Aries–Libra

Aries is born to develop a self-determining individuality and sprint ahead of the pack. Aries must learn courage, dare to break new ground, fight for a cause or for the underdog and put herself first without apology. But when she disengages from her birthright, Aries settles into a place of laziness where she expects others to provide maintenance (the worst of Libra). Staying in someone else's shadow or acting as a perpetual supporting player, she refuses to blaze her own trail. When she is afraid of going it alone and engaging in healthy conflict, she turns into an apologetic sheep desperate to please and appease.

Libra (the polite Aries) is born to be the strategist, the mediator, the peacemaker. He learns to bring a balanced objectivity to situations. Forever the bridge-builder, Libra irons out disputes in a diplomatic, fair and civilized way: decisions are based on reason, unhampered by emotion. At his worst, Libra loses his cool and creates conflict – often in order to resolve it. When anxious and insecure, Libra separates people, keeping them to himself to maintain his position as top dog. Thus Libra turns into a biased, intolerant, disruptive, or divisive troublemaker who relishes rudeness and lives to provoke.

Taurus–Scorpio
Taurus is born to be the 'rock', the stalwart and constant upon which others can rely. Her job is to preserve and sustain, demonstrate faithfulness and stay 'for the long haul'. A sensualist, she enjoys and revels in the pleasures of life. Taurus builds foundations to last and amasses something of material value that will weather the storm. At worst, there's a covetous attachment to what's not hers and a fanatical obsession with sexual or emotional situations, particularly with people she can't control. Recognizing her innate power and the dependency of others on her, she holds loved ones to ransom to get what she wants.

Scorpio is born to become the alchemist, the potent healer and the unflinching investigator of life's mysteries. He lives to explore the deeper meaning of existence, the dialectics of nature, the taboo and forbidden. But the shadow side of Scorpio cannot see that the biggest mystery of his life is, in fact, himself. He refuses to shed light on his hidden realms or soar to a higher level of consciousness. Instead, he stays in a comfort zone – free of risk and imagination – focusing on the physical, acquiring possessions and accumulating wealth (the worst of Taurus). Afraid of his own codependency, Scorpio becomes intolerant and scornful of others' weaknesses.

Gemini–Sagittarius
Gemini is born to spot patterns, to connect people and ideas. Gemini seeks to communicate, understand and articulate – and to offer options and other viewpoints for consideration. She melds aspects of numerous philosophies to create her own eclectic system of thought. At worst, Gemini becomes a fundamentalist who has discovered 'The Truth'. Moving from an objective information gatherer, she revels in superstition rather than facts, or becomes a know-it-all with a condescending attitude or moral arrogance – claiming God, education, or the righteous path for her own.

Sagittarius is here to aim high, ask the big questions and explore the possibilities beyond the facts. A natural evangelist, he ignites other people's interest with great enthusiasm. Born with a voracious appetite for knowledge and living, he welcomes all philosophies and never stops learning. At worst, Sagittarius focuses on gossip and superficial information or becomes overly logical, reporting the evidence but missing the significance within. He loses any hard-won integrity by becoming the hypocrite, the name-dropper or the silver-tongued confidence trickster, living on his wits and taking any advantage he can (the worst of Gemini).

Cancer–Capricorn

Cancer is a romantic, wistful and poetic sign born to help others connect to their heritage and treasure their past – without becoming a slave to it. She is the midwife, guiding people through life's emotional conflicts and rites of passage. At worst, Cancer uses emotional manipulation to advance causes close to her heart, which soon hardens with ruthless ambition. Believing that blood is *not* thicker than water, she reinvents her past, or disconnects from it, and strives to attain rank and position. She can get toxic: seething with resentment over others' achievements, bitter at her early struggles or exclusion from 'the system'.

Capricorn is born to rise above initial hardship, endure a long apprenticeship and attain a position of respect and authority – a monument to individual achievement. On this path towards mastery over his environment, he is challenged to work within a rigid hierarchy, guard his principles and retain a moral code that is beyond reproach. He loses the grip on all he has worked for when he is driven by an underlying, repressed emotional fanaticism where the end justifies the means. He fails when he loses track of goals, fears success, or retreats to wallow in self-pity (the worst of Cancer).

Leo–Aquarius

Leo is born to recognize the power of her individuality, one that stands apart from family and overbearing patriarchal influences. Her personal journey is to discover her creative potency and to explore the divine child within – ideally before she becomes a parent and 'encourages' her child to act this out for her. Wallowing in her opposite sign, she turns to an audience to provide the approbation she craves. In the spirit of narcissistic entitlement, she uses others without giving due credit and she begrudges them *their* time in the sun. She slavishly follows science, theory and ideology rather than art, heart or passion.

Aquarius is born to provide a clear, original perspective on social issues of justice and responsibility (the spirit of *liberté, égalité, fraternité*). Initially a people-pleaser, he must eventually assume his own authority and see his separateness as a strength. But when he's unable to see that everyone is special yet also equal, he operates from an egocentric, autocratic standpoint where 'some are more equal than others'. At worst, Aquarius fights for the group but secretly feels superior and despises commonness. Desperate to be adored and singled out as special, he employs prejudice, favouritism and preferential treatment.

Virgo–Pisces
Virgo is born to be the craftsman and the specialist. A natural harvester, she separates the wheat from the chaff and her interest lies in getting to the heart of the matter. Her challenge is to balance mind, body and spirit. Focusing on details that are useful and essential, Virgo aims to create systematic order and make the world a better place. When she is unproductive, Virgo wallows in confusion, wastefulness and chaos (the worst of Pisces). Running from her mundane commitments, Virgo acts indiscriminately and wanders aimlessly, becoming a martyr and blaming others for her fatalistic worldview or for feeling victimised and abused.

Pisces is the Good Samaritan, born to offer service, empathy, altruism and compassion. Aware of the interconnectedness of all life, he teaches others about the universal joys *and* sufferings of the human condition. He is the choreographer of humanity's dance with its higher self. When not following this spiritual journey, he becomes critically destructive, attacking others' faith and pouring scorn on attempts to understand life's mysteries (the worst of Virgo). When he feels undervalued, he becomes obsessed with controlling the inconsequential, fussing over hygiene, becoming addicted to rituals, or simply 'sweating the small stuff'.

A Chart Example

The word 'polarity' suggests principles that are diametrically opposed, yet each pair of opposing signs represents two sides of the same coin. The very nature of an axis is to make us aware of both sides – to be conscious that they are inseparable and interlinked. An emphasis on one side of the seesaw always affects the other. This is most noticeable with in-sign planetary oppositions.

Singer Karen Carpenter was born with the Sun in Pisces conjunct the Midheaven (MC). Karen became the first high-profile (Sun–MC) celebrity to fall victim (Pisces) to anorexia nervosa. To the public, her struggle with the disorder and her tragic death at age 32 are inextricably linked to her wholesome image and pristinely pure voice, with its instantly recognizable, melancholy timbre. She is both tragic and magical.

The Sun on the MC is not always the blessing it seems, particularly for a shy, sensitive and susceptible sign like Pisces. At its most visible and public, the Sun has nowhere to hide – and the stronger the light, the darker the shadow. As a result, those with the Sun conjunct the Midheaven are often very private, reclusive types who have a strong desire to withdraw periodically from the glare and demands of the spotlight. Karen was only 20 when she and her brother Richard topped American pop charts in 1970. Not feeling pretty or slim enough, she was only comfortable singing behind her drum kit, but the audience wanted her out front and centre stage (Sun–MC).

Karen's Sun is opposed by Saturn in Virgo, suggesting a strong work ethic and her workaholic nature. There was much to prove to the world – but would she ever be perfect? It has been argued that Karen felt largely ignored by her family and that she was brought up to support Richard's prodigious talent (the family had moved to California to help his musical aspirations). Karen hero-worshipped Richard (note that her Mercury, which rules siblings, is conjunct god-like Jupiter) but she was an obsessively protective sister, jealous of women who got too close to him: her Moon–Pluto opposes the Mercury–Jupiter and they all fall across Richard's Ascendant–Descendant axis. She (s)mothered him.

Anorexia is known to be the curse of high achievers. Arguably, through strict dieting, Karen sought to maintain control (Saturn)

Karen Carpenter

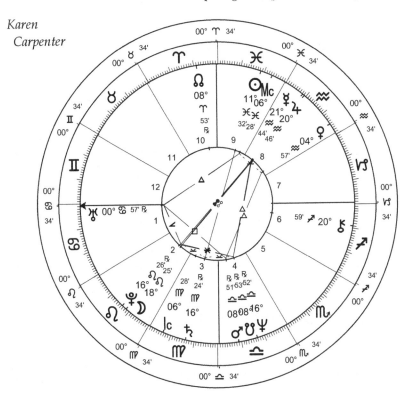

of her perfect public image (Saturn in Virgo opposite Sun–MC) and the disorientating, chaotic nature of fame (Pisces). (Saturn in Virgo opposite the Sun suggests malnutrition, a *denial of nutrition*.) It was her defence mechanism amid the pressures of non-stop touring and unrelenting public scrutiny – and a sad reflection of her low self-esteem.

Chapter 2

DEFINING CHARACTER, BEHAVIOUR AND PERSONALITY: CLUES TO THE DIFFERENCES BETWEEN THE SUN, MOON & ASCENDANT

Very often, the first 'way in' to reading a horoscope – or to grasp its essence quickly – is to consider the Big Three: the Sun, Moon and Ascendant, either individually or as a trio. Together, these three complexes (their sign and house position and aspects from planets) form the fundamental components and core dynamics of a birth chart and act as excellent starting points for following trails and spotting chart themes.

When beginning to synthesize these areas, it's vital to keep in mind that the meanings of the Big Three are not interchangeable: the Sun in Taurus is not the same as the Moon in Taurus and when Taurus is placed on the Ascendant, it is quite distinct from its role as the Sun or Moon sign. The characteristics of Taurus (the *how*) will be present when it's the sign of any of the trio, but the *why* (the driving force, energy, motivation) and possibly the *where* (the area of life affected) will be different.[1]

So, what are the main distinctions between the Sun, Moon and Ascendant? One way of considering the Big Three is to examine the differences between the meanings behind the words 'character' (the Sun), 'behaviour' (the Moon) and 'personality' (the Ascendant). These words are often used interchangeably, but a deeper exploration of their meanings can shed light on interpreting this astrological trio.

Character: The Sun
Our essence, vocation, type of 'heart'
The Sun reveals our main life purpose, core reasons behind why we've been born and what we're in the process of becoming. When we express our Sun complex (its sign and house position and aspects), we are acknowledging our birthright: the opportunity to manifest our individual life path and potential. Each Sun sign

and Sun–planet combination is an *archetype* (a pattern or a set of symbolic images) that each of us can strive to embody.

Interestingly, the Sun is often reduced to a *stereotype*, thanks to an oversimplified formula of adjectives and keyword traits used to assist chart interpretation. Although these keywords can be helpful, the Sun's meaning invites a more subtle interpretation. It shows how we envision our individual life path and what essentially are the most important things in life to us.

Our character is a collection of fundamental, integral philosophies that we have gathered over time. I link the Sun to the process of the *development of character*. Character is an *accumulation* of traits, responses and behavioural patterns (underscored or challenged by other parts of the chart) that becomes the *central direction, focus and set of beliefs* in a person's life. The embracing of character (the Sun: its message, its archetype) leads to healthy self-esteem and a path of integrity and wholeness (again, concepts linked to the Sun placement, through which we are encouraged to 'follow our bliss'). Character is more difficult to ascertain in ourselves and others, and like the sometimes elusive nature of the Sun in our horoscope, it takes time for us to uncover it – and time for it to reveal itself.

Behaviour: The Moon
Our needs, habits, sensory input and impressions
The Moon complex reveals our fundamental relationship needs, drives and expectations. It shows our innate responses to everyday life. At worst, this can be habitual behaviour that we are slaves to, or a 'default' position where we simply absorb experience passively or become little more than 'a bundle of reactions'.[2] The Moon can reflect our most tender, vulnerable and immature side – a storehouse of emotions. The Moon speaks of what we're attached to, what we need to feel safe and rooted.

Our behaviour is a collection of instincts formed to create a complex pattern. It is an interconnected web of habitual responses – with the chief aim of remaining safe and being looked after. Here, we recognize some of the key functions of the Moon. For instance, the Moon in Gemini learns to be informed on a variety of topical issues – ready for exchange and discourse – in order to be, and feel, needed. For the same reasons, Taurus learns to be the loyal, dependable rock, to build ties that last and to embody a set of firm guiding principles.

Behaviour is how we *conduct* ('bring together') ourselves to create a range of responses in ourselves and those around us. Another word that is descriptive of the Moon, astrologically, is *temperament*, which is often linked to the four elements (the four 'humours' that were said to make up our disposition). But the Moon is a mix of elements of the emotional realm; it reveals our emotional nature.

Personality: The Ascendant
Our approach to life, interactions, a role/part we play

The Ascendant is a symbol of our one-to-one, meet-and-greet personality that we rely on to socialize. It is a vehicle we use to interact with others – our personal interface, a cloak we wear to 'appear' to others when we walk out of our front door. I like to think of the Ascendant as our opening position and overt agenda (quite different from the hidden, sometimes painful agenda revealed by the Moon).

Essentially, the Ascendant is a collection of expectations we have of the world and our immediate place in it. The Ascendant reveals the first impressions we make and receive – and these start as early messages about our behaviour ('good/bad' and 'right/wrong') and how we attempt to meet the expectations of others through our actions as children.

The personality is seen in the Ascendant complex (most importantly its sign and major planetary aspects to its degree). It is the *variable means by which we negotiate* our needs with others (as seen by our Moon) and formulate or build something we can identify as character (as seen by our Sun). In other words, the Ascendant acts as an interface between the Sun or Moon (or other parts of the chart) and the immediate world around us.

With 'personality', there is *energy* – a particular attitude, humour, engagement and interaction. This energy is quite different from the accumulation of early (lunar) behaviours or the formation of (solar) character.

Personality is easy to pick up on, quick to read and decipher – usually upon first meeting someone (Ascendant). I've found that it shows up in personal mottos (e.g., 'No pain, no gain,' says the

Scorpio Ascendant person; 'If you want it done, you have to do it yourself,' the Aries Ascendant realizes) – although the *combination* of Ascendant and Midheaven signs is often more descriptive of lifelong mottos or creeds.

Personality traits have little to do with our true character. They are what we show to others (our appearance, in many ways) and the means we use to get through life. Astrologically, the Ascendant is often seen as the vehicle by which we reach the Sun's destination (i.e., our life goal). It is the route to getting our needs (Moon) met in relationship and how we negotiate these personal needs in a one-to-one environment.

So, here is a quick summary:

- The Sun (core character) is linked to our central purpose, goal, focus and life path; a *journey* of self-discovery – the process of becoming whole.

- The Moon (behaviour, temperament) speaks of our needs and habitual responses to everyday life; our emotional nature: a bundle of reactions and a storehouse of feelings.

- The Ascendant (one-to-one personality) reveals our approach to life; the tools we use to interact with others; our first impressions (made and received).

The Sun is the very heart of our horoscope, but the Ascendant and Moon say more about our personality and behavioural traits. These two chart factors are of far greater importance when considering how people come across, behave, react and interact in life. Both are key to relationship patterns and dynamics that start early in childhood with family members and schoolmates, and form the basis of expectations (and roles played out) in love, work and friendship. The Sun is more concerned with a journey, a path of self-discovery and our major life statements. It is the ultimate path, the archetype that we are here to embrace and embody.

In short, the Sun–Moon–Ascendant trio offers a quick 'way in' to the major traits of a person – their character, behaviour and personality. How do the Big Three work together in a horoscope? And how can they provide trails to discover key themes?

The Original Dreamgirls:
The Sun–Moon–Ascendant Combinations of the Supremes

Let's consider the Sun–Moon–Ascendant trio in the horoscopes of the most successful girl group in music history, the Supremes.

Who would imagine that three young women would have such different destinies? One would stay with the group to the bitter end 18 years after it started, one would die tragically at age 32, and one would achieve stratospheric success as a solo artist – and bear the brunt of the other girls' relative post-group failures.

In the 1960s, the music scene was defined by the Beatles, Elvis, Bob Dylan, the Rolling Stones and three innocent girls-next-door from Detroit: Diana Ross, Mary Wilson and Florence Ballard. They formed the Supremes and their music was the soundtrack to the 1960s era of social change. Diana, Mary and Florence were role models of African-American empowerment – their appearance on *The Ed Sullivan Show* was a landmark moment for 'coloured people' on American TV. Diamonds in the rough, the Supremes were polished by Berry Gordy's Motown hit factory, and each singer morphed into the epitome of sequinned star power: glamorous and elegant, with poise and panache.

Diana Ross, with impatient ambition and single-minded focus, was promoted to lead singer. The group first hit the Top 40 charts in June 1964, when Uranus transited over Diana's Midheaven (MC). Soon Diana was having an affair with the married Gordy (apparently consummated on 15 April 1965, as transiting Saturn conjoined her Venus, and Uranus opposed it).

Over the next few years, the group had a string of hits that topped the charts and they became world-famous. But before long, Gordy was grooming Diana Ross for solo stardom; it seemed that Mary and Florence has become little more than excess baggage. Diana Ross went solo in January 1970 and Gordy washed his hands of the original group, choosing to focus on steering Diana's music and film career.

Diana
Ross

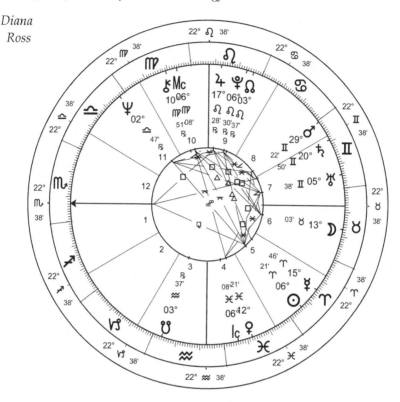

Diana's first audition for Gordy had been in the summer of 1960, when transiting Pluto was conjunct her MC. Aptly for the transit, Gordy would become Diana's professional father, controlling mentor, lover, and father to her first-born. She nicknamed him 'Black'. His tunnel vision about Diana and his Svengali-like control (Pluto) over her can be seen by his natal Moon in Scorpio, his Venus on Diana's Ascendant, and his Saturn exactly opposite her Mars.[3]

Let's take a look at the Sun–Moon–Ascendant combination for each member of the trio.

Diana Ross
Sun in Aries, Moon in Taurus, Ascendant in Scorpio
Two of Diana's Big Three are in fixed signs (tenacity, staying power, persistence), and there's a Mars–Pluto theme with Aries and Scorpio highlighted (drive, combative energy, selfishness,

power). The latter signature is underscored by its links to the Big Three:

- The Sun in (out-of-sign) square to Mars;
- The Sun in exact (partile) trine to Pluto;
- The Ascendant ruler, Mars, in the 8th House;
- The Moon in square to Pluto.

In addition to Diana's trio being Mars- or Pluto-themed, the Sun is in the 5th (by Equal houses, and on the 5th cusp by Placidus) and opposite Neptune. Neptune is that intangible, special 'something' that suggests star quality – the X factor. In a performer, it is charisma, stage presence, magical allure, longevity and – most importantly to the music moguls – the promise of mainstream commercial success that transcends all cultural barriers. The Sun in Aries in the 5th opposite Neptune suggests an illusion of warmth, intimacy and approachability (the diva wanting to 'reach out and touch' her audience's hands). With this placement and the Moon square Jupiter in Leo, Diana personifies the modern-day idea of diva-hood: the demands, perfectionism, fashions and all-consuming vanity. In short, the haute and hauteur.

The Supremes were the first glamorous African–Americans sold to a white, pop music audience – a lacquered Neptunian fantasy. They created a bridge between white conservatism and black radicalism at a time in the mid 1960s when the Uranus–Pluto conjunction opposed Saturn. But it is Ross's Neptune- and Mars-tinged horoscope (absent in the charts of Wilson and Ballard) that indicates her ability to project glamour to the masses (Sun opposite photogenic Neptune) and channel her ferocious drive to attain excellence (Mars) and realize her dreams (Neptune). At times, Neptune has also been evident in her struggle to maintain control (Scorpio), personally and professionally.

Neptune's downside is the backlash of scandals and allegations, of being tarnished by rumours. Public perception of Diana's temperamental behaviour brought unparalleled criticism, thanks to Mary Wilson's disingenuous book (published in October 1986, as transiting Neptune conjoined Diana's Solar Arc Ascendant). Music historian David Nathan wrote, 'Diana personified a myth … [a powerful woman] to be scorned, disliked and diminished.'[4]

Perhaps she has never overcome the public's inability to reconcile her soft onstage image and Venusian voice with her ruthless Martian drive: 'The lure and slink of the kitten, and the claw of the tigress.'[5] Her wispy, sensual, coquettish voice and waif-like appearance (the Venusian and Neptunian feel to the chart) are at odds with her dynamic ambition and self-centredness (Mars, Aries, Scorpio). It seems women are seldom forgiven for going after what they want.

Diana Ross is a living embodiment of the power of positive action – a testimony to dedication, hard work and self-belief. With the support of Gordy, she created an image and nurtured her talent and willed herself to become the first female African–American global superstar. In 1976 and 1996, *Billboard* magazine named her Female Entertainer of the Century. The Sun in Aries and Moon in Taurus combination is suggestive of the childish stubbornness she showed during her early fame, being a 'chiffon battering ram', having grit and grace, or, as one critic put it, 'part guts, part geisha'.

Mary Wilson
Sun in Pisces, Moon in Leo, Ascendant in Taurus
Wilson's Big Three attest to her enduring (Taurus) theatricality and drama (Pisces, Leo) and a tenacious spirit (fixity). Through books, fashion exhibitions, and line-ups of new Supremes members, Wilson has soldiered on (Taurus) to keep the magic of the Supremes alive (Pisces) – a proud keeper of the flame (Moon in Leo). Now a goodwill ambassador and motivational speaker, Mary Wilson offers her 'Dare to Dream' lecture, which emphasizes the need for personal perseverance (Taurus Rising) in order to achieve goals and dreams (Sun in Pisces).

With the Ascendant in Taurus, Mary Wilson has been territorial about the group and, since its dissolution, she has *stood firm* to keep hold of her part in the *rightful ownership* of the brand: she spent many years fighting Motown for the right to use the name of the Supremes in her concerts (whereas Ross was automatically granted that privilege), and she has helped to create legislation that prohibits impostor groups from using the names and likenesses of famous acts.

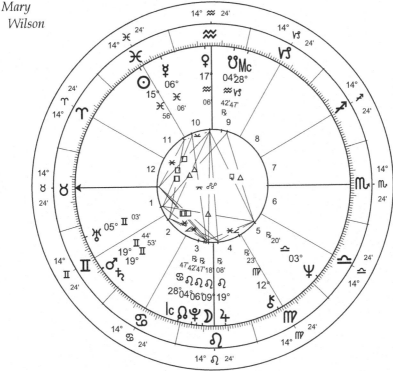

Mary
Wilson

But with the Sun in Pisces, Wilson seems to have become a living, suffering martyr to the Supremes' cause, someone who felt (justifiably, perhaps) wronged by Motown, pained by Ross's attention-grabbing antics, and overlooked by music historians. Holding on to resentment (fixity, Moon–Pluto in Leo) for being in the shadow of her more luminous rival, Wilson seethed through two volumes of autobiography, painting Ross as vain, selfish and ruthless. (Her Sun squares Mars–Saturn in Gemini, suggesting a journey of learning to speak up for herself, as well as the bitter war of words between her and Diana.) Tellingly, her Ascendant is conjunct Diana's Moon in Taurus, and the pair share fixity (obstinacy, firmness, attachment to unwavering principles), Mars in Gemini and a Moon–Pluto aspect. Mary appears to relish her role as a persistent thorn in Diana's posturing, preening side, and seems determined to keep the (one-way?) vendetta alive.

Florence
Ballard

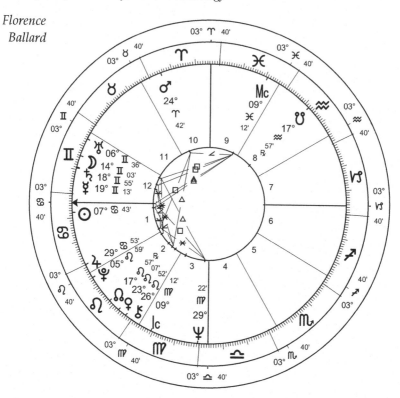

Florence Ballard
Sun in Cancer, Moon in Gemini, Ascendant in Cancer

Flo Ballard's Big Three lead us to the major dynamics of her chart: the focus on the Water sign of Cancer and its powerfully placed ruler, the Moon, which is conjunct Uranus, Saturn and Mercury in Gemini. In her short life, Ballard went from celebrated Supreme to an erratic, defiant nuisance who was ejected from the group (on 1 July 1967) for gaining a reputation for unreliability and a dependency on alcohol (note the Pisces MC and Neptune square the Ascendant). The following year, she attempted a solo career and began legal wrangles with Motown (both in vain). By 1975, she was on welfare to help feed her three young children. When Ballard died from a blood clot on 21 February 1976, she was only 32 years of age.

In truth, Flo felt abandoned and betrayed (Moon–Uranus) by her former friends and, even up to her untimely death, could not let go of the pain she felt (Cancer). 'Flo could seamlessly slip into moody silence, her eyes haunted by something unspoken.'[6]

Both haughty and earthy, Ballard was the group's original lead singer – a proud, regal woman who was nicknamed 'Blondie' (Sun Rising, Venus in Leo). Aggressive and sassy on the surface, Ballard was a seething soul, tortured by her past. Just prior to signing with Motown, she was raped at knifepoint (in early autumn 1960, as transiting Uranus crossed her Venus–Chiron, and Solar Arc Pluto approached her Venus). Mary Wilson wrote of how this event turned Flo sceptical, fearful and cynical. Mary also observed (picking up Flo's Sun Rising/Moon–Cancer emphasis): 'Everything about [Flo] was big. When she was happy, it was contagious ... She was terribly moody, constantly up and down ... She'd be in some dark mood, and then, miraculously and suddenly, it was over.'[7] Writing of Flo's tragedy and depicting her as a victim of Gordy's exclusive focus on Diana Ross and Diana's own ambition, Mary has kept Flo's contribution to the group alive (aptly, Wilson's Sun–Mercury flanks Ballard's Midheaven in Pisces).

Like the Big Three, the lives of the Supremes are exemplars of compatible and contradictory goals, temperaments and attitudes; the ability of each member to deal with the unnatural state of celebrity (where stardom can easily become a narcotic); and the disorientating fall-to-earth that follows life after intense fame. We can also see each member of the Supremes as the epitome of one of the Big Three:

- Diana as the Sun (in Aries, the pushy go-getter out in front: the charismatic, limelight-stealing lead singer with a direct line to the boss);
- Florence as the Moon (in Gemini, besieged by Uranus and Saturn: the sensitive, forgotten 'soul' of the trio whose sudden reversal of fortune began her demise);
- Mary as the Ascendant (in Taurus: the 'glue' who attempted to keep the Supremes – and the old grudges – going).

References and Notes

1. I recently rediscovered a gem in my library: Donna Cunningham's *How to Read Your Astrological Chart* (Weiser, 1999), which I highly recommend as a book that looks at this trio in some depth. Cunningham also labels it the 'Big Three'.
2. This is an interpretation proposed by Dennis Elwell who, in a 1999 interview with Garry Phillipson, spoke of the Moon as having the potential to be 'almost the Achilles heel' in the horoscope. See www.astrozero.co.uk and www.skyscript.co.uk/elwell.html
3. A gambler and visionary dream-maker, Gordy was born with the Sun, Mercury and Mars tightly conjunct in Sagittarius opposite Jupiter in Gemini. The Sun–Mercury–Mars conjunction opposes all three Supremes' Uranus and closely trines Gordy's own Uranus in Aries.
4. David Nathan, *The Soulful Divas*, Billboard Books, 1999, p. 148.
5. Mark Ribowsky, *The Supremes*, Da Capo, 2009, p. xvii.
6. Ibid., p. 16.
7. Ibid., pp. 78–79.

Chapter 3

PLANETARY TYPES: IDENTIFYING THE KEY PLAYERS

As we interpret more charts and research more life stories, we begin to realize that the horoscope reveals the qualities, motivations and passions that lie *beneath* a person's work and life, rather than their actual job. The horoscope can reveal drives towards a particular vocation in the broadest sense (umbrella terms such as 'educator', 'communicator' or 'researcher' are useful) – but there's no part of the birth chart that unequivocally identifies someone as, for instance, an astrologer, a chef, a builder, or the next pop idol. Birth charts of those in one particular profession are as varied as the motives, styles and skills of their owners.

While repetitive patterns in a chart incline us more towards a particular way of expressing ourselves in life (given the opportunity and dependent upon a number of external factors), *specific* jobs don't appear to be written in the same way.

Perhaps some years ago, pinpointing or identifying a person's job from their horoscope was easier. Options were limited. But now, people feel less condemned to accept their lot and follow in their family's footsteps and, in the West, we're reminded of a need to pursue work that expresses who we are. At times, the ways to do this seem almost innumerable.

The more extensive our research into how people manifest the potential in their horoscopes, the more we realize that set astrological 'signatures' – decreed a long time ago about which chart features make a successful actor, chemist, or politician, for instance – do not stand up to scrutiny.

The Gauquelin Research
Michel and Françoise Gauquelin understood that their research (comprising the birth data of tens of thousands of eminent professionals) produced significant results only when studied in great numbers. Yes, Saturn was statistically more likely to be in

a 'Gauquelin Sector' or 'G-Zone' (around the four angles, particularly in the Placidus cadent houses: 12th, 9th, 6th and 3rd – see diagram, right) in the charts of hundreds of noted, top-ranking scientists. But when looking at the charts of individual scientists, they saw that the effect was hit and miss.

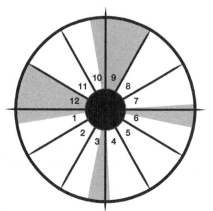

The Gauquelins realized that Saturn types (those who had Saturn in one of the four G-Zones) would enter the field of science and excel at it because the personality model needed for a successful scientist was similar in nature to that of astrological Saturn. In other words, the position of Saturn at birth in a G-Zone was linked to the temperament found in eminent scientists (the same was found for Mars with sports champions, top executives and military leaders).

But more compelling (and arguably more useful to astrologers) was the Gauquelins' character trait research, which comprised keywords from biographies describing the *natures and personalities* of these professionals. If a natal planet were in a G-Zone, the Gauquelins found that biographers would use certain character trait descriptions linked to that planet. (Saturn traits discovered include *conscientious, methodical* and *observant,* which fit the general model of a scientist's personality.) This method – proving more helpful on an individual, chart-by-chart basis – allows us to see *variance* within a profession. Put another way, a successful scientist of a Jupiterian nature may be in the statistical minority among his eminent colleagues, but upon closer inspection of his character, as defined in biographies, we would (and could) expect to see keyword traits of a Jupiterian nature (among these, *conceited, lively, proud* and *worldly*).

Identifying Planetary Types

The Gauquelins' compilation of keywords also allows us to define and *refine* the character of the planets. For me as an astrologer, it highlighted the obvious: all planets by way of *planetary types* are represented in every profession. Although the Gauquelin model takes into account only the diurnal position of a lone planet, in my experience the easiest way to tell a planetary type is to consider any planet:

- In a Gauquelin Zone – conjunct the four angles or further into the Placidus cadent houses;
- Greatly involved in the chart's action – i.e., heavily aspected or the apex of an aspect configuration;
- Standing apart from the other planets – e.g., the handle of a Bucket chart;
- The dispositor of several planets (particularly the inner planets) – e.g., a number of planets in Gemini and Virgo would increase Mercury's importance.

All Planetary Types in Major Life Areas

Let's consider the planets we might expect to be strong in politicians' horoscopes. Could it be the Moon (being in touch with the public pulse and reflecting the mood of the people), Jupiter (a need for prominence, the do-gooder), Saturn (civic responsibility and an aptitude for working within the system), Pluto (gravitating towards power, influence and control) – or another?

In reality, we find that there are Saturn-prominent politicians like Richard Nixon (Saturn in a G-Zone; the Sun, Jupiter and Chart Ruler Mercury in Capricorn; the Moon in Aquarius) and Margaret Thatcher (Saturn Rising), whose ambition, work ethic, control-freak rigidity and conservatism defined them.

While Venusian politicians Bill Clinton and John F. Kennedy (with an emphasis on Venus, Taurus and/or Libra) brought allure, charm, likeability and an insatiable sexual appetite to their posts, they also came as double acts with their potent wives (Venus/ Libra).

And there are charismatic Jupiterian or Neptunian political figures who embody hope, make promises in times of despair and subsequently disappoint many, such as Barack Obama (Jupiter in a G-Zone, opposed by Mercury, and an elevated Neptune square the Sun and Mercury).

Of course, many of these example politicians have other planetary themes in their charts, too: Kennedy's Mercurial

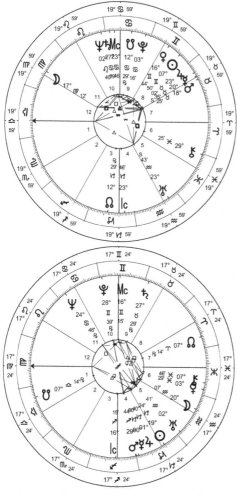

overtone (Gemini planets and the Moon in Virgo) reflects his oratory skills and mastery of the sound bite. (**Kennedy's** chart is on the left.)

While **Richard Nixon's** elevated Pluto (opposite Mars–Mercury–Jupiter) suggests that this Saturnian politician was held in the clandestine and vice-like grip of suspicion, paranoia and control. (His horoscope is below.)

By gaining a sense of a politician's astrological 'signature' (be that of one or a few key planets), we have an inside view into their defining traits and life stories, their predominant talents and foremost needs. We should not lose sight of the other placements and subtle shades seen elsewhere in their horoscopes, but it is important to know the major planetary players in any drama.

If we consider another field, such as music, we might immediately think of the Moon, Venus or Neptune as the significator. Neptune is often the planet linked to musicians but, in my research, it is prominent only when the character and life events of that musician are Neptunian. Perhaps there are enigmatic roles played, chameleon-like or mysterious personas adopted, various addictions, much glamour, or an attempt to transcend mundane reality and convey a spiritual message. Iconic Neptunian music figures include Boy George (Neptune on the Descendant opposite Venus Rising), David Bowie (Neptune squared by Mercury, Mars and the Sun), Alice Cooper (Neptune Rising), Marc Bolan (Neptune conjunct an elevated Sun and Venus), and Cat Stevens (Neptune Rising square Mercury). Sometimes they have worldwide appeal, saturate the market, are 'sold' to all genres and demographics – or, to borrow an overused Neptunian Internet expression, they 'go viral' (Justin Bieber has the Sun, Venus and Saturn in Pisces, with the Moon square Neptune; while Susan Boyle has a Grand Trine between Chart Ruler Mercury in Pisces, Mars and Neptune).

Areas of life are too broad to assign to one planet only. For some, Jupiter 'rules' religion, and others see it as Neptune's domain. But do people who are described as 'religious' have either planet prominent (or significantly placed) in their horoscopes? Under the umbrella of religion, astrological Jupiter has links to faith, belief and the idea of an almighty, powerful, benign deity. For the Jupiterian type, life is an expansive quest and the hereafter a transition – the beginning of another explorative journey.

But would Jupiter be strong in the chart of someone described as religious who is involved in organized religion and believes in the concepts of guilt, being born into sin, karma ('we reap what we sow'), atonement, confession and penance? This God-fearing person might better fit the Saturn-type personality and have a chart that backs this up.

The nature of Pluto through the lens of religion would suggest cults, hidden aspects of religion and powerfully transformative belief systems, while countercultural Uranus could range from the person being anti-religion or atheist to having a perspective (their 'truth') that theirs is the 'only way'.

In any case, planetary placements of real people, rather than significators based on *affinities*, should back up the assertions we make. By all means, we should question birth data and sources, but when the evidence piles up and our theories don't stand up to closer scrutiny, it's time to put aside our preconceptions of what a certain person's chart *should* look like, and face up to the evidence in the horoscope in front of us. And we learn far more when we look for common astrological links in the charts of people who share a set of traits (or life experiences), rather than starting with a narrow frame of reference such as 'all astrologers should have/do have/need a strong Mercury (or Uranus), etc.'

A Mercurial Example

In consultation, I've always found it useful to locate the essential, primary themes in the horoscope and unlock the key drives in the client's nature – in short, to identify the client's planetary type(s). When we're asked to look at a client's professional potential, a fundamental understanding of one's talents, interests and aptitudes is perhaps the most worthwhile starting point.

A Mercury-type client of mine – with Gemini Rising, the Sun and Mercury in mutable Virgo in the Equal 3rd House square Neptune in the 6th – has never found it easy to stay on a particular career path and often feels anxious (Virgo) and of two minds (Gemini) about the 'right' course of action in his life.

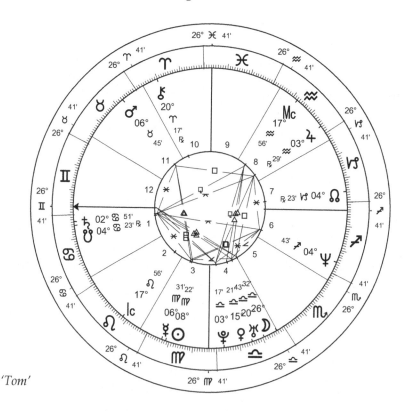

'Tom'

When 'Tom' (a pseudonym) spoke of his work, what became noticeable from the chart were his use of his Virgo editing skills, diligence and an interest in honing his craft. He began work in local and hospital radio stations, cataloguing TV shows in a library, and then video mixing. He continued his apprenticeship as a TV researcher and later became a producer of lifestyle, news, and current affairs shows. Tom is now producing a live debate and discussion show – a platform for young people to voice their concerns on issues affecting them.

We can 'hear' the Mercury overtone in his work and in his tendency to change jobs every few years. Yet, in consultation, he also spoke of a need to search for something less mundane and more meaningful (6th-House Neptune's square to the Virgo planets). He is currently looking to lend his skills to charitable work, which 'coincides' well with transiting Neptune in Pisces moving closer to aspect these planets.

Considering this pivotal square aspect (with its repetitive Mercury theme) in Tom's birth chart, an interest or career in the media might spring to mind. But more importantly, we as astrologers can identify the interest in (and talent for) variety, industry, information, communication, discrimination and helping others – all suggested by the emphasis on Mercury, its houses and the sign of Virgo – and encourage him to pursue work where these traits can be brought to the fore. This aspect also suggests that settling down and having a dependable 9-to-5 job from graduation to retirement are not familiar facets of his character or life script. (Looking further into the chart, we can note that the Moon conjunct Midheaven-ruler Uranus underscores this message, but there's also a conflicting need for security, as seen by MC co-ruler Saturn in Cancer on the Ascendant.)

Since I understand Virgo's temptation to downplay its achievements and talents, part of my job in consultation might be to emphasize and have Tom articulate, appreciate and assign value to those 'little things' that play vital roles in his working life: the concern to perfect a skill, to develop precision, to contribute something useful and to be of service. In our work as astrologers, it proves worthwhile to recognize a key overtone – a planetary type – and then to assist clients in identifying, following and being true to their fundamental character.

Chapter 4

GETTING STARTED WITH NATAL CHART ASSESSMENT

In this chapter, I'll be looking at how to dissect a horoscope, discover its key areas and then find signatures (repetitive patterns, 'overtones') that reveal a chart's dominant themes. This is not an essay on the interpretation of the various pieces of the astrological jigsaw. Instead, what I've compiled is a three-step guide to Types, Trails and Themes that I have found helpful for students to use when evaluating the principal and supporting players and pinpointing the key themes in a natal chart. It is not my intention to reduce the chart to a handful of factors and miss the more subtle aspects of the chart (and its owner), but the following guide offers *one way* – and by no means the only way – to *locate* and *prioritize* the primary, significant players in the horoscope.

It is, of course, essential to have a firm grasp of the meanings of the planets and to know the range of their expression in the signs, houses and aspects (when they are in combination with each other). There is no definitive way to delineate a horoscope. Each of us has our own method, which says much about our own chart and the way we see the world. With a good vocabulary and effective technique (plus much practice in reading charts and researching life stories), all roads can lead to Rome.

Yet, any system of chart assessment we choose must be flexible and remain open to the evolution of ideas. Natal astrology calls for fluid skills and an understanding of human nature, not an archaic or inflexible system that rubber-stamps charts or attempts to fit set 'rules' onto a person's character, prospects and 'fate'. A strict allegiance to any method can reveal more about an astrologer's need to be right and to latch onto a system that is unfailingly reliable. When dealing with natal astrology, there is no 100% certainty. We're fortunate that it works as well as it does! Blind adherence to any astrological system may be comfortably reassuring (albeit static) for its practitioner, but it does little for the clients and their development.

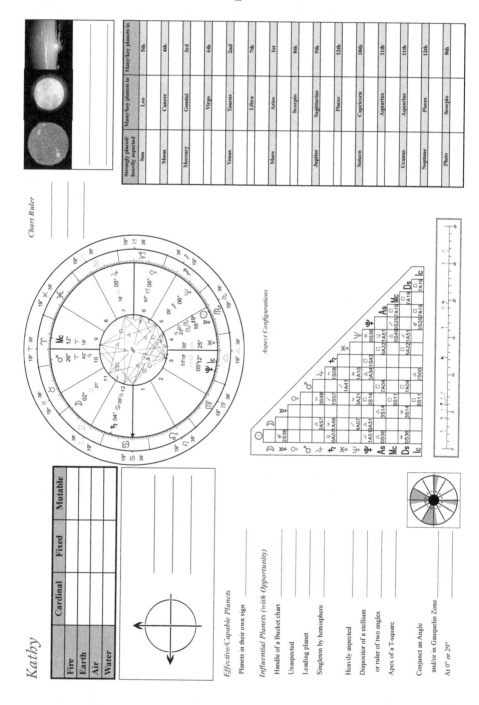

Katby

Chart Ruler

	Cardinal	Fixed	Mutable
Fire			
Earth			
Air			
Water			

Aspect Configurations

Strongly placed/ heavily aspected	Many/key planets in	Many/key planets in
Sun	Leo	5th
Moon	Cancer	4th
Mercury	Gemini	3rd
Mercury	Virgo	6th
Venus	Taurus	2nd
Venus	Libra	7th
Mars	Aries	1st
Mars	Scorpio	8th
Jupiter	Sagittarius	9th
Jupiter	Pisces	12th
Saturn	Capricorn	10th
Uranus	Aquarius	11th
Uranus	Aquarius	11th
Neptune	Pisces	12th
Pluto	Scorpio	8th

Effective/Capable Planets

Planets in their own sign _____

Influential Planets (with Opportunity)

Handle of a Bucket chart _____

Unaspected _____

Leading planet _____

Singleton by hemisphere _____

Heavily aspected _____

Dispositor of a stellium _____

or ruler of two angles _____

Apex of a T-square _____

Conjunct an Angle _____

and/or in Gauquelin Zone _____

At 0° or 29° _____

Opposite is a sample form (with an Equal house chart) that I print out when teaching this area of synthesis.

Before we look at the steps in detail, here's a quick overview of the three sections introduced in this essay:

Types
> Assessing Imbalances
>> (The Elements and the Modes)
> Discovering the Orientation of the Compass
>> (The Four Angles)
> Assessing Planetary Strength
>> • An Effective Planet
>> • An Influential Planet
>>> *Influential by Isolation*
>>> *Influential by Integration*
>>> *Influential by House or Zodiacal Position*

Trails
> Understanding and Synthesizing the Big Three
>> (The Sun, Moon and Ascendant)
> Highlighting the Major Aspects
>> (The conjunction, square and opposition; the trine and sextile)
> Singling out Aspect Configurations
>> (The T-square, etc.)

Themes
> Spotting Signatures
>> (Repetitive themes from planets, signs and houses)

TYPES
Imbalances • Orientation • Planetary Strength

1. Assessing Imbalances

Getting a handle on the elemental and modal distribution of planets can be a good start to any evaluation. Sometimes these are more or less equal, but often there is an imbalance. Identifying a lack is as important as recognizing an emphasis. For instance, there may be no planets in the Fire element, or many planets in the fixed mode. Emphases and lacks show up as basic factors in our psychological make-up. 'Weighting' these reveals how and where our fundamental nature may be in or out of sync.

The **elements** reveal: what we're motivated and driven by; what acts as an incentive; where our enthusiasm lies; the type and source of our energy.

- Dominant Fire seeks glory, excitement, challenge, greatness and elevation. Fire is motivated to enthuse and inspire and to maintain a playful, vibrant lifestyle.

- Dominant Earth seeks expediency, tangible results, the routine of the familiar and physical activity/sensuality. Earth is motivated to offer rock-like support and gain pleasure from a job well done.

- Dominant Air seeks variety, travel, space, exchange and dialogue and a rational perspective. Air is motivated to question, analyse, debate and to find patterns.

- Dominant Water seeks harmony, flow, emotional connections and to be of service to the human condition. Water is motivated to perceive (and respond to) that which has not been verbalized.

Elemental lacks indicate that this motivation is unconscious; under the surface, there is a drive to experience this missing element in obvious or unsophisticated ways. We may seek partners who embody our missing element, or we'll be highly sensitive about the traits suggested by the element and find a way to overcompensate.

For example, if we lack Air, we might fill our house with books and maps and enrol in many courses to actively engage in 'gaining knowledge'. With a lack of Earth, we might be prone to ostentatious displays of wealth (see Donald Trump's chart over the page) or even marry 'Mr/Ms Earth' – a financially secure or practical, reliable person.

The **modes** reveal: our style of expression, our *modus operandi*; our way of negotiating conflict and expressing the energy represented by the elements.

- Dominant cardinality is active; it initiates and creates change, makes things happen, encounters/engages in conflict. The energy is *directed*.

- Dominant fixity is durable, loyal, attached and principled; it accumulates and seeks ownership; it resists change and digs its heels in. The energy is *sustained*.

- Dominant mutability is flexible, adaptable and in constant flux; it questions, researches, learns; it avoids conflict and responsibility. The energy is *disseminating*.

Tips
- Use a total of 9 points: 7 bodies (Sun to Saturn) and 2 angles (Ascendant and MC).
- Expect an average of 2 or 3 placements in each element and 3 in each mode.
- Only take into account an emphasis (4+ points) or a lack (0 or 1 point), but give more weight to an element or mode that contains 2 or all 3 of the Big Three (the Sun, Moon and Ascendant). Saturn, on the other hand, can often feel like a 'lack', a minus in the assessment.
- You may wish to mark each emphasis or lack with a + or – next to the element or mode, for easy reference.
- Consider the signature and anti-signature. The signature is the sign that's made up of the strongest element and mode (e.g., dominant Fire and mutability = Sagittarius). The anti-signature is the least/ missing element and mode combo (lack of Water and fixity = Scorpio). Usually the signs of the signature and anti-signature are next to each other or in quincunx.

Visually, it's helpful to create a grid that can be read by column or row in order to spot emphases and lacks. It's also good to see how the planets and angles can be grouped. In the element/mode table (below the chart opposite), the luminaries are in mutable signs and the angles are fixed.

2. Discovering the Orientation of the Compass

Next, consider the two axes that comprise the structural foundation of the chart: the four angles. Are they of a particular mode? Perhaps all four elements are found on the angles. Or the angles have planetary rulers in common (as they do when the mutable signs are on all four angles – see the diagram on the right), and these rulers may be in aspect, making this an important planetary combination in the chart.

All Mutable
All four elements
Rulers: Mercury, Jupiter

The four angles represent a highly personal compass, showing how we view, negotiate and interact with our immediate and broader environments. They are also the badges we wear: our identity, meet-and-greet badge (Ascendant), our advert for (or label we assign to) an 'other' (Descendant), our social status or professional CV badge (MC), and our family coat of arms (IC). Noting the *orientation* of our compass is key to understanding our stance in personal, relationship, social and family settings. Are these in harmony with the personal planets and key themes of the chart?

In the horoscope of Donald Trump (opposite page), we can immediately see that all four angles are fixed, but the luminaries are mutable. This suggests that, at heart (Sun), he needs (Moon) variety, space and flexibility. Trump is a natural salesman who loves promoting his grandiose visions (Gemini, Sagittarius). But the way he interacts with the world is to develop, build and sustain permanent constructs (fixed angles). That's his stance, and he wants his four lenses – the 'windows of his world' – to be immovable, secure, anchored. (People with the reverse – strong fixity but mutable angles – might have trouble reconciling their natural need for stability and attachment with the shifting goalposts of their environment.)

Donald
Trump

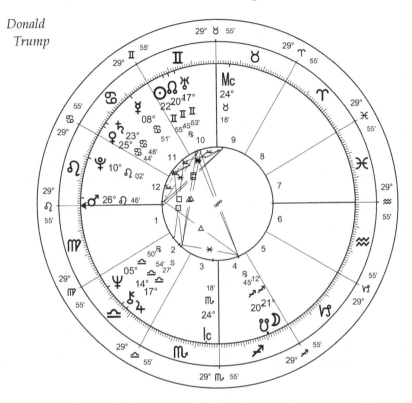

	Cardinal	Fixed	Mutable
Fire		♂ ASC	☽
Earth		MC	
Air	♃		☉
Water	☿ ♀ ♄		

Two of Trump's angles (the Ascendant and MC) form his *public persona,* and we can see how clearly his 'permanent constructs' appear in this Leo–Taurus mix. Trump is a celebrity (Leo) businessman (Taurus) whose famous name (Leo) brings value (Taurus). His real estate holdings and buildings (Taurus) bear his name (a Leo Rising businessperson *is* the product!) and are imposing, permanent fixtures (fixity) around the United States.

This innate PR man with big dreams (Gemini–Sagittarius) has a level of charisma that engenders belief from others (Leo) – they see him (his construct) as a solid investment (Taurus, fixity).

3. Assessing Planetary Strength

To assess whether a planet plays an important role in the chart, I believe there needs to be a distinction between *effective* and *influential* planets. Both fall under the umbrella of judging 'planetary strength' but are quite different in practice. Horary astrologer Deborah Houlding makes a similar distinction, labelling planets with *capability* (to do the job written 'on the tin' – effective) and those with *opportunity* (to be major players in the nativity – influential). For the purposes of this essay, I'll be describing effective planets first, then influential ones. But in my experience and in practice, it is important to pinpoint the major, *influential* players in the horoscope first, and then to look at their quality and style (ways in which they are *effective*).

An Effective Planet

This is, in essence, about a planet's condition – its ability to carry out the job it is naturally inclined to do. An effective planet is one that is found in a sign that resembles its key principles and themes (e.g., Mercury placed in Gemini or Mars in Scorpio). Here, planet and sign share an affinity; they speak a similar language. The manifestation (effect) is clear and straightforward without a conflict of interest.

But that's as far as it goes. Every planet-in-sign combination has a *range* of expression and possibility – talents and problem areas. Combinations that aren't traditionally 'effective' (i.e., in the sign of rulership) simply do jobs differently or have an unconventional agenda. In *natal* astrology, simply classifying planets as being in *rulership, detriment, exaltation,* or *fall* can obfuscate interpretation and lead to the incorrect assumption that some planet-in-sign positions are plainly 'better' or 'worse' than others. We fail as astrologers when we don't recognize the potential inherent in a 'foreign' placement. Just consider how capable Mars in Libra can be in times of war: a cool-headed strategist with peace on the agenda who excels in the art of negotiation, someone who can look *beyond* the simple act of warfare. A study of leaders with Mars in Libra reveals a track record of dynamic leadership. The placement is an important alternative to 'natural' Mars expressions in hot-headed Aries or volatile Scorpio.

Basic, traditional classification also leaves many planets without assignation. I think that we would all benefit from considering the similarities and differences (and areas of compatibility and friction) in *every* planet-in-sign scenario. What do Saturn and Virgo have in common? How would Jupiter be explored in the sign of Scorpio?

The more charts we read, the more we realize that successful *and* unfulfilled people have every possible planet-in-sign combination. People accomplish extraordinary things with so-called debilitated positions, where planets that 'should' signify success in their field don't have the 'required' dignity, while people with planets in 'pristine' condition can choose paths, or encounter limiting external factors, in which these 'advantageous' placements languish or stagnate. This is where the second classification (below) becomes important, and describes whether a planet's job (regardless of its sign position) is an *influential* one in the horoscope.

An Influential Planet
This term relates to a planet's involvement and position in the chart (through aspect or noteworthy/remarkable position in the horoscope). An influential natal planet is one that dominates, receives singular recognition, or is set apart from other planets (as opposed to any planet being activated in forecasting, whereby it assumes importance during that period). Such a planet is a leader in the chart, a dominating force in the person's life stories, traits, encounters and experiences. Once an influential planet has been determined, the *quality and style* of that impact (its anticipated expression and manifestation), however, is seen in the planet's position by sign, house and aspect.

Influential by Isolation
- The planet as a 'handle' of a Bucket-shaped chart shows what we 'hold on to'. It is often a focus of activity (a *raison d'être*) to the point of compulsion or fixation and at the expense of other planets. It can either result in an extraordinary accomplishment, or act as a millstone or an 'excuse' for neglecting other areas of our life.

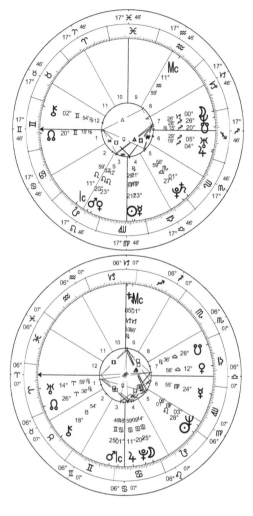

- <u>An unaspected planet</u> is one that can function autonomously and in an all-or-nothing manner.

- A 'leading' planet is the first to rise after much unoccupied space. It is a driving force, a frontman. (See Uranus in Donald Trump's chart on page 41.)

- <u>A singleton by hemisphere</u> (less so by element or mode) is a standout planet. This is particularly noticeable when above or below the Ascendant/Descendant axis, where it represents the only planet that is either 'seen' externally (above) or hidden beneath the surface (below). Sometimes there are two, and their combination tells a story, too.

Notice the visible Moon–Neptune in the 7th House, the only planets[1] above the horizon in the chart of **Amy Winehouse** (top chart, above). Much of what the public witnessed was the saga of Amy's symbiotic relationship with her ex-husband and the addictions that bound them – all played out daily (Moon) in soap-opera style in the tabloids (Neptune). For **Princess Margaret** of England (second chart, above), the two planets above the horizon are Venus in Libra in the 7th (widely) square Saturn on the MC in Capricorn. Biographers and the media have portrayed her as a woman forced to make an unenviable decision (Libra) between romantic love (Venus) and her duty to the British throne (Saturn, Capricorn).

Influential by Integration
- A <u>heavily aspected planet</u> becomes a key figure because it is in dialogue with much of the chart's action.

- <u>The dispositor of a stellium or the ruler of two angles</u> becomes an 'ambassador' – a representative with authority that describes the impetus behind much of the chart. (Stick to traditional rulerships, saving modern rulerships – the outer planets – to show links to wider generational themes and higher levels of mass consciousness.)

- <u>The focal planet ('apex') in a T-square</u> becomes a powerful, principal point of release and a 'solution' to the dynamics of the configuration.

Influential by House or Zodiacal Position
- <u>Conjunct one of the chart's four angles and/or in a Gauquelin Zone</u> (especially around the Ascendant or Midheaven (MC), or behind them in the cadent 12th or 9th House, respectively). This is where the planet is at its most prominent and its characteristics most noticeable in the life and 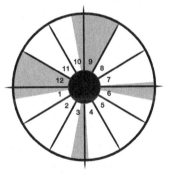 to others. (See diagram on the right.) The importance of planets placed in cadent houses in quadrant systems goes against much traditional opinion, where angular houses take precedence.[2]

- <u>At 0° or 29° of a sign.</u> At 0°, a planet acts out the most obvious and familiar traits, but there's a fresh, raw, unstudied quality or naïveté. At 29°, there's a knowingness (and skilful mastery) of the sign's dynamics and the planet may exhibit the sign's most challenging, extreme facets.[3]

TRAILS
The Big Three • Major Aspects • Aspect Configurations
---

1. Understanding and Synthesizing the Big Three

The Sun, Moon and Ascendant are arguably the most important positions in the horoscope. The Big Three are excellent entrance points into the chart and are areas we engage with most frequently. Ask yourself how they work together, what they have in common and where there may be conflicts of interest.[4]

- The Sun – *core character:* our fundamental mission, individual role, life purpose and vocation; what we're in the process of becoming; our essence and inner identity; our type of 'heart'.

- The Moon – *behavioural traits:* our habits; our fundamental relationship needs and impressions; innate responses to everyday life; our 'backpack' of emotional experiences that have been stored since childhood; our feeling nature and vulnerable side; who we are 'behind closed doors'; our hidden agenda.

- The Ascendant – *personality characteristics:* our approach to life; our meet-and-greet function and the role(s) we play to navigate our journey; our overt agenda; mottoes for survival and interaction; first impressions made and received.

How are they linked? Do two or three have an element or mode in common? In addition, their trails can lead to discovering a key aspect or focal point in a chart.

Example: **Jacqueline Stallone**, with the Sun and Moon in Sagittarius, Ascendant in Libra (see the chart on the opposite page). The Libra–Sagittarius combination stirs up ideas of international partnerships; opportunities through influential social or legal associations; speaking out about relationships, equal rights and issues of justice; and even beauty in sport.

In the chart of this flamboyant businesswoman and astrologer (and mother of film star Sylvester Stallone), all of her inner planets

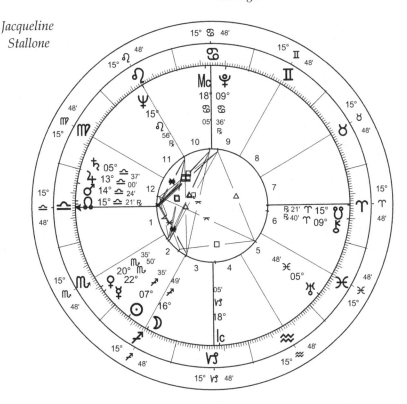

Jacqueline Stallone

are in either Sagittarius or Scorpio, and ruled (i.e., disposited) by Jupiter and Mars, respectively. The trails of the Sun, Moon and Ascendant (its ruler is Venus in Scorpio) lead back to her Mars–Jupiter conjunction (on an angle), making this the most influential aspect in her chart.

2. Highlighting the Major Aspects
Aspects show a dialogue and a flow of energy between planets (or between planets and angles). These help us to zoom in on the main life scripts and dynamics of the personality. The three major aspects to consider are the conjunction, square and opposition.

- The conjunction is a focal point in the chart; a powerful merging of energies that never act alone. A script/dynamic that is obvious to others.

- The square is an area that requires action, effort, striving and stretching. A script/dynamic manifesting as challenges that 'build character'. A tension that creates excellence, while fostering achievement and mastery.

- The opposition represents a face-off between conflicting parts of our nature most often seen in relationship patterns. A seesaw script/dynamic demanding that we integrate parts of ourselves through relationships, rather than disowning or projecting them.

The other aspects can be ignored at this stage. The influence of 'soft' aspects (e.g., the trine and sextile) can be overwhelmed by the main three above. I'd only consider very close trines and sextiles (no more than 2 or 3 degrees), but would stick to 8° orbs for the major aspects and include out-of-sign (dissociate) aspects.

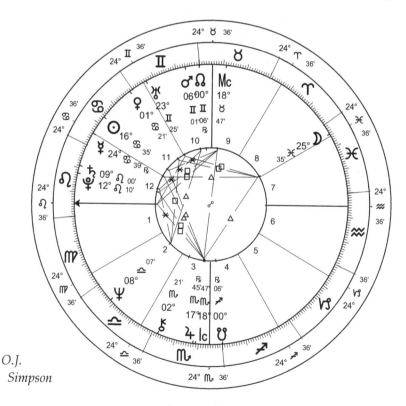

O.J.
Simpson

The 'minor' aspects (e.g., the quincunx, sesquiquadrate, semi-square) so often describe a specific theme or script rather than a condition met regularly in life. Add aspects to Chiron and any other bodies you use, but I would not recommend listing/interpreting aspects between the planets from Jupiter to Pluto (e.g., natal Saturn square Pluto). These assume importance only when drawn into the main action by aspecting inner planets or angles. Sticking with the major three and very close soft aspects, we should have a list that looks like this:

Example: **O. J. Simpson** (see chart opposite)

The major, hard aspects:
- Moon square Venus
- Moon square Uranus
- Venus conjunct Uranus
- Venus square Neptune
- Jupiter conjunct IC
- Pluto square MC/IC

Close soft aspects:
- Sun trine Jupiter
- Moon trine Mercury
- Mars sextile Saturn
- Mars trine Neptune

These pivotal aspects certainly reflect Simpson's charm as an entertainer and his charismatic sporting persona, along with the domestic drama that wrecked his reputation. The female 'relating' planets (the Moon and Venus) receive challenging outer planet aspects, while the Jupiter–Pluto links to the MC/IC axis suggest his remarkable rise and fall, and how his double murder trial was of significance to the US and its African-American community.

The close soft aspects (and their natal positions) such as Sun–Jupiter, Moon–Mercury, and Mars–Neptune point to the 'lucky' elements of his life, from his athletic talent and early charismatic standing/fame, to product endorsements and his post-sports career in film, to his mid-1990s legal escape, thanks to an eloquent Dream Team of lawyers.

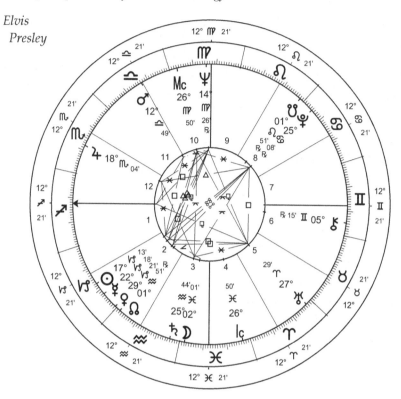

Elvis
Presley

3. Singling out Aspect Configurations

Planets that interlock by forming geometrical configurations, such as the T-square, Grand Trine, or Yod, usually dominate the birth chart and overshadow other placements. The actual aspects (e.g., the three trines of the Grand Trine) define the *nature* of the dialogue, while the planets (and their sign and house placements) describe the players involved in the creative tension and activity. You may wish to search for the 'Alpha', driving planet in any configuration, as outlined by astrologer Donna Cunningham.[5]

Example: **Elvis Presley** (chart above) with a cardinal T-square of Mercury conjunct Venus, both opposite Pluto, and all square to Uranus, the apex. On one level, this configuration manifested as a voice (Mercury) that was rich, powerful, soulful and possessed great range (Pluto). Presley's was a melodic, sensual instrument (Venus) that changed and greatly impacted his generation (Pluto).

He was a country boy who introduced rhythm and blues (Pluto) to white America – a taboo (Pluto) in the 1950s. In the process, he revolutionized (Uranus) rock music and popular culture (Venus). Falling across the 2nd and 8th Houses, this 'cash cow' aspect also speaks of the enormous financial wealth he generated for those around him, particularly after his death, and the tight control the executors have had over his estate.

The apex is Uranus in Aries in the 5th. Aside from Elvis's much-rumoured sexual predilections, this placement suggests his exciting and dangerous, playful and sexual way of performing. He was full of youthful vigour and testosterone – and hip-shakingly rhythmic. As astrologer Wendy Bristow notes, '[His] sexy moves were an accident. Elvis was … hyperactive … He just couldn't stop himself jiggling.'[6]

Elvis also shook up the establishment and turned people on to a new wave of music – he was an early pioneer of rock 'n' roll (note the term's sexual Aries/5th-House connotations). His music gave birth to the rebellious teenager, and Elvis was rock's first sex symbol and most influential star.

THEMES
Spotting Signatures

Here, we're looking for repetitive statements and patterns – what we might call signatures or overtones. It is often said that a major statement will be written/expressed in at least three ways in the birth chart. For example, a horoscope may have a *Capricorn* Ascendant, plus a Sun–*Saturn* conjunction, which is opposed by the Moon in the *10th House*. These three placements would suggest a Saturn/Capricorn/10th-House signature. We might spot a Venusian emphasis – but is that Venus/Taurus/2nd, or Venus/Libra/7th? Or perhaps there's a mix, e.g., *Libra* is on the Ascendant, and the Sun is conjunct *Venus* in *Taurus* in the 7th.

Here is a simple way of approaching this: start with each planet and its associated house(s) and sign(s). For instance, is there a focus on the Sun (major aspects to it, particularly conjunctions, squares and oppositions), the 5th House (at least a few planets posited there), and/or Leo (ditto)? This is a systematic way of

'Luke'

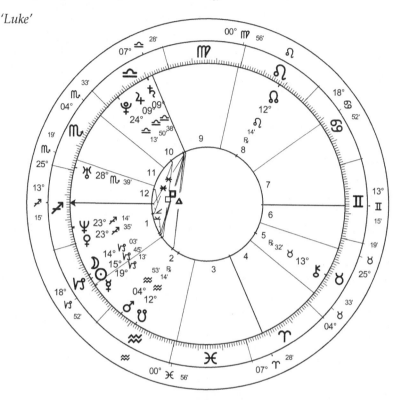

looking for <u>planets</u> that are strongly aspected or positioned in the chart (linked to other planets or the angles), <u>signs</u> that have many planets posited, and <u>houses</u> that contain many planets. It's a bit laborious, but once you've done this a few times, you'll be spotting themes quickly without the need to do this step by step.

Above is the horoscope (calculated with Placidus houses[7]) of a client, 'Luke' (a pseudonym). Let's go through the process of looking for an emphasis, which I've underlined in the table opposite. The *sign* placements of the outer planets are generational, not personal, and have been put in parentheses.

A Brief Analysis of Findings

This table confirms that the Sun–Moon–Mercury triple conjunction is influential, but its associated signs (Leo, Cancer, Gemini, Virgo) and houses (5th, 4th, 3rd, 6th) are not dominant. What transpires, though, are the following:

1. A Jupiter–Sagittarius signature (the emphasis on Sagittarius and an elevated Jupiter aspecting the Sun–Moon).

2. A Saturn–Capricorn–10th signature (three planets in Capricorn, and Saturn on the MC aspecting the Sun–Moon).

3. A lesser, Venusian 'sub-tone' (two planets in the 2nd House, and three planets – two social, one outer/generational – plus one angle in Libra).

Where a planet, sign or house is strong, it has been shaded in the table opposite. The Jupiter and Saturn signatures are reinforced by their own elevated (and tight) conjunction at the MC, and by the fact that the Big Three are either in Sagittarius or Capricorn. Between them, Jupiter and Saturn disposit six of the ten planets (including, traditionally, the Aquarius Mars) and rule the Ascendant.

Strongly placed/ heavily aspected	*Many/key planets in*	*Many/key planets in*
Sun	**Leo**	**5th**
conj. Moon, Merc; sq. Jup, Sat, MC		
Moon	**Cancer**	**4th**
conj. Sun, Merc; sq. Jup, Sat, MC		
Mercury	**Gemini**	**3rd**
conj. Sun, Moon; sq. Plu		
	Virgo	**6th**
Venus	**Taurus**	**2nd**
conj. Nep; sext. Plu		Merc, Mars
	Libra	**7th**
	Jup, Sat, (Plu), MC	
Mars	**Aries**	**1st**
		Sun, Moon, Ven, Nep
	Scorpio	**8th**
	(Ura)	
Jupiter	**Sagittarius**	**9th**
conj. Sat, MC; sq. Sun, Moon	Ven, (Nep), ASC	
	Pisces	**12th**
		Ura
Saturn	**Capricorn**	**10th**
conj. Jup, MC; sq. Sun, Moon	Sun, Moon, Merc	Jup, Sat, Plu
	Aquarius	**11th**
	Mars	
Uranus	**Aquarius**	**11th**
	Mars	
Neptune	**Pisces**	**12th**
conj. Ven		Ura
Pluto	**Scorpio**	**8th**
sq. Merc	(Ura)	

Looking closer, it's the Capricorn–Saturn–10th signature that dominates the chart because three 'inners' – the Sun, Moon and Mercury – are placed in Capricorn, linking the sign to the client's inner identity, life purpose and vocation (the Sun), his habitual behaviour, needs and temperament (the Moon), and his ways of expression/reasoning (Mercury). The dispositor of these three planets, Saturn, is powerfully placed on the MC and in its natural house, the 10th (along with Jupiter).

There is also a Libra/2nd-House influence, with two planets in the 2nd House (four by Equal houses) and four points in Libra, suggesting a Venusian sub-tone to the chart. Venus is involved in a very close conjunction with Neptune, but this is placed in Sagittarius, underscoring the Jupiter signature (which in itself says much about his outlook on life and approach to people – Ascendant/1st House).

When there are a couple of signatures, consider these to be *a bit like* a planetary pairing in aspect (e.g., Jupiter–Saturn). There may not be a dialogue/aspect between these two planets in the horoscope, but the main themes and thrust of the birth chart are *of the nature of both planets*. When those two planets happen to be in aspect with each other – as they are in the example above – the theme is strengthened.

By spotting a planetary signature, we uncover a key part of the life story/character. We can then go deeper and assess the 'condition' of that planet to pinpoint themes, life issues and needs. This method is not about reducing the chart and avoiding its complexities. It's a technique that can help us get to the very heart of what the chart and person are about – their driving forces and key life experiences.

We need a method to investigate and identify the patterns that form in the horoscope – a way to follow the trails and recognize the chart's major themes. It's essential that we keep this relatively simple: a proliferation of techniques can overwhelm the astrologer and result in muddled messages that leave the client perplexed.

Although much of our work with clients is Mercurial (we observe, assess, interpret and then articulate these symbols in a language that the client can understand), our job as consultant astrologers is also Jupiterian: to transcend the technique, to explore the significance and meaning in these symbols, to discover the narrative that has formed as a result of these patterns. We embark on this journey *with* our clients, gaining much from dialogue and listening to how they use a particular aspect or placement. Only with their help can we truly bring the chart to life. In doing so, we open their minds to the various routes available and possible destinations ahead.

References and Notes
1. If you use Chiron in a natal chart, then its presence in Winehouse's horoscope (in Gemini in the 12th House) could speak of the pain of addiction/loss of control that acted as a source of her creative writing. Being in the 12th suggests that Chiron's message was clearly visible to others yet it was tough for her to take control of.
2. For more on the Gauquelins, see Chapter 3.
3. See Chapter 16 and Chapter 17.
4. See Chapter 2.
5. See Donna Cunningham's article 'The Alpha Dog Planet in a Stellium or Major Configuration' in *The Mountain Astrologer*, June/July 2013.
6. Wendy Bristow, 'Elvis and the "X" Factor', in *The Astrological Journal*, March/April 2009, p. 32.
7. As the article first appeared in *The Mountain Astrologer* with Placidus houses, I've kept this. In Equal houses (my preference), the house emphasis shifts from the 1st House to the 2nd House, but little else changes.

Chapter 5

SPEAKING YOUR CHART:
THE ESSENCE OF A PLANETARY PLACEMENT

The following is an edited, shortened version of my opening plenary at the 2012 Astrological Association Conference. Some of the text is adapted from my textbook, Getting to the Heart of Your Chart *(Flare, 2012).*

One of the reasons I wanted to give this presentation was to show how we all 'speak our charts', sometimes profoundly, sometimes very simply or casually. We can all improve our astrology by paying attention to what people say about themselves.

'Speaking your chart' means to describe yourself or your life in such a way that you are articulating planetary placements in your horoscope. Here, I want to have fun looking at some quotes from people – and how these reflect their horoscopes.

When clients or public figures speak their charts, we collect gems that inform our practice as astrologers. These gems:

- Consolidate our understanding of astrological principles in practice;
- Broaden or refine our knowledge of astrology;
- Reveal the function of a planetary placement in that person's life;
- Guide us towards the key themes of the person's chart (or current focal points in the client's life).

I loved learning astrology with a biography in one hand and a birth chart in the other – and continue to do so. In fact, my interest in particular well-known entertainers, politicians, criminals, sportsmen and religious leaders often stemmed from finding their horoscope first (God bless Lois Rodden and the team of data collectors!), being curious as to how that sign or planet manifested – and then reading about them.

The fact is, the more charts we study, the less we are inclined to rely on a narrow model of presumed astrological signatures. We sometimes follow what astrologers have said in the past and keep applying these 'rules' or observations without question, but I believe that we learn so much more about what astrology means in the modern world by researching the lives of people who interest us, and listening to the people around us speak their charts.

By listening to our clients, favourite public people and our loved ones, it reminds us not to impose a set of pre-determined interpretations onto a client – we must avoid fitting a chart rigidly onto a person ('Ah, you have Sun–Saturn, so you must be X, Y and Z'). I prefer to turn it around – to listen to how it manifests, to consider what I know about them, and *then* look for it in their horoscope. This is one of the key ways to get students to learn astrology for themselves – to participate in this process of discovery and embrace their own findings.

If we don't listen, we never really know how people 'inhabit' their horoscopes, how relevant our assumptions are, or how the major themes of their birth charts play out in their lives. This process gives us a chance to redefine and often refine astrological placements for ourselves – to build an arsenal of observations and traits.

Just as astrologer Sue Tompkins links Pluto to dogs, Aquarius to birds, and Uranus transits to major moves to Australia, we can all make our own observations, preferably based on a wide range of charts. (Although we should be rigorous and realize that two instances don't make a tenable theory. It brings to mind someone in a talk of mine who suddenly declared, 'Virgos don't pee until 2.30 in the afternoon.' For some reason I doubted the authenticity of her research ... But hey, maybe I'm wrong, and maybe that's why Virgos are so irritable in the morning ...)

For example, over the years, I've seen that Sagittarius (or a strongly-placed Jupiter) is often linked to depression (born from a disappointment that people or life doesn't give back as much as they put forward). While, to me, Virgo is the great eccentric – very idiosyncratic and the obsessive controller of its environment. I link the Taurus–Scorpio axis to gardening and the Virgo–Pisces axis to dance. We all have these observations – some trivial, some profound – that can be tested when we meet new clients.

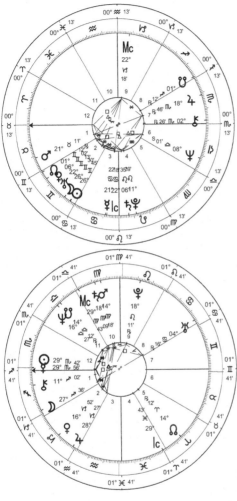

Looking at specific degrees, I've found that 24-25 degrees of the mutable signs have a strong connection to the issues of hearing, harmonics and deafness, while 26-27° Sagittarius appears to be an area of the cosmos linked to Islam.

I've been led to the latter observation because soon after the Saturn-Uranus conjunction at 27° Sagittarius in 1988, *The Satanic Verses* was published. Author **Salman Rushdie** (chart, top left), was issued with a *fatwa* and condemned to death a few months later. He was born with the Sun-Moon at 26° Gemini. When Pluto reached 27° Sagittarius, he was knighted and this provoked further threats and protests.

The most vocal of anti-Muslim protestors is **Pat Condell** (chart above), whose Moon is at 27° Sagittarius. He began his YouTube videos (where he proclaims himself 'godless and free') when TR Pluto was conjunct his Moon at 27° Sagittarius.

I'm interested in specific degrees and their meanings, and this research is at its very early stages – so I don't know yet whether this degree relates to the Islamic faith or more specifically to blasphemy of the Qur'an, as perceived by followers of Islam.

Richard Swatton, in *From Symbol to Substance* (Flare, 2012), informs us that correspondences can be read on numerous levels: as objects, principles, feelings, emotions, attitudes, places, actions, professions and people. In *The Contemporary Astrologer's Handbook* (Flare, 2006), Sue Tompkins reminds us that the cosmos is jokey and cosmic correspondences can be great fun to spot. Sometimes we are able to understand a facet of a sign in a roundabout way or via unexpected trails.

Here's one that falls under the seemingly trivial: I used to wonder why so many Sagittarians (Sun or Ascendant) wore headbands! This fashion was at its height in the 1970s/early 1980s when Neptune – the planet of fashion trends – moved through Sagittarius! (These are things astrologers wonder about in cinemas when others are just watching the film!)

Here are a few who are famous for wearing them – they are all strongly Sagittarian: Jacqueline Stallone (Sun and Moon), Jimi Hendrix (Sun, Mercury, Venus, Ascendant, and, actually, he wore a bandana), Brigitte Bardot (Ascendant), and country singer Janie Fricke (Sun, Mercury, Jupiter, Ascendant), who said it was a sad day when fashions changed and she had to hang up her headbands. At 91, Jackie Stallone had a major makeover (check this out for yourself online) and you'll notice that her headband is now where her lips used to be.

This may all seem jokey, but why Sagittarius? The Greeks and Romans wore laurel wreaths (in honour of the son of Zeus/Jupiter) as a sign of their achievements, rank, status and education (we are also warned not to 'rest on our laurels'). They were woven into a horseshoe (Sagittarius) shape. Caesar proclaimed the laurel wreath to be a 'symbol of the supreme ruler'. (This, I believe, gives us an insight into the true nature of the Jupiterian and Sagittarian.) And the laurels were later used to crown victors at the Olympic Games. (I associate Sagittarius with the Olympics – the international event, the sporting excellence, the spirit of competition, and the torchbearer carrying the Olympic Flame.)

When we listen to life stories, we don't have to look far to see these in the person's horoscope. As we might expect, the Moon complex (its sign and major aspects) is 'heard' most clearly when clients describe their emotional needs and responses, their early shaping experiences, their gut instincts and general temperament.

When clients reveal their personality characteristics – those employed to meet and greet the world one-to-one – and their agenda, plus early messages about behaviour, they're speaking their Ascendant and any planets conjunct that angle.

The Sun is often expressed by clients as an inner awareness of a specific identity or calling (their vocation). The Midheaven is often how they are described by others in a 'social shorthand', what they aspire to be, and one facet of their social persona.

So, when singer Diana Ross (see her chart on page 20) was described as 'a complex, voracious personality that could find happiness in no other way than to be loved by millions', we are drawn to the word *voracious* (and might think of greedy, ravenous or devouring). As astrologers, we could go straight to her Jupiter in Leo square the Moon (an insatiable appetite to be loved and applauded) – and we could consider her Sun in Aries in the 5th House opposite Neptune.

In interview, she has described herself as a 'chronic list-maker' and others have called her 'very much a perfectionist and always anxious to be the best at her craft'. 'Chronic', 'anxious', 'perfectionist' and 'list-maker' are all words that, with an astrological ear, lead us to her MC in Virgo – suggesting how she is perceived by others and how she attempts to gain control of her professional life and reputation.

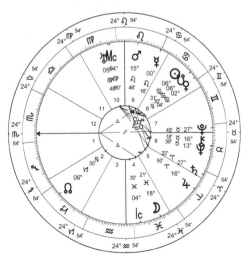

One of the most remarkable educators of the twentieth century was **Helen Keller** (chart on right), who became a world-renowned lecturer and writer despite being struck deaf and blind by an illness at nineteen months of age. When she wrote, 'I long to accomplish a great and noble task but it's my duty to accomplish small tasks as if they were great and noble,' we can hear the essence of her MC in Virgo and its ruler, Mercury, at 0° Leo.

We can also hear **Margaret Thatcher's** Virgo MC (and her Saturn Rising) in this quote: 'Look at a day when you are supremely

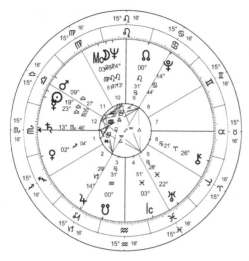

satisfied at the end. It's not a day when you lounge around doing nothing; it's when you've had everything to do, and you've done it.' Her chart is pictured on the left.

Libra is a fascinating sign and I think it's often misunderstood or simply labelled 'indecisive' or 'appeasing'. As a mediator to warring sides, Libra understands the art of diplomatic negotiation and arbitration. But Libra knows that the concept of compromise is overrated: no one gets what they really want. (Jimmy Carter – Sun in Libra and Libra Rising – once said, 'Unless both sides win, no agreement can be permanent.') Libra is a cardinal sign and, upon closer inspection, has an agenda. Libra seeks agreement through the full acceptance of its needs by the other. At first, it attempts to have those needs met through the line of least resistance – gentle, logical persuasion and charm (Libra sends you to hell in such a way that you actually *look forward to the trip*). But when faced with stubborn obstruction or an impasse, Libra reveals itself to be an iron fist in a velvet glove by sending in the troops.

And what comes through in the chart of **Karen Carpenter** (chart opposite page, top) when we hear this quote about her?

> On one level, Karen was ebullient, pretty and wholesome as mom's apple pie; on another she was obsessional, immature and bizarrely jealous of any woman who had an affair with [brother Richard].[1]

Karen adored and elevated her brother – here we note Mercury–Jupiter are conjunct – and, as Richard said, 'She was unnaturally possessive of me … she was mothering me all the time.' Here we can see Moon–Pluto in Leo in opposition to Mercury–Jupiter. The successful brother became the focus of her attention. Sadly, as it turned out, Richard was unable to have a relationship until Karen passed away at age 32 from anorexia.

The wholesome image is, in part, suggested by the Cancer Ascendant, and it was noted that, 'She had built a wall around herself so that it was difficult to penetrate her emotional defences.'[2] And we can start to link perfectionism and part of the psychology of anorexia nervosa to a strong Uranus.

We don't always get an automatic 'hit' when we see someone's Ascendant. Remember British actor **Kenneth Williams** (chart on right), best remembered for the Carry On film series? We might remember his flaring nostrils and obsessive talk about his bowel movements and haemorroids, and his love-

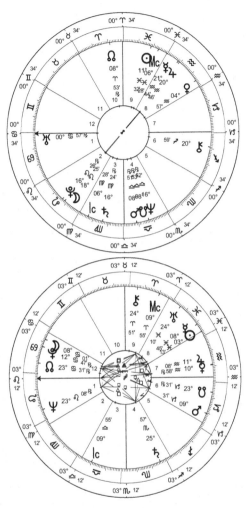

hate relationship with his mother who lived next door (note the Moon–Pluto in Cancer having just risen into the 12th).

He doesn't seem to be Leo Rising until we remember his 'sneer', the narcissism and the disdain he felt when the public was over-familiar. There's a wonderful quote about him: 'He felt he didn't belong [with his family]. He felt a bit like a changeling, a little prince of higher birth accidentally dropped to this low-life family.'[3]

Without knowing it, clients have a way of spotting or emphasizing which part of their chart they want to talk about.

Words spoken during a consultation are the client's way of letting us know which area of their life and chart has assumed particular importance at the time of their appointment. In other words, clients lead us directly to the most important areas of their horoscope.

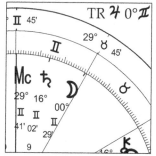

One recent client (chart on left) spent a few minutes in the consultation trying to find the right words for what we wanted in life. He kept coming back to 'needing more' … 'more from life'. 'I just need more!' he said. At the time of our consultation, transiting Jupiter was on his Moon in Gemini in the 9th. As an astrologer, I was obviously being guided towards this transit and this natal placement – and the consultation developed down that avenue. (This reminds me of a client who said, 'I have difficulty expressing myself. I'm just not very … very … ' 'Articulate?' I interjected. She said, 'Yes, I just don't have a way with … a way with … ' '*Words?*' I offered.)

Moving on. Have you ever noticed how people with mutable signs prominent (especially on the Sun, Moon or Ascendant) use the word 'sorry' so often? They are always apologizing – you soon discover that it's not because they're terribly contrite, it's because 'sorry' is the easiest way around any difficulty – it gets them out of a commitment or conflict they want to avoid. Whereas some heavily fixed people would rather burn in hell than apologize because what they say and do is so often inextricably linked to their sense of self. 'Failure' (i.e. getting it wrong) means so much more to them than it does to mutables. And what about those of us who are cardinal signs? We're just always 'in the right', aren't we? Simple as that. End of discussion.

I have a friend with a strongly Sagittarian/Jupiterian chart (pictured, right). Jupiter is the Chart Ruler and square to the Moon in Sagittarius in the 9th. I always laugh when she describes ugly people as being 'unfortunate looking'. It's so apt for her chart! It's as though – from her Jupiterian standpoint (on a high horse) – ugliness is unlucky, ill-fated, highly regrettable. *Unfortunate.*

I've always loved aphorisms – they often get to the heart of an astrological concept in a way that pages of interpretation simply cannot:

A strong Venus: *I'm going to be assertive, if that's OK with you.*

What Gemini won't tell you: *Conversation is a contest in which the first person to draw breath is declared the listener.*

How Aries gets his point across: *Will you stop talking while I'm interrupting.*

What Scorpio knows: *Silence may not be the best defence, but it is certainly the most annoying.*

But in all seriousness, we do start to see that the signs are more than just a collection of adjectives or even motivations; they're a particular approach/stance that has specific routes through life.

It's often the humorous quotes that really get to the heart of an astrological placement. In my research for my booklet, *Humour in the Horoscope* (Flare, 2014), most often I found Uranus strongly placed (contacting the angles or personal planets by hard aspect), and personal planets in Aquarius and Capricorn. There was a preponderance of Mercury–Mars and Mercury–Uranus aspects. These, I've found, are the most common in funny people's horoscopes.

So, Mercury–Mars contacts might conjure up:

- Sharp, incisive thinking; rapier wit; caustic;
- The desire to communicate, to get a message across quickly; straight talk; a desire and ability to 'cut the crap';
- Verbal dexterity; fast talkers; the cut-and-thrust of vicious verbal exchanges; rudeness and vulgarity.

It's not surprising to find that many comic masters – who excel in this type of humour – have this combination. Comedy writer and actress Caroline Aherne's Mercury–Mars conjunction in Capricorn first came in the guise of simple-voiced senior citizen Mrs Merton. She was able to shoot down snobbery or pretension (Capricorn) in celebrities with some barbed, to the point questions:

> To the magician's assistant Debbie McGee: But what first attracted you to the *millionaire* Paul Daniels?

> To astrologer Russell Grant: Do you think they'll ever find a man on Uranus?

Others include outrageous actress Tallulah Bankhead and offensive stand-up comedians Chubby Brown and Bernard Manning, as well as various lead actors in *Ally McBeal*, *Friends* and *The Golden Girls*.

'Fast-talking' is also the terrain of Mercury–Mars, and Ben Elton (Mercury in Aries square Mars in Cancer) made his name in the 1980s in leftist political stand-up comedy. The two embodiments of motor-mouth teenage chavs – Vicky Pollard (from *Little Britain*) and Lauren (from *The Catherine Tate Show*) – were created by Matt Lucas and Catherine Tate, both Mercury–Mars comedians. I've always loved the wit of country singer-songwriter Dolly Parton, known as much for her songs as her wonderful down-to-earth one-liners. In her chart, Mercury in Capricorn opposes Mars, and she quipped: 'I look just like the girls next door … if you happen to live next door to an amusement park.' She was also mischievous enough to enter a drag queen Dolly Parton lookalike contest. She came in third.

If we take Saturn and study quotes and biographies from those who have a strong Saturn overtone in their horoscope (including the sign Capricorn), we can start to grasp the essence of the planet and its sign.

Researching the life of actor **Anthony Hopkins**, we encounter the solitary, inhibited and melancholic side of Saturn and a liking for the spartan, bleak or austere. Hopkins is a double Capricorn with Mercury and Venus there, too. He grew up hating authority figures and left school with a drive to achieve fame and money, to be a 'somebody'.

Anthony
Hopkins

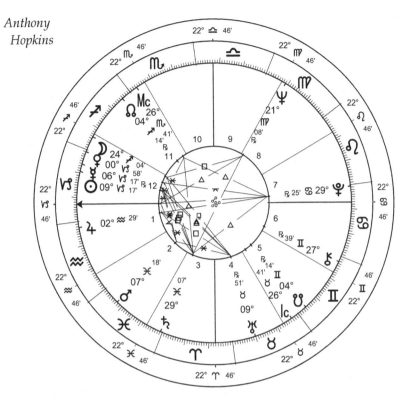

My research suggests that Saturnian personalities must often
struggle on through an early 'lack' or handicap – a feeling within
that they are without something automatically afforded to others.
(Capricorn knows little of the nepotism employed by its polar sign
of Cancer.) Hopkins has said:

> I love the bleakness [of travelling by car across America]
> because it is part of myself. I love the coldness of life. I love the
> inevitability of it all. When I went to school I discovered I was
> on the wrong planet because I was so academically retarded. I
> guess I misused my education … I was the one who didn't fit
> in … It's a romantic fantasy I have of the loner, the lone wolf
> who doesn't need any affection. That's part of my life, actually,
> I think I can do very well without any affection and love … I
> am capable of withdrawing from people and closing myself
> off. Maybe it's a form of martyrdom.[4]

In this quote, Hopkins articulates his chart's Capricorn emphasis and ruler Saturn in Pisces in the (Equal) 3rd House.

When director Oliver Stone was casting the actor for his biopic *Nixon*, he sought Hopkins for the part because 'the isolation of Tony is what struck me. The loneliness. I felt that was the quality that always marked Nixon.'[5] It's not surprising that Nixon's Capricorn planets (see page 30) line up with Hopkins's chart.

Saturn types aim to redress early hardship by becoming an established authority in their field. Capricorn knows it must endure a long apprenticeship and hold in check the personal needs in order to attain the rank and respect it craves. In 1996, Hopkins shared some insights into his psychology with *Vanity Fair*:

> I think success has been very important to me. I wanted it
> to heal some inner wound of some kind. I wanted revenge; I
> wanted to dance on the graves of a few people who made me
> unhappy – and I've done it.[6]

Hopkins would later achieve great recognition in Merchant–Ivory films by playing emotionally repressed characters determined to ward off intimacy (Saturn), and he has also excelled in creating portraits of simmering, smouldering restraint and terrifying menace (note the Scorpio MC, too, which is descriptive of his most famous portrayal – the psychiatrist and killer Hannibal Lecter in *The Silence of the Lambs*).

When we 'hear' Saturnian people talk, we encounter patience, prudence, sobriety, control, shrewdness, ambition, a methodical approach and the priority of duty over pleasure. Biography reveals an innate reserve, a need for privacy, an aloof self-containment and a desire to be an authentic person of 'substance' and character.

And finally. I love tennis. Watching it, playing it. I've understood that, on court (as well as on any stage), a player's Ascendant comes to the fore. Consider the following:

- **Roger Federer** (chart on opposite page, top left) – his graceful technique and finesse and tidiness, white cleanness! He has Venus Rising in Virgo and he never looks as though he's broken into a sweat.

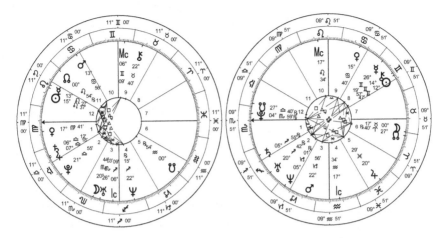

- **Rafael Nadal** (chart above, right) – we note his single-mindedness, powerhouse strength and fixed stare. Nadal was born with Pluto Rising in Scorpio.

- What of **Martina Navratilova** (chart below, left) and her serve-and-volley attacking style, muscular/intimidating presence on court? She also wore her emotions on the surface, often moaning when she didn't get close to perfection. She was born with the Moon Rising in Aries. Her great rival **Chris Evert** (chart below, right) was an unflappable, steely 'ice princess', defensive baseliner and counterpuncher. She has Moon–Saturn–Venus on a Scorpio

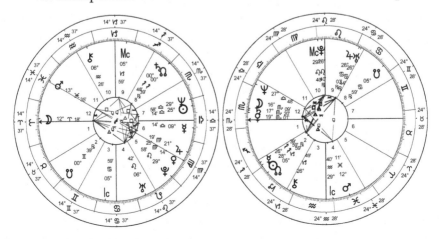

Ascendant. Steffi Graf was known for her commanding, majestic presence, speed and agility, as well as her mane of hair. She has the Sun Rising in Gemini.

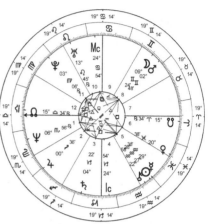

• As for **John McEnroe**, although Libra Rising suggests disputes over line calls were about issues of fairness, we have to look a bit further. We really 'hear' the bad behaviour of Moon–Mars in Gemini (verbal emotional outbursts) opposite Jupiter (exaggerated) and T-square Pluto (full of rage). With Saturn in Capricorn in the 3rd, he was famous for crying at the umpire (Saturn), 'You *cannot* be serious!'

There is much debate over what can or cannot be 'seen' in the horoscope but the chart is simply a moment of time – it could be a chart for anything. (It might be fairer to say that our chart does not belong to us, we belong to it – that moment of time.)

The astrologer must have *context* in order to read the chart appropriately – and, even then, it contains numerous symbolic possibilities that could play out in all manner of ways. Engaging with the client – hearing them speak their most important aspects and placements – is a fundamental, invaluable step towards understanding their particular perspective and their own ways of using their birth chart.

References and Notes
1. Corinna Honan, *Daily Mail*, 10 December 1994.
2. Ray Coleman, *The Carpenters: The Untold Story*, Boxtree, 1994.
3. Russell Davies quoted in *Kenneth Williams* on *The Biography Channel*.
4. Hopkins quoted in BBC's *Omnibus: A Taste of Hannibal*, 2002.
5. Oliver Stone quoted in *Newsweek*, 11 December 1995.
6. Hopkins quoted in *Vanity Fair*, October 1996.

Chapter 6

SEARCHING FOR PARENTAL SIGNIFICATORS
IN THE NATAL HOROSCOPE

Where are our parents shown in the *natal* chart? Are they described by planets placed in the 4th and 10th Houses, the signs on the cusps of these houses, and/or the planets ruling them? Or are they somewhere else?

It is often quoted that the 'shaping' parent (the one who most prepares or conditions the child for the outer world) is indicated by the 10th-House complex, while the more 'hidden' parent is linked to the 4th. Some texts state that the father *is* the 4th House because – in spite of natural links to the feminine, maternal (fourth) sign of Cancer – this is the house associated with where we've come from (the father's 'seed') and the family name.

It may be important, even vital, to assign parents to specific houses when practising horary astrology but in my view, a house in natal astrology does not govern a specific person. Each house represents a *place* of activity, an *area* of life. Planets in signs show the players and their motivations, while aspects between planets reveal the storyline possibilities, but the houses show *where* on the set the performance will take place. People may be 'projected' onto – or encountered in – a particular house (area of life), but their influence can be seen elsewhere, too.

If we are products of our parents (and ancestors), then their influence, ambitions, desires and fixations – the various examples they set in our lives – should be seen *throughout* our horoscope in quite specific ways. For example, if our attitude toward money is formed by interaction with one or both parents, this will be seen by our natal 2nd-House complex (planets in that house, the sign on the cusp and its ruler) and possibly by transits, progressions, or directions at the time when issues involving money arise. By studying this house, we can uncover our attitude toward assets, earnings and possessions, much of which may have been shaped by our parents. (Planets in signs, of course, play a major role in behaviour: the Moon reveals attitudes towards everyday spending and what we consider necessary purchases for comfort, survival and shelter, while Venus shows the ways in which we spend money on indulgences – the type of goods we splash out on to pleasure ourselves.)

If we attempt to assign a parent to a house, it's important to remember that parents usually come in pairs. For example, some cookbook interpretations would consider Neptune in the 4th House to indicate the possibility of a child having an absent father. But what of the child's mother? Perhaps she longed (Neptune) for a better life or resigned (Neptune) any hope of fulfilling her own ambitions. Is her life (or at least the image of her life as seen by the child) illustrative of Neptune, too? Was she perceived as feeling lost or victimized when her husband left? Was there an attempt to blot out the misery of her less-than-ideal life? Did she consider herself a martyr or yearn for life to be more magical? Perhaps she searched for greater meaning or spirituality. If we were to assign one parent to a house in this circumstance, which one would it be?

When I began researching parental significators, a student of mine, **Mark** (chart opposite), with Mercury in Aquarius in the 4th House told me the story of his childhood. His father was a Socialist who had Marxist literature around the house and often engaged the family in political discussions and social debates. His mother was a 'very sociable person who often invited friends over to the house', where they would chat about anything and everyone. Here, the 4th-House Mercury in Aquarius appears to reveal the influence of both parents. But more significantly, it tells of his *home environment*; it speaks of his perception of home, the activities taking place and the messages received there.

I started to collect parental stories and these kept leading back to the luminaries (the Sun and Moon) and the signs on the MC and IC, rather than the entire 10th and 4th Houses themselves. Images, impressions, facts and descriptions of our chief caretakers, Father and Mother, are best seen by the Sun and Moon, respectively. They describe our perception and awareness of our parents, how they impacted our life and what we feel/felt was important to them. In addition, the dispositor of the Sun and Moon is a planet *in operation*, functioning to 'serve' the luminary by carrying out *specific* tasks.

'Mark'

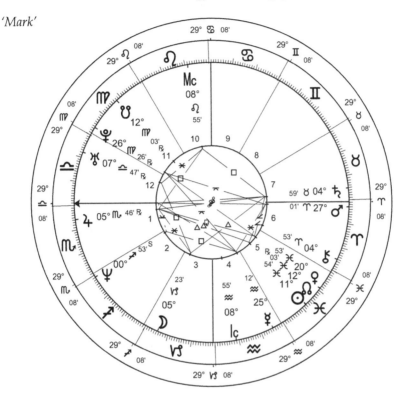

The MC/IC axis speaks of messages that we receive from parents/parental figures that create personal, deep-rooted principles (IC) and the social ethics and work philosophies shaping our place in the world (MC). Looking back, our first image of success (MC) comes from our parents: how they compared to other children's parents 'out there' in the world, how their own aspirations blossomed. Whether or not their tree was 'in bloom', the seeds of their experiences were planted in our IC, and this nurtures, cultivates, shackles or delays the development of the foliage and fruit that appear at our MC. What is inherited and instilled at the IC is called upon to be manifested through the social- and work-based lens of the MC.

Some Stories

The father of **'Adam'** (chart on following page) was shut out from Adam's early life by his mother, and both mother and son were

'Adam'

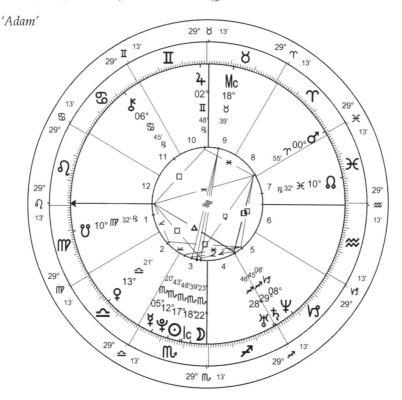

dominated by her own father. The grandfather attempted to dictate Adam's every move, even sleeping in the same bedroom as the teenager. In Adam's chart, the Sun (father) is contained (trapped on either side) by Pluto and the Moon – all three are in Scorpio and conjunct the IC. There are often early experiences of powerlessness and a lack of control over one's 'destination' when Scorpio is on the IC. A way forward may be to cultivate a professional life that is profitable, steady and secure (Taurus MC). Those with this potent axis often work to amass something of material value and permanence, to fend off the waves of emotional crises that are anticipated and feared. Adam's Scorpio planets are disposited by Mars in Aries: the boy's outlet was sport, but this was thwarted by a series of accidents to his ankles and knees on the football field (Mars squares Saturn–Uranus). Injured, he later trained as a mechanic and began teaching football to earn enough to leave home and gain a firm footing in the world (Taurus MC).

'James'

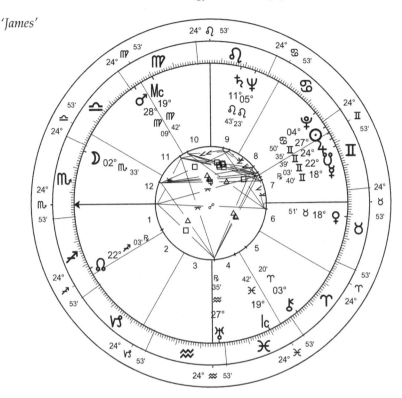

'James' grew up in dire poverty with an alcoholic mother who took an intense dislike to him (one manifestation of his Moon in Scorpio square Neptune in Leo) and a philandering father whom James nevertheless admired and elevated (Sun conjunct Jupiter in Gemini). With limited schooling available, his father encouraged James to read and educate himself (Sun–Jupiter in Gemini), learn a craft (Virgo MC), and move beyond the limits set by the religion that engulfed his community (Pisces IC).

An early school event changed James' life. His father, when asked by the headmaster what he thought young James could do with his life, hadn't considered any options – so he didn't speak up! This enraged the young Gemini, who was an exceptional student; it had been a chance for him to be given some help and direction before he left school. Instead, he spent the next three years on the streets selling newspapers and later bitterly regretted it. This is one of the life messages for Gemini: this sign encounters people who

'Grace'

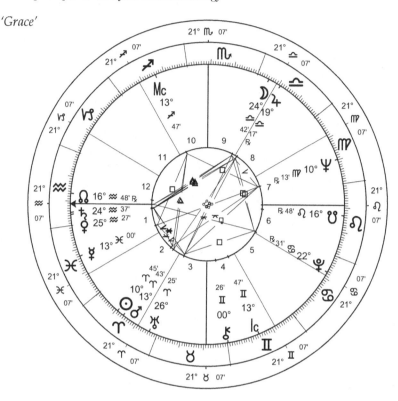

stay silent or don't understand, so the Gemini person's motivation becomes a desire to communicate, to be heard and understood. With a mutable Pisces IC and Virgo MC, James took to cycling and, for a while, gambled to escape the hardship and penury of his life. He later trained as an engineer and technician (Mars is near the MC in Virgo). While learning his craft, he became a union representative who fought and 'spoke up' for the rights of his fellow workers.

For **'Grace'**, her father and the subsequent men in her life are described well by her Sun conjunct Mars in Aries: her dad was a pioneering radiologist and dentist who had been burned on the brain by X-ray equipment, which caused rages and blackouts. Grace would later get involved with three men who were either aggressive, philandering or physically abusive partners. If Aries is a sign of violence, Grace's Moon in Libra describes her mother, who would run away from the home following a confrontation with her aggressive husband. This happened from the time Grace was three (note the Moon–Jupiter conjunction opposite Uranus and various 3° orbs in the chart that would have been triggered by Solar Arc at age three: Sun–Mars, Ascendant–Saturn, Mercury–Neptune, Neptune–MC) until her mother's final departure eight years later. Grace's childhood had many unanswered questions (Gemini IC). Missing a mother, she had no one to teach her about menstruation, sex and hygiene. And the big unanswered questions were 'Where did my mother go?' and 'Is she coming back?'

With Mercury opposite Neptune T-square the MC in Sagittarius, Grace recalls a time when, after she was naughty, her father said, 'As long as you tell me the truth about what you did, you'll be OK with me.' But she wasn't. She confessed and was punished. So, she learned to lie to avoid her father's wrath and a repeat betrayal.

Later, Grace spent much of her marriage not trusting her husband's words and suspecting him of affairs, subtly trying to discern the truth and read between the lines/lies. The mutable (= avoidance) T-square speaks of, among other things, deceit, illusion, the distortion of facts and concealment of the truth, yet the Sagittarius MC as the apex points to discovering her own truth out of these mixed messages (Gemini IC).

She found her calling late in life as a Justice of the Peace, deliberating on criminal cases (Moon–Jupiter in Libra) from an elevated position of authority (Sagittarius MC). In the UK, a magistrates' court deals with 'small' crimes such as petty theft, deception, trespass, stalking and illegal use of motor vehicles – apt therapy for Mercury in Pisces opposite Neptune in Virgo.

After a life of many unanswered questions, Grace was able to use her talent for spotting the details in evidence to reveal the truth and reach her own conclusions.

Chapter 7

TEARING UP SCRIPTS: THE MOON, SATURN AND THE FEAR-DRIVEN PATTERNS OF CHILDHOOD

WRITTEN WITH LYNNE WILSON

The principles of 'Script' were devised and developed by spiritual teacher Barbara Muhl, who ran workshops in the 1980s and wrote a book about it entitled *Script, Kid and Fantasyland*. A script is a fear-based belief and conclusion we've made about ourselves and our world, such as 'I will always be rejected in love' or 'I will never get it right'. It's a hidden, emotional mantra that describes what we believe will happen to us — it is the driving force behind many of the miserable events in our lives.

A few years ago, I was introduced to this concept by my friend and colleague, Lynne Beale (later Wilson), who is an astrologer and metaphysician. It spoke to me immediately and appeared to mirror facets of astrological Saturn and the Moon. So, in late 2011, Lynne and I put together a seminar to play detective and see whether or not the scripts described by attendees could be revealed by these planets in their charts. And the MC/IC axis – the natural rulers of which, in quadrant house systems, are linked to 'caretakers' Saturn (Capricorn/10th-House cusp) and the Moon (Cancer/4th), respectively – was it implicated, too?

The Principles: What Is a Script?
All scripts begin with extreme statements like 'I will always ... [be betrayed by those I trust]', 'I'm always ... [to blame]', or 'I will never ... [be taken care of]'. *Always* (an unwelcome commitment) and *never* (the denial of a need) are the sources of the fear.

Scripts were written by us when we were ignorant, immature children with undeveloped consciousness. These scripts/conclusions/beliefs later go on to control our behaviour and sabotage our relationships. They manifest as events that trigger emotions and keep us stuck in a rut of self-fulfilling prophecies.

Here, we can see sides of the Moon and Saturn at work. Scripts become our scaffolding (Saturn) and safety blankets (Moon). Fatalism and clinging to the discomfort of the familiar (Saturn–Moon) create a safe prison, which perpetuates unhappiness and impedes growth. But as with astrological Saturn, these scripts become our life work to address and overcome.

In truth, a script won't stand up to rational examination in adulthood, because the rational mind was not involved when we wrote it as a child (Moon). Back then, based on limited information, we interpreted an event and came to a conclusion that was crystallized (Saturn) into a belief and rigidly maintained.

The Process: Defence Mechanisms

Rejection is the fear underlying the scripts we write. We grow up carrying these beliefs/scripts and are terrified to let others see them, going to great lengths to ensure that our scripts don't get read. We develop behaviours to prevent others from discovering what we think is the 'truth' about us – the fear of having our scripts read is sometimes so extreme that it feels tantamount to facing death.

We then engage in resistance behaviour (Saturn–Moon), mistaken in our thinking that these are survival techniques. For instance:

Fear of Being ...	Resistance Behaviour
Unaccepted	We become indispensable.
Judged, criticized	We become our own boss to avoid being put down.
Ignored	We become someone who can't be ignored.
Abandoned	We leave relationships before others do.
Rejected	We become people-pleasers or do-gooders.

The one fear we all share, that underlies all scripts, is 'I will never be good enough' – and this can result in workaholism, where we labour in order to prove our worth.

Along with resistance behaviour, we create fantasies to make our script-ridden life more tolerable, hoping that the result will bring the script to an end. One example could be dreaming that we will meet someone who won't ignore, ridicule or abandon us. Yet, replacing the script with a 'fantasy script' gives us false hope and distracts us from the real problem, thereby helping to sustain the main, original script. For instance, we might return to the same abusive person over and over again, hoping that they'll provide what we need this time. Another potentially endless cycle would be attempting to seek love from parents who have demonstrated for years that they are incapable of delivering it.

Engaging Others in the Script

Despite our dread of scripts becoming known, they are magnetic and attract people ('Readers') who will unintentionally read them out to us (and we, in turn, unintentionally read theirs). Barbara Muhl says that a script creates 'an auric field': we unconsciously seek out relationships where the other person will engage in a dialogue to confirm our incorrect beliefs, e.g., the fear that we are being ignored, betrayed or abandoned or that we'll never get it right or be good enough.

How does this work? We hear others say (or see them do) exactly what the script declares. In doing so, they confirm our worst, terrifying fear: that the script is who we are underneath. But this fear is really F.E.A.R. (False Evidence Appearing Real). In astrology, we see this with placements and aspects: Moon–Uranus people develop a great sensitivity to rejection and will often find themselves in a situation where they meet exactly that – or their compensatory 'resistance' behaviour (e.g., being too clingy or needy) triggers the same result.

The Sequence

Scripts are the cause of our negative behaviour. And then the behaviour sustains the script, others confirm it and it is reinforced. Using an example from Lynne's casebook, 'Antonia' (a pseudonym), the circularity runs like this:

1. **Early childhood experience/event** Antonia's younger brother was born when she was three-and-a-half years old. When her mother couldn't cope, Antonia was moved out of the family home and looked after by her grandparents for several years.

2. **Interpretation** In the battle for mother's love and attention, Antonia lost out to her brother. 'I am not as loved, important, or wanted as my brother.'

3. **Conclusion ('always/never') – this forms the script/belief** 'I'm never chosen. I'll always be second. I'll never be good enough.'

4. **Development of resistance behaviours and/or creating a fantasy (false hope) to escape the script** Resistance: Antonia became obsessed with looking perfect and being desirable to potential suitors in the hope that she would win their attention. Fantasy: 'There is someone who will make me #1 and desire me the most above all others.'

5. **Unconsciously attracting a Reader** Yet, she found herself attracted to and pursuing men who were unavailable or who had other priorities. (Here, she is setting herself up for a competition, re-enacting the earlier sibling situation.)

6. **Receiving the Reader's confirmation** The men would tell her they didn't want to be in a committed relationship – or the indirect message was that they were choosing work, friends, or a partner over her.

7. **(Over-)Reacting to the confirmation (being 'in script')** Antonia would respond with temper tantrums; she would give mixed messages (coming on strong and then backing off) and participate in acts of self-degradation to win her man's favour.

8. **Reinforcement of the belief** 'Someone else will always be more important than I am.'

9. **Result/further manifestation (repeat of the script)**
   'I'll keep competing until I win that man who will choose
   me and place me first.' *Then back to No. 4. Development of
   resistance behaviours and fantasy scripts.*

It's no surprise to learn that Antonia has Saturn in the 3rd House
of siblings widely conjunct Venus (comparisons, relationships),
with both squaring unavailable, sacrificial Neptune. Note that
her brother was born when she was three-and-a-half: the orb of
the Saturn–Neptune square is 3.5°, as is that of the Sun–Mercury
conjunction, indicating the importance (Sun) of the sibling
(Mercury). The Moon in Virgo closely squares her Ascendant/
Descendant axis, suggesting that she is highly critical/obsessive
of her (and her partner's) appearance, over-analytical of the
relationship and can adopt a role of servitude, victimization or
self-sacrifice in relationships.

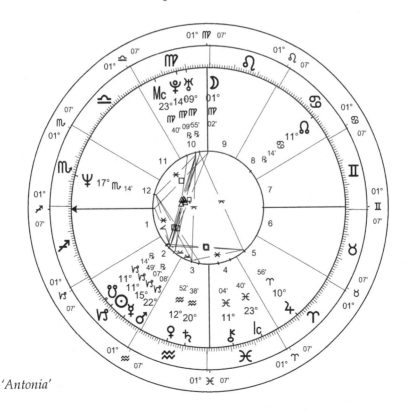

'Antonia'

'Anthony'

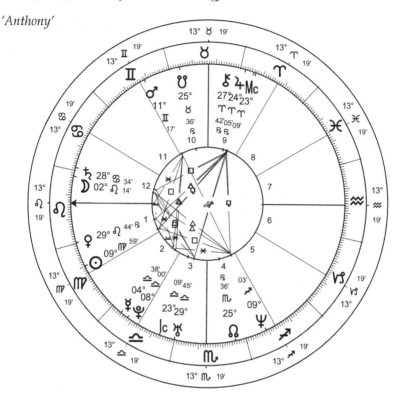

Another Case Study

In the seminar Lynne and I held, several students offered examples of scripts in action. 'Anthony' spoke of his irritation and fury when letters go astray or e-mails don't arrive; his Midheaven (MC) ruler, Mars in Gemini, opposing Neptune offers one astrological significator for this. Looking further into his issue, he complained of often feeling left out – not being privy to certain facts – and sometimes 'irrationally' suspicious that others were withholding or concealing information from him. (Note, too, Mercury conjunct Pluto.)

Looking back to his childhood for a time when he may have written such a script, Anthony remembered the same emotion of being excluded when he was three years old. He and his mother were involved in a minor car crash; upon arriving home, she sent him to bed and told him to sleep. Instead, he sat by his bedroom window watching the car being fixed and neighbours gathering to discuss the drama. To him, it felt like a party. He was furious at being left out of the spectacle outside.

By being packed off to bed, Anthony interpreted this as his being ignored, marginalized or excluded because he was an inconvenience. His mother hadn't said this, but it's what he had concluded.

As we can see in his chart, the Moon in Leo needs to be important and can be extra sensitive to being ignored and missing out on the fun. How frustrating for a young Leo Moon child to have a drama and not be allowed to take centre stage! We notice the Moon and Saturn conjunct within a 3.5° orb in the 12th House. This aspect (along with an aptly suspicious Mercury–Pluto conjunction) would have perfected by Solar Arc direction around the time of this seemingly minor but script-making event.

Rather than seeing that his mother was acting as a caretaker (Moon–Saturn), Anthony wrote a script that concluded that her actions and the resulting 'missing out' reflected something about him. (With the Moon–Saturn conjunction in the 12th, he admitted to feeling 'almost locked in prison' in his bedroom that evening.) Anthony also stated, in the seminar, that part of his frustration was at not being able to care (Moon) for his mother at that moment because he'd obeyed (Saturn) her order to go to bed.

So, the conclusion/script may be that he will 'always be excluded and miss out'. Events and people in adulthood will 'conspire' to reinforce that belief.

And what does Anthony now do for a living? He works as a hygiene health inspector for restaurants. Note that the Sun in Virgo is in a T-square to the Mars–Neptune opposition, and Saturn in late Cancer conjoins the Moon. A stickler for details and correct information, he is in charge of ticking off the boxes and controlling the data so that no information evades him. But this won't tear up his script and his complaints about mislaid letters and withheld information at work betray this.

Tearing Up the Script

We create events and experiences based on our beliefs. Put another way, our life mirrors our mind and thoughts. Tearing up our scripts requires much work. Astrologically, we are not talking about the Sun: the architect of our aspirations, the power to choose consciously and the solar principle of 'becoming who we were born to be'. Instead, we are dealing with the painful, dark side of the Moon: an attachment to unconscious scripts written early in life. The Moon is the container – a storehouse – of experiences, our memory bank of responses. And along with the lunar principle, we have to contend with Saturn, which crystallizes these early experiences into a hardened shell that resists change.

There are three steps to tearing up scripts:

1. **Identify the scripts and corresponding resistance behaviours** To identify scripts, we must look for patterns in the most painful of our life experiences: to look specifically at what was felt, what we told ourselves and came to believe. For instance, if we were let down or ignored, our script may be 'I am not worth spending time with'. Our experiences later could be that people cancel on us, or we sense that they really want to be anywhere than with us. We must then look at our resistance behaviour – for example, going overboard, being indispensable, or trying too hard to be liked so that others want to spend time with us and not reject us. These behaviours never create the desired result. We still have the initial script read to us: others may avoid us because they find us too intense or smothering.

2. **Recognize which events in our lives are script events** We must be aware enough to question the script, go deep and describe what it feels like each time we're in the middle of it. One way to recognize that we're having a script event is to identify feelings of anxiety, fear or threat. There is an emotion present; we're having a reaction and take it personally, often to an irrational or exaggerated extent. Feelings are real – the real 'us' in any moment. But emotions are *feelings plus mental dialogue* – things we tell ourselves about the feelings. Emotions are conditioned responses based on old conclusions (scripts) from past experiences. One way of seeing the difference is to remember the adage: 'Pain [a feeling] is inevitable; suffering [an emotion] is optional.'

3. **Accept 100% responsibility for our own scripts**
Healing often starts with slowly diluting the intensity of the
script's power over us, recognizing a script in action and
slowly backing off from reacting to this with emotion. The
next step is to correct the false beliefs that our scripts are
based on. This is done by forgiving the ignorant child in us
who wrote it when we were young. Then, we can forgive
others for powerlessly reading the script to us (we choose
them to do so!) and we can refrain from participating in
anybody else's script.

In Anthony's case, rather than seeking to blame his mother for
leaving him out of the drama (Saturn conjunct the Moon in Leo),
as an adult he could seek to understand that he made a choice
at that time, one based on limited experience. And what did he
value more? He valued sticking to the rules, keeping harmony
and not disappointing his mother – this was his reaction then, it
doesn't have to be a perpetual response today. (This is perhaps
where the MC in Aries versus the IC in Libra comes into effect:
the challenge to do your own thing rather than keeping the peace
and pleasing others.) The emotion linked to the event is perhaps
annoyance at his decision not to break the rules and his inability
to do what he wanted. Back then, anger won over as he sat
cloistered in his (12th House) room, fuming at being left out.
As an adult, he's taken a position where he administers the rules
and has the power to penalize those who break them. Yet, he's in
a system that is rule-laden and he's not breaking any, so it seems
that he is still perpetuating the cycle.

A script can be torn up by recognizing it while it's happening
(rather than resisting it or indulging in fantasy behaviour). We can
then get to the root of the fear (Saturn) and correct the false beliefs
and behaviours (Moon) it is based on. We need to accept that
we have created the script from limited information and that
when we know better, we do better. Only we can resolve/eliminate
it and feel real – liberated – when we finally tear it up.

It is also helpful to start eliminating the 'always' and 'never'
mantras by remembering the times when scripts didn't come to
pass in the negative way we expected. (This reminds me of the
actors who confess to reading ten reviews, but ignore the nine

good ones and only remember the critical one.) We can also start listening to and believing those who work with us positively and don't read our scripts back to us.

Scripts remind us of the powerful conscious and unconscious decisions we make concerning the major facets of our horoscopes – and how easy it is to turn an aspect into a negative state of being. Subsequent research since the seminar suggests that working with a client's Saturn and Moon patterns will reveal their scripts and as astrologers we can help them to focus on new, positive ways of exploring these placements.

About the co-author: Lynne Wilson (née Beale) studied at the Centre for Psychological Astrology (CPA) in the early 1990s and qualified as a metaphysical practitioner with the Metaphysical Society for the Expansion of Consciousness in 1995. She teaches across England and runs her own practice in Eastbourne.

Chapter 8

THE SUN, MOON AND MIDHEAVEN IN VOCATION

The birth chart offers clear signposts that reveal vocational drives, career choices, work avenues and employment options. In this essay, I'll be looking at three areas in the horoscope, ones that I most associate with vocation, everyday work routines and making an individual contribution to society. These are:

- The Sun – our calling;
- The Moon – our daily work needs;
- The Midheaven (Medium Coeli, the 'MC') – our social/ professional persona and contribution.

These three parts of our chart can point us towards paths of personal success and professional fulfilment. In order to make the most of each, we should consider:

- Following our Sun – by engaging in activity suggested by its placement and aspects, for we receive internal nourishment and external recognition by doing this;
- Feeding our Moon – by ensuring we are surrounded by nourishing people and supportive environments; and
- Directing the Sun through our Midheaven – by expressing our fundamental self in the outer world, building a legacy and contributing to a larger goal/greater good.

There are other areas of the horoscope that relate to work and career – from the Earth houses (2, 6, 10) to the Ascendant (our agenda and one-to-one interactions) and Mercury (our mental aptitudes) – but even though the chart should always be read as a whole, this essay focuses chiefly on the Sun, Moon and the Midheaven.

A vocation is something that gives our life meaning and significance; it occupies a place in us of creativity and fertility. It is something we feel compelled and 'called' to do (from *vocare*, to call, and *vocationem*, spiritual calling). The vocation is a fundamental area of our life to which we are dedicated. It may have little to do with our basic job or how we earn a living. Our vocation lies *within* us; it is at the core of our reason for being/ living. It is understandable then that some astrologers, including me, link vocation to the astrological Sun rather than a house or horoscope angle.

Its link to the Sun in our horoscope suggests that our calling is something 'deep down inside ourselves' striving to appear, to make a significant personal statement and to stamp an individual mark (the Sun) in some way onto the world around us. In his eloquent and poetic publication, *An Astrological Guide to a Fulfilling Vocation*, astrologer Brian Clark writes:

> Vocation is an aspect of our fate, an integral part of our character which seeks expression … In contemporary terms we can imagine vocation as the calling to one's authentic role in the world. It is a calling from deep inside the self, an internal voice. The language of the soul speaks through images and feelings, not with literal words. Hence this inner voice, this calling, is often felt as a yearning to fulfil one's self creatively. The language of images needs to be engaged with, not deciphered. A vocation is not a literal pathway already existing in the world, but rather something that is shaped over the course of our lives as we come to know ourselves. Vocation is the calling to attend to soul in the world, not a literal mission.[1]

A calling appears to be beyond any single profession or line of work. The vocation isn't a clear job definition. It is what lies at the heart of the matter, the purpose behind the activity. Writing or composing is not a vocation per se; the vocation is the *life force and energy behind* the composition, the motivation that prompts a desire to write and communicate one's message. Astrology isn't a vocation either; it's a vehicle – a language, method, tool – to help us *fulfil our calling*. Each astrologer becomes a specific type of practitioner and for very different, individual reasons (as seen in their natal horoscope). We have astrologers who are researchers, counsellors, the answerers of questions, wannabe gurus ...

Consider these three questions: Have you discovered your own vocation? Are you actively engaged in this? And are you earning a living by following this calling exclusively?

The reality is that most of us don't work in the field that truly expresses who we are or want to be. We are on automatic pilot. Most of us are not aroused by the work we do. It's a means to an end and perhaps that end is getting to the point of retirement in order to follow a cherished dream. It's no disgrace to earn your living without following your vocation, but it is a disgrace to put it off and wait 'until there's more time'!

Do we all have a vocation? In *The Soul's Code*,[2] James Hillman writes that each of us has a 'daimon', a guardian angel or spirit, that endeavours to help us fulfil our calling. Some of us have a very strong sense of vocation, often from early on in life. In the horoscope there is usually a repetitive pattern – a theme that recurs in so many ways that we cannot ignore it and have little choice but to express it. Perhaps the more contradictory overtones and 'choices' there are in our charts, the more likely it is that we won't feel compelled to explore our vocation until later in life, if at all. One thing is for sure: people don't feel as condemned to accept their lot nowadays and are more aware of a need to pursue work that expresses who they are (whether this is a hobby or paid employment).

As I wrote in *The Mountain Astrologer* (Oct./Nov. 2010):

Getting in touch with our calling is a matter of defining it and being in a time/place/environment that allows it to be nurtured into manifestation and to bloom ... Looking back on a life we may discover, as James Hillman wrote in *The Soul's Code* (Warner, 1997), that events have conspired to bring our particular calling (as carried by the daimon) to the fore to fulfil its function.

Elemental Considerations

There is no placement or planetary combination that says 'plumber', 'astrologer' or 'politician' or one that identifies us as the next 'pop idol'. (Although astrologers had a somewhat easier job a hundred or more years ago when there were fewer professional choices.) Trying to pinpoint an actual job for a client might be a thankless and unproductive task. It is better to work on identifying their needs, their talents and goals than to create a list of specific job roles.

We can ask the client what excites them, what they are drawn to and ask, for example, whether they consider themselves a:

- Communicator
- Educator/teacher
- Seller/agent/go-between
- Manager/organizer
- Constructor/builder/developer
- Maintainer
- Protector
- Campaigner
- Server/supporter

The horoscope reveals the motivations, qualities and passions that lie behind a person's work. For instance, here in the UK, barristers do a different job from solicitors. They have the 'right of audience' in court and, instructed by a solicitor, they are in the business of advocacy – pleading, arguing – before a judge. Although Mercury may 'govern' advocacy, the birth charts (and Mercurys) of these barristers will be as varied as their own individual motivations, professional styles and communication skills. These drives, styles and potential skills, rather than the actual jobs, are the parts that I believe can be seen in the horoscope.

Why the person is doing their job is always more important than *what* they're actually doing for a living. (The 'why' can be seen in repetitive chart themes, key planetary placements and elemental balances/imbalances.)

For instance, consider the elements of the Sun, Moon and MC signs. Is our calling (the Sun) an Earthy one? Does our daily working environment (the Moon) need an Airy outlet? What is the fundamental motivation behind gaining recognition and contributing to the world around us (the MC) – does it come from Fire, Earth, Air or Water? Perhaps one element dominates the trio.

The elements reveal what motivates us – what stimulates, inspires and spurs us on towards goals and personal fulfilment: our incentive.

Fire ignites in fields offering challenge, competition, excitement and risk. Fiery people seek glory, greatness and recognition of their individuality rather than money or position; they wish to enthuse others and are fuelled by passion and optimism. They are hustlers, (self-)promoters, evangelists, visionaries, inspirational teachers or leaders/motivators/life coaches/instructors.

Earth works well in fields offering safety, expediency/ usefulness and tangible results. Earth signs wish to leave the world a better place than they found it. They seek routine and a steady income; they stay with the known and familiar and are security-conscious. Gaining pleasure from a job well done, Earthy people are reliable providers, dependable 'rocks' and productive, purposeful 'realists'. They are craftsmen, builders (of anything, from homes to empires), lovers and supporters of their countryside; they are sensualists and work directly with their bodies (sports, physical work).

Air comes alive in fields offering exchange, dialogue and debate. These individuals seek interaction, variety and travel; they want to learn, read, question and communicate. Air people are interested in theory, concept, the abstract, formulas, patterns; they analyse, deduce and reason. They are fascinated by *people* and make natural communicators, salespeople, persuaders and advocates.

Water seeks work in fields offering an emotional connection. Water people focus on human values and aim to be of service to the human condition and endeavour to help, care and develop emotional ties. They perceive that which has not been verbalized and connect to that which cannot be articulated. Water signs are empathetic and sympathetic; their antennae scan atmospheres and pick up nuance; they have spot-on judgements and gut instincts. They are the carers, counsellors, therapists and intuitives.

Before we look at the Sun and Midheaven as principal components of *realizing* and *manifesting* our vocation, let's look at the Moon and its role in our working life.

The Moon

- Our 'backpack' of needs
- The working environment
- The routine job and our attitude towards it
- Fundamental relationship needs

What do we need at work? What kind of work will *feed* us on a daily basis? What sort of environment will make us feel comfortable, safe and secure? The Moon has much to say about our daily rhythms, feelings and habits. And, as most of us spend one third of our adult life at work, the Moon is a fundamental consideration. The office needs to be a place we want to go to in the morning!

Noel Tyl has written of the planets and 'need fulfilment' and the Moon sign being the 'reigning need' of the personality. In his chapter from *How to Use Vocational Astrology for Success in the Workplace*, he writes:

> Fulfilment of our personal reigning need in life must somehow be abetted by the work atmosphere, pace, energy, growth stimulus and image trappings of our job, cued by the Moon and its sign ... We see how important it is, indeed, that the job situation assimilate, support and/or reward the need fulfilment behaviours.[3]

The Moon indicates what we're *sensitive* to. It's fascinating how some people are drawn to (or compelled to engage in) daily routines that challenge this most vulnerable area of their lives/ charts. Some of my actor and singer friends and clients have Moon–Uranus contacts, suggesting that they rebel against (Uranus) sedentary 9-to-5 office work (Moon) and are sensitive (Moon) to rejection (Uranus). Yet many have to audition or perform on a daily basis, where the threat of rejection or a pie in the face is forever present. Somehow they gravitate towards a scenario that pushes their most sensitive of buttons. Here we can also sense the calling (Sun) being stronger than simple daily needs (Moon).

If we wish to consider the most suitable environment at work, we must look to the Moon complex (its placement and aspects).

What is our favoured working habitat? A Moon sign in Air needs light, space and an airy office – without being swamped by emotional, clingy co-workers. Fixed signs need a permanent desk, not some swap-and-change office environment! The Moon in Aries needs a busy environment and the autonomy to make decisions, to spearhead their own ventures and to set targets. The Moon in Cancer needs a nest, to feel a sense of belonging at work. The Moon in Libra favours a working environment of discussion, debate and joint decision-making, where there is respect for each other's opinions. Astrologer Faye Cossar suggests that we go further by considering lunar synastry with a company's horoscope to see whether we will feel 'at home' there.[4]

The Moon represents the level of deeper communication between co-workers, those non-verbal interactions that make up a relationship and go beyond the exchange of information, facts or gossip (Mercury) or the pleasantries (Venus). It is essential to help a client acknowledge their Moon, which will give them permission to want (and ask for) more at work. Identifying their office needs is often a client's first step towards improving their daily working lives.

A few years ago I read Judith Hill's book *Vocational Astrology*, which presents a wonderful collection of 100 horoscopes of individuals who have successful jobs *and* enjoy their work. I started to realize the importance of the Moon and its dispositor in describing the work, routine and rhythms that *nourish* us. For instance, if the natal Moon is in Scorpio, the daily job and regular activities need to allow some room for penetrating, probing analysis. People with the Moon in Scorpio want to engage in the investigative process; they are drawn to everyday work that is deep and in which they can express passion. Often they are involved in work that regularly brings up life-or-death matters, crisis-driven situations or political undercurrents.

The Moon's dispositor (i.e. the planet that rules the Moon sign) provides additional, specific information about what lies behind our working needs. Continuing with our Moon in Scorpio example, Mars and Pluto become the dispositors (but I'd recommend leaving Pluto for more generational matters, and focusing on the placement of Mars). If Mars were in Virgo, this would suggest a craftsman-like approach to tasks and a need to be helpful/useful in whatever penetrating, probing work (Scorpio) is pursued.

So, what do Scorpio and Virgo have in common and how do they differ? Both signs are concerned with research, service, perception, control and health matters (the sickness and the cure) – Scorpio from a Watery, emotional perspective, Virgo from an Earthy, practical and expedient angle. Scorpio seeks respect and privacy but has a strong instinct to merge with another, while Virgo works well in a cloistered environment and is comfortable with its aloneness, cherishing periods of solitude.

One example I have of this combination belongs to a client born with Moon–Neptune in Scorpio (and Mars in Virgo) who looked after his sick mother in the family home for twenty-nine years. She had had a stroke when he was thirteen years old and, rather than becoming a flight attendant and travel the world (a childhood dream), he trained as a nurse – partly in order to attend to her.

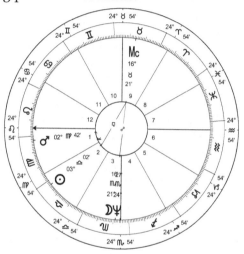

Over the years he quite literally saved her life on a number of occasions, *moving mountains, against the odds* (Scorpio) when she became sick (Virgo) and doctors held out no chance of survival. For my client, the reason behind (dispositor) the desire to engage in deep, transformative work (Moon in Scorpio) was a need to get things back in order and functioning efficiently ('healthily') again (Mars in Virgo). Put another way, an innate desire *to be in control* of one's daily environment (Moon in Scorpio) stemmed from a deeper fear of chaos or sickness (the dispositor Mars in Virgo).

The Sun

- What makes our heart sing
- Labours of love
- Following our inner self and sense of purpose
- What we were born to do
- Vocation

The astrological meaning of the Sun is often dismissed or simply reduced to adjectives and keyword traits of its sign position. Perhaps this is because one's *core* is more difficult to capture, articulate and elucidate. Yet those adjectives hammered into us early on in our astrological education are useful here. Each sign's characteristics are valuable when remembering the qualities we can bring to our professional lives.

What are we *really* here to do? The Sun says much about our true purpose in life and what we're striving to become. The focus we place on the Sun in Western astrology suggests how much we value the idea of having an individual purpose, a destiny to discover or a life path that is special and unique in its message. Perhaps the reason Sun-sign astrology (in columns and books) is so popular and widespread is that it puts us at the centre of our universe, serving as a daily reminder of who we essentially are, our identity, life force and individual journey – what makes us special and different from the crowd. Yet astrology's enduring appeal lies in its ability to combine this specific sense of individual destiny with particular birth chart groupings (e.g. Air signs), signatures/overtones (e.g. Mercury-themed charts) and types (e.g. Geminis), so we know we are not alone in this pursuit of a unique path.

Astrologer Kim Falconer reminds us that:

> We don't automatically have all the solar traits indicated by our Sun sign. It is much more an assignment than a published thesis, and we have to work hard for most or all of our lives to complete it … Understanding our solar needs can go a long way toward developing natural abilities.[5]

One of our jobs as astrologers is to speak to the very core of who our clients are, to illuminate their Sun, to share what astrology says about who they were born to be; we must help them recognize and live out their Sun archetype. It is often said that we shine and feel alive when we engage in activity suggested by our Sun. This process of helping clients to rekindle their life mission should take into account the Sun's complex: its sign and house position, as well as aspects.

The Sun is our type of *heart*. For instance, the Sun–Neptune person needs to connect to a spiritual centre, to follow their compassionate, intuitive and empathetic heart – one with heightened sensory ability, colour, flair, art and imagination.

When we define the natal Sun, we and our clients can begin to *realize* and *manifest* this most personal and compelling of journeys. Ideally we can do this for ourselves, rather than having someone act it out for us (e.g. marrying someone who epitomizes our Sun complex). And if we don't constructively engage with the messages of our Sun sign, we languish in the opposite sign. The warning is to follow your Sun or wallow in the worst of its polar opposite!

The Midheaven

- The best pathway to recognition
- Our definition of success
- A facet of our public persona; our reputation
- Making a contribution to the world around us
- Aims, direction, status, goals

The Midheaven shows the qualities we admire, elevate and wish to emulate. It can also be a 'social shorthand' for the ways in which we describe to others what we do and, in turn, phrases that are used by others to introduce and describe us. As the most elevated point in the horoscope, the MC is the route up from our inner, private world (IC) and out into the world. We put ourselves 'out there' through our MC sign, whether that's in society, in a local group or on national TV. It is descriptive of our reputation. Rather than our character (Sun) or personal temperament (Moon), the MC reveals our image and, along with the Ascendant, it informs how we 'dress ourselves up' and construct a public persona.

Success in the horoscope is symbolized by the MC – it's the attainment of a goal and some form of recognition for our strivings. In *Money: How to Find It with Astrology*, Lois Rodden describes the MC as the best pathway to social recognition and worldly success – the conduct we need in order to succeed and achieve status and recognition. She writes, 'Success is shown in a chart by the extent to which we assume the role symbolized by the MC voluntarily and constructively.'[6] In essence, the MC says much about how and where we can express professionalism (literally *to declare aloud or in public*, to profess one's vows).

The MC–IC axis reveals the early messages we received from parental figures about 'the big world out there' – ones that relate to personal, deep-rooted principles (Imum Coeli, the IC) and social/work philosophies that affect our place in the world (MC). The axis says much about what was stressed as important by our parents. The MC is a call to leave the comfort zone and 'family name' of the IC and branch out on our own, to dare to create our own name and reputation. What is instilled early on in life at the IC (ideas, belief systems, messages from parents) is called up to be manifested in the world through the MC.[7]

The MC is very different from the zenith (90° from the Ascendant), although they can occasionally share the same degree. The zenith (the cusp of the 10th House by Equal house division) and the subsequent 10th House relate to mundane work and career matters. A transit/progression/direction to the zenith (nonagesimal) degree brings up important work developments, while the same to the MC will coincide with something more meaningful about life direction and will have an impact on our reputation and perception of our social role. The MC is a more personal point that has links to deep-seated drives to achieve something significant in the outer world and resolve parental influences later in our social life.

Directing the Sun through the Lens of the Midheaven

Ideally, once we've identified and started attending to our daily needs (the Moon), we can concentrate on the bigger yet more intimate picture: fulfilling a personal, creative desire (the Sun as our vocation) and sharing this 'mission' with the people around us (the Midheaven).

The MC is the culmination and summit of the chart (literally and figuratively, as the most elevated point a planet can reach in its daily cycle). It is the means by which we can channel other features of our horoscope (revealing our talents, needs and desires) into society or a public/social/work arena.

Working the message of the Sun (the inner light) through the filter/lens of the MC (the external prism) is a way of fulfilling our destination/destiny/role in a social or public context. It is not necessarily about achieving acclaim or public renown – or even earning a living in the area of our vocation. It is about finding a way to project our solar philosophies, purpose and creative endeavours through the lens of the MC and make a meaningful, personal contribution (the Sun) to the world around us (the MC). It's about 'putting our vocation' *out there* and inspiring, helping, awakening, supporting and educating others. The MC complex is the signpost to how we can do this successfully and have others recognize our contribution.

Consider the Sun like a 'beam of light' (the colour of this light is seen by the sign placement, the motivation by the element of its sign, the force/energy by aspects from the planets). Imagine it when projected through the prism of a particular MC – when it's refracted into society. The MC is the most ideal way of actualizing potential (the Sun) in order to 'become ourselves' in society – it shows how we can bear fruit socially and professionally. How we manifest in society what we feel summoned to do is shown by how well we are able to integrate the MC complex (its sign and aspects) with the Sun complex. Are these points immediately compatible? Is their conversation fluent, the message easily accessed and understood? Or perhaps these two complexes require more effort and awareness to make manifest one's essential 'heart' (the Sun) and receive some sort of recognition and validation.

The MC, like the other three angles, is linked to the path of the Sun. The Sun is on the MC around noon each day, so many people born in the late morning/early afternoon will have both Sun and MC in the same sign, suggesting that their purpose, calling and innate qualities (as shown by the Sun) can be 'seen' and recognized easily 'out there' (MC). In other words, their essence is on display, their reputation (MC) clearly linked to their calling (Sun).

For most people, the Sun and MC signs are different and our job as astrologers is to blend these two signs (and complexes) and articulate their range of possibilities to clients. We must ask ourselves what these signs (and complexes) have in common and what they, in combination, can create that is fruitful. For instance, it might be 'easy' for someone with the Sun in Aries to shine this through an MC in the fellow Fire sign of Leo, but how can someone with the Sun in Cancer shine through an MC in Aquarius? Still, any combination, no matter how disparate, is capable of working together and producing something remarkable and individual!

Combining the Three Points – Some Client Stories

Brian: Sun in Sagittarius, Moon in Aquarius, MC in Aries

Sagittarius, Aquarius and Aries are signs that value freedom, independence and have a desire to speak up, speak out and *experience* life to the full. Each of the three has opinions on how the world can be improved! Sagittarius is a natural front-of-house meet-and-greeter. It is a sign linked to publishing, sport, sales and promotion. In Brian's chart the Sun is in the 5th House: he's a playful, free spirit and a man-boy in his late 30s who has never quite grown up. But the Sun makes a tight opposition to Saturn in Gemini: he has always spoken of a need to prove himself to, and impress, his father, who is an established name in publishing (Sagittarius).

This opposition saw Brian follow his father into magazine publishing as an office worker who spent his days on the phone selling advertising space in a small, traditional firm. On a daily level this job suited Brian's friendly nature and desire to chat with strangers and regular customers (Moon in Airy Aquarius conjunct the Descendant) – the only

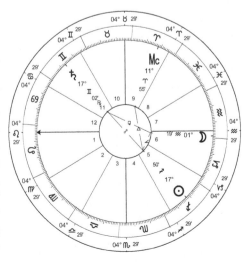

concession was taking out his earring before he walked through the door each morning! – and he stayed in this role for a decade (note the fixed Moon). But working for someone else in an establishment-type, 'serious' job to please his father (Sun–Saturn), where there was no room for promotion or self-determination, never really appealed to his Aries Midheaven. Eventually he got in touch with this MC by becoming a personal trainer. Aries is a sign of the motivator. Aries needs targets and goals, to pit itself against some form of opposition. It is a sign at home with provoking others into taking control of their own lives. Aries offers a minimum-step program (it couldn't abide *twelve!*) and wouldn't have the patience to put up with someone who returned each week just looking for a sympathetic ear. It needs to see results fast. Aries wants to breathe new life into an existing idea, to race in front of the pack and get *ahead*. Like the Sun, the Midheaven sign can take some years to fully express its many facets. With Brian, he expressed his Aries MC as a rather cocky, sex-driven teenage 'lad' – impulsive and a bit reckless, leaving a trail of one-night stands behind him. Later, his contagious enthusiasm proved essential to his success as a trainer.

Kim: Sun in Taurus, Moon in Virgo, MC in Virgo

When the Moon and the MC share the same sign, the parts of life that provide succour, comfort and nurturance can be areas that one becomes known for in one's professional or social environment (MC). Often, what is naturally done well at home can be of benefit to the person and others in the outside world. In Kim's chart all three vocational components are in the element of Earth. She is, at heart, a collector, a hoarder, someone who wishes to build something of enduring, practical value (Sun in Taurus). At

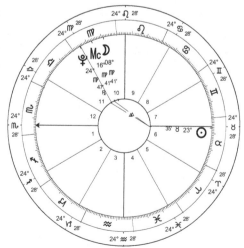

her home I encountered her Moon. I remember being struck by the large collection of bottles and jars stacked away in cupboards in her kitchen. And they were all labelled (Virgo) or in the *process* (mutable) of being labelled (Virgo's work is never done!). Over the years I have marvelled at the time she has dedicated to specific tasks (Earth is *slow*) and she told me recently of an Alice in Wonderland party she had at her home – one that took *twelve months* to plan. At work (five years as a Creative Director of music videos), Kim used these natural tendencies (Moon), and her attention to detail, efficiency and kindness (Virgo) were personal traits that media clientele admired in her. Together, these created her reputation for excellence (MC in Virgo). Later, Kim became a full-time artist and has since staged a number of award-winning exhibitions. One of her most memorable pieces of artwork is truly Virgoan: 800 antique test tubes (filled with resin and inks referencing colours and forms of *bacteria*) set within a large white frame in a circular, mandala pattern. Her website lists the key themes inherent in her artwork (revealing her Taurus–Virgo combination, plus the Pluto overtone of Scorpio Rising and Pluto on the MC): preservation vs. organic decay, rhythm and repetition, the precise vs. the organic, bacteria as life-enhancing/life-destroying. She writes, 'Labels are used for defining and identifying; bottles distil or preserve' (Virgo–Taurus).

Amy: Sun in Pisces, Moon in Aquarius, MC in Gemini

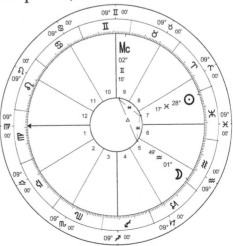

Two of Amy's vocational trio have mutability (Sun, MC) and Air (Moon, MC) in common, underscoring the Gemini MC placement and a fundamental desire for variety, movement and space (mutable Air). Amy is, in essence, a rescuer who needs to be of service to others, particularly in the emotional realm (Sun in Pisces in the 7th). During the time I've known her, she has counselled people, devoted time to charities and supported sick friends. Amy needs breathing space in her daily working life and has lived alone for many years (Moon in Aquarius). Originally an office PA for a banker in the City of London (MC in Gemini), Amy gave up this well-paid job when she felt called to pursue studies in metaphysics and tarot (Pisces). A period of learning numerous, related subjects turned into a multi-faceted career as a teacher–consultant–supervisor facilitator of many mind–body–spirit disciplines (Gemini MC has a hyphenated reputation!). She now runs her practice in two towns and travels to and from them regularly (Gemini). Pisces has an instinct to save, empathize and merge. It seeks an emotional connection and spiritual exchange that Airy Aquarius and Gemini can't fathom. But Aquarius (along with Gemini) stands back, observes and clarifies from a rational, detached viewpoint. It avoids getting swamped or smothered by the needy. This Sun–Moon blend could suggest a struggle to find a freedom–closeness balance in personal relationships (for the longest time, her two cats have been Amy's only companions). But at work she has used this combination to develop a reputation by word-of-mouth (Gemini) of running workshops in her home (Moon) with groups who share her interests (Aquarius), articulating a variety (Gemini) of metaphysical ideas and spiritual practices (Pisces), including inner-child therapy (Moon in the 5th).

Heather: Sun in Gemini, Moon in Taurus, MC in Leo

Heather worked for many years to combine her dual interests (Gemini) of music and astrology, writing songs about her own horoscope. When I knew her, she spent much of her time talking about herself and bolstering an overblown but perhaps fragile ego (Gemini, Leo). Heather's key pursuits appeared to be fame and recognition (Sun–Jupiter conjunction, Leo MC) – and her pushy personality generated much publicity and fanfare for her ventures but provoked much opposition and scorn from others. A natural deal-maker (Gemini, plus Scorpio Rising) and delegator (Leo has a knack of 'encouraging' others to take on Leo's workload!), she ran a business promoting a select group of psychological astrology consultants that thrived for a short while. But Leo MC is not a team player, and the business fell apart amid personality clashes (Leo) and disputes over rightful shares of daily income (Moon in Taurus). The Moon in Taurus showed itself in Heather's need to accumulate money and, with Sun-Jupiter in the 8th, she had a philosophy that warned 'what's mine is mine, and what's yours will soon be mine!' With good investments and support from her husband's job

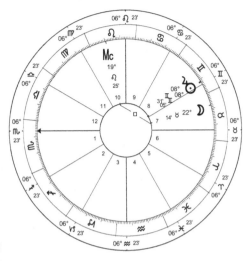

(Moon in Taurus in the 7th), she built a nest egg that enabled her to move to another country and set up a health and beauty spa to pamper clients (Taurus, Leo).

Sally: Sun in Pisces, Moon in Libra, MC in Cancer

With two vocational points in cardinal signs and two in Water, the vocational message is to seek challenge, make things happen and initiate (cardinal) matters of an emotional nature where human values and being of service to the human condition (Water) are prerequisites. With strong cardinality, Sally needs

to be in charge, ideally in joint-charge (Libra) with someone who does a different, valuable job in the office. At best, Water people have gut instincts that turn into spot-on judgements and work well for them. At worst, there can be a series of emotional crises, an attraction to emotional leeches or an over-attachment, dependency and unhealthy symbiosis in personal and professional relationships. Sally is a personal injury lawyer who has a reputation for caring, supporting and guiding injured clients through their emotional turmoil (Cancer is the midwife, Pisces is the rescuer). She is a born strategist who can bring balance and objectivity to her daily work life (Moon in Libra). On both the occasions she worked for someone else, she encountered an imbalance of power and daily conflict (Libra) from difficult, irrational and sometimes tyrannical bosses. Sally's Moon in Libra was called upon to mediate, calm, appease and restore harmony. When she worked for herself, she ended up supporting both (male) personal partners. Libra needs to be liked and have its ideas accepted – but when confident, it begins to rely less heavily on others and uses charm and persuasion manipulation to have its *own* needs met. Here, the Moon in Libra (conjunct Uranus) is far less malleable or emotionally attached than people think or the Pisces–Cancer might suggest.

Follow Your Chart and Your Heart
We do our best work as astrologers when we encourage clients (and ourselves!) to follow the messages written in their horoscopes. I'm thankful to astrologer Faye Cossar for introducing me to the work of Barbara Marx Hubbard, who said, 'The vocation is the genius of the individual wanting to be expressed.' Hubbard uses the term 'vocational arousal' to describe that powerful spark that gets ignited when someone you meet *moves you forward* in a powerful way towards your own calling. This is what we have the potential to do as astrologers.

Some become nurses, teachers or fundraisers because 'good people do that'. Others are embarrassed to take up a pursuit because of what friends and family might say. This reminds me of the month in 2011 when my Ascendant (representing one's physical environment/surroundings) moved into regal Leo by Solar Arc (where it will stay for 30 years). I was asked to give consultations at the lush, splendid and salubrious Royal Crescent Hotel in Bath, England, and invited to stay over in one of their thousand-dollar-a-night suites (I could certainly get used to that for the next 30 years). With my new environment (Solar Arc Ascendant) now in Leo, I encountered three (of the six) clients that first afternoon who had acting ambitions (Leo), all of whom felt that such things were flights of fancy – silly and childish. Part of each of the sessions dealt with the possible ways they could learn to act and, when I returned earlier this year, two of the three had joined amateur dramatics groups and were loving it to bits!

One of the attacks on modern astrology by some astrologers is that we encourage people to become *anything* they like. We do have our limits and certain practical considerations must be taken into account. But the key to our work as modern astrologers is to help clients discover what they truly love and encourage them to pursue it one way or another. It may not matter whether they win awards or are judged successful by others – what matters is that they love what they do, which brings its own feeling of accomplishment.

At one conference I remember being horrified to hear an inexperienced astrologer recall discouraging a client from following a cherished dream because her chart didn't show *eminence* in that field. The astrologer had missed a chance to encourage the client to pursue it anyway!

Despair, it is said, comes from choosing to be someone other than ourselves. Being an Aries, I'm all for 'self-centred astrology': doing what makes us happy. We should encourage our clients to do the same. Remind them of who they were born to be – they already know this deep inside. They'll hear your words and recognize that special, burning desire they perhaps set aside many years ago … a fire that is still simmering. They just might need someone to open up avenues, possibilities and passions that they hadn't dared to consider – or rekindle.

Novelist Edith Wharton wrote, 'There are two ways of spreading light: to be the candle or the mirror that reflects it.' We astrologers can do both jobs in consultation. We're the mirror (the Moon) when we're able to speak to our clients, reflect their inner drives and talents, and then 'turn them on' to their calling. And we're the candle (the Sun) when we personally demonstrate what it is to work in a field like astrology – to engage in a true labour of love. In doing so we create an energy around us that brings opportunity and advancement for us all; it inspires others to stay with what truly makes them deeply happy – to 'follow their bliss', as Joseph Campbell often said.

In my book *Palmistry 4 Today*, I wrote of the three Ds: discipline, determination and drive, and the need for courage. **Courage + Talent + Energy = Success in Life**.

> Courage is essential ... We need courage to channel our energies in order to explore our talents and express ourselves. We must never lose sight of the wonderful realities in our lives as well as our dreams – a loyalty to both keeps us alive. We must always dare to travel uncharted waters, to take risks, to grow, learn and live. Success starts with a way of thinking and being ... None of us can change the past, but past circumstances and choices have helped to bring us to the place where we stand today. In knowing this, we can cast aside regret and expectation, and create our future by working now – in the present – to reach out and experience challenges, adventures and relationships. And it's never too late to start over.[8]

References and Notes

1. Brian Clark, *An Astrological Guide to a Fulfilling Vocation*, Astro*Synthesis, 2010, pp. 3-4.
2. James Hillman, *The Soul's Code*, Warner, 1997.
3. Noel Tyl, *How to Use Vocational Astrology for Success in the Workplace*, Llewellyn, 1992, pp. 42-3.
4. Faye Cossar, *Using Astrology to Create a Vocational Profile*, Flare, 2012.
5. Kim Falconer, *Astrology and Aptitude*, AFA, 2001, p. 90.
6. Lois M. Rodden, *Money: How to Find It with Astrology*, Data News Press, 1994, p. 191.
7. Transits, progressions and directions that ingress into our MC sign or Sun sign can signal periods of activation – times when we are most easily able to reconnect with our aims, goals and calling.
8. Frank C. Clifford, *Palmistry 4 Today*, Flare, 2010.

Chapter 9

JUPITER: A NEW TAKE ON AN OLD CON ARTIST

Jupiter's placement in our horoscope says much about where we invest belief and meaning in life. The Greater Benefic's message is one of exploration, growth and the broadening of horizons. Wisdom and blessings fall under the auspices of Jupiter, and our own natal placement reveals how and where we're blessed – so much so that we can inspire others with its message and give freely and generously of our gifts.

The Jupiterian personality is said to be optimistic, hungry for knowledge, hopeful and expansive: an embodiment of the power of positive thought and a belief that the Universe will provide.[1]

The Real Nature of Jupiter?
The Gauquelins' research into character traits (see pages 27–8) showed that planetary keywords given by astrologers matched biographical descriptions of those born with that particular planet in one of the Gauquelin Key Sectors (Zones). But in Jupiter's case, particularly with positive descriptions of the planet, the results were weak. In fact, the Gauquelins discovered that keywords for the Sun were more often linked to biographies of those with a prominent Jupiter. Could it be, then, that the Jupiterian, rather than the solar, personality is the one that stands out as being authoritative, brilliant, influential, powerful, vital, successful?[2]

In my own work, I've seen Jupiter, rather than the Sun, powerfully placed in the charts of those who command respect and dominate through charisma and force of personality. It appears that a strongly placed Sun, particularly near an angle, puts us under the glare (and pressure) of the spotlight – we are on display and are noticed, we 'shine' and gain attention. But it is a strong Jupiter that suggests a personality type with a desire for (and belief in one's) prominence, distinction, power and influence.[3]

Interestingly, the Jupiterian individual (perhaps more so for those with the Ascendant or Moon in Sagittarius) often suffers from depression. Not depression born from half-full, 'just being practical', Saturnian cynicism, but from disappointment that others haven't shown the same level of energy, heart and dedication. Easily deflated by others' lack of commitment or the world not promising all that was hoped for, these Jupiterians allow both disenchantment and despondency to creep in. British astrologer Roger Elliot, with Jupiter conjunct the Midheaven, once wrote that everything he touches 'turns to gold – 9 carat gold plate that eventually comes off on your fingers.'[4]

The Shadow Side
And what of the less exemplary and even darker sides of Jupiter? What of the times when morality and ethics are cast aside and promises reneged upon? When the philanthropic or evangelical urge – the talent to inspire or to promote a cause – becomes a need to play God, guru, starmaker, or Svengali? When one develops an inflated sense of importance? When blessings, good fortune and abundance turn into greed and a thirst that is never quenched? There are murky, sinister sides to Jupiter and its signs (Pisces the Piranha and Sagittarius the Holier-than-thou Hypocrite) that don't make it into most of the textbooks!

Evangelists ('messengers of good news') were originally travelling preachers – crusaders and zealots who sold their vision of God in order to convert and to save others. This is chiefly the function of Jupiter: to reach out, publicise, promote, persuade and inspire a religious conviction. (Neptune aims for the moving mystical connection, to become 'at one' with a higher power, while the mutable signs are all messengers of some kind.)

But for many years, evangelism has meant big business for these proselytizers who, particularly during the 1980s Capricorn era of conspicuous consumption, sold salvation via their TV shows and infomercials, while indulging in lifestyles befitting potentates. They cashed in on God through the power of broadcasting (Jupiter) and then swapped allegiance to worship the almighty Dollar. Appropriately, with the Achilles heel of Jupiterians – being elevated to godlike status only to believe their own publicity – many ended up with the wrong type of

convictions. Here are key features of some evangelists'
horoscopes (note the Neptune theme, too):

- **Jim Bakker**: Mars in Pisces conjunct Jupiter in Aries, both
  opposite Neptune, T-square Mercury in Sagittarius. Pisces
  Rising, Sagittarius on the MC.

- **Tammy Faye Bakker** (later Messner): Sun in Pisces square
  Jupiter on the Descendant, Sagittarius Rising.

- **Jimmy Swaggart**, whose condemnation of the Bakkers was
  overshadowed by his own tearful admissions of solicitation:
  Sun in Pisces exactly trine Jupiter, Sagittarius Rising. Jupiter
  square Mercury.

- **Oral Roberts**, who famously asked his followers for $4.5
  million otherwise the Lord 'will take my life': Sun opposite
  Neptune and closely trine Jupiter. (Mars as the T-square
  apex of a Moon–Pluto opposition to Mercury.)

- **L. Ron Hubbard**
  (chart on right),
  an evangelist of a
  different kind – went
  from writing pulp
  fiction to publishing
  the highly influential,
  controversial self-
  improvement, meta-
  physical manual
  of mental health
  'auditing', *Dianetics*. It
  was published in May
  1950, with Jupiter in

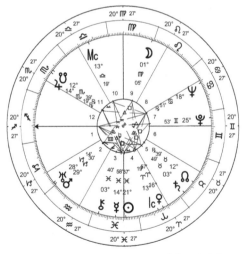

Pisces and transiting Neptune having just crossed his MC.
L. Ron Hubbard created his own religion (The Church of
Scientology) three years later. He was born with the Sun in
Pisces and Sagittarius Rising. His Sun–Mercury conjunction
is in a Grand Trine with Jupiter and Neptune.

- Finally, **Billy Graham**, for so long untainted by scandal and considered a moral compass for other erring evangelists, has a similar Jupiter–Neptune theme (although the major thrust of his chart is Martian with Aries Rising, Mars–MC and a strong Scorpio/8th House theme). Graham has the Sun closely trine Jupiter and square to Neptune, plus Moon–Mars in Sagittarius on a Capricorn MC.

Maintaining Integrity

It is no small irony that where we have Jupiter natally is where our morality or ethics can be questioned, especially when we've veered off the road of integrity, cut corners, or dined out too often on someone else's reputation (or credit card). Jupiterians will, at some stage, have to take a stand and fight for their principles.

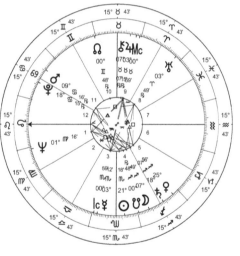

Michel Gauquelin (chart on right), who was born with Jupiter on the MC in Taurus, loved astrology from childhood. He built up an enormous collection (Jupiter) of hard facts (Taurus) that the scientists couldn't ignore … so they had to challenge him and falsely replicate his findings to disprove him. But he stood firm against decades of scepticism by maintaining a stubborn belief in his findings. (Note his Mercury in Scorpio – the researching, penetrating, political mind.)

Jupiterian professions include the priesthood, law, politics and publishing (all of these once considered professions for the noble gentleman and educated few). These vocations were seemingly beyond reproach but are now most often under attack because of abuses 'allowed to go on' behind the scenes when absolute power corrupts absolutely.

Neil Hamilton, the disgraced Member of Parliament, who was accused of taking 'cash for questions' and fought unsuccessfully for many years to clear his name has Jupiter on the MC. The scandal erupted when transiting Uranus and Neptune crossed over his Jupiter–MC conjunction.

Attracted to confidence schemes or grand theft, the Jupiterian criminal is often charismatic, given more credit than he deserves, and (rarely a suspect) roams free to get away with murder, sometimes literally. He evades the authorities through lucky escapes, oversights, or careless mistakes by the police. That is, until his luck runs out – usually for Jupiterian reasons: feeling invincible, tripping up, or making errors in judgement.

The mobster **Lucky Luciano** (chart on right) is considered the father of modern organized crime in the United States for splitting New York City into five different Mafia crime families. In 1929, Luciano was forced into a limousine at gunpoint by three men, beaten and stabbed, and then dumped on a beach on New York Bay. He somehow survived the

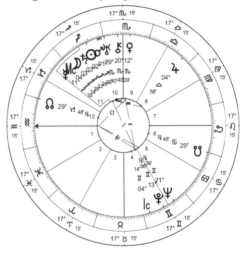

ordeal but was forever marked with a scar and droopy eye. His survival earned him the name 'Lucky'. His chart has five planets (and the MC) in Sagittarius and Jupiter sextile most of them.

Another Jupiterian who pushed his luck was documentary-maker Morgan Spurlock, born with Jupiter conjunct the Sun, Venus and Mercury in extreme Scorpio (all opposite Saturn in culinary Taurus). For his much-hyped film, *Super Size Me* (2004), Spurlock ate three McDonald's meals a day every day (and nothing else) for 30 days. It was mandatory that he take the 'super-size' (Jupiter) option whenever it was offered. Before starting, Spurlock was of 'above average' health and fitness; by the end of filming he was said to have gained 25 pounds (11 kg), become quite puffy and suffered liver dysfunction and depression.

Divas Don't Do Stairs

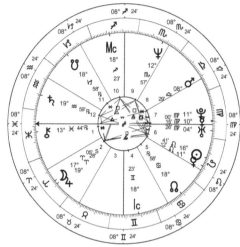

Although the word 'diva' is casually applied to anyone nowadays who can hold a note, research shows that the diva temperament is a truly Jupiterian expression. Here, we enter the realm of the imperious, privileged and pampered princess – a monument to hauteur and high drama – who expects (by divine right) that the world will serve her own needs and indulge her excessive demands. When we hear monstrous (perhaps exaggerated) stories of temperamental, self-centred divas flaunting outlandish behaviour, we encounter a prominent Jupiter, usually in a Gauquelin Zone or conjunct a personal planet (the Fire signs are present more than usual, too).

Consider a handful of examples of those whose shenanigans have contrasted with the standards expected of mere mortals: Maria Callas (Jupiter in Sagittarius conjunct the Sun, both in a G-Zone); Diana Ross (Jupiter in Leo in a G-Zone, Aries Sun, see page 20); **Whitney Houston** (Jupiter conjunct the Moon in Aries, in a Grand Trine with the Sun in Leo and the MC in Sagittarius, chart above); Mae West (Jupiter in Aries in a G-Zone trine the Sun in Leo); **Elizabeth Taylor** (chart on right, Jupiter in Leo square the Moon and trine her Sagittarius Ascendant); and Demi Moore, famously dubbed 'Gimme Moore' (Jupiter in a G-Zone).

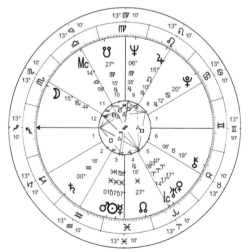

Another interesting discovery is that we can personify our Jupiter sign to the extent that we become overblown parodies of that image. Not surprisingly, Jupiter is often the key synastry link between comedy impersonator and subject/victim where there needs to be an *exaggeration* of mannerisms.

Consider two of the entertainers who played Margaret Thatcher (Scorpio Ascendant people are easily impersonated!): Janet Brown and Steve Nallon. Impressionist Janet Brown, who for so long gave the acceptable 'impersonation' of Thatcher, was born with Jupiter Rising in Sagittarius. She was the former PM's favourite and the synastry is revealing: Brown's Jupiter is on Thatcher's Venus, and Brown's MC ruler Venus is on Thatcher's pivotal Jupiter–Pluto opposition.

Steve Nallon offered a less forgiving portrayal – that of a militant Iron Lady who handbagged everyone into submission for TV's *Spitting Image* – and he was born with Jupiter–Saturn flanking the MC in Capricorn (at the same degree as Thatcher's axis).

Thatcher's own Jupiter (in Capricorn in the 2nd House) describes much of the *expansion* that took place while she was in power: a focus on young entrepreneurs, aspirational Yuppies, privatisation of industries, owning shares, and even the stone-cladding (Capricorn) people put on their houses.

Investing in Confidence

The word 'hyperbole' encapsulates much that is Jupiterian. Auto executive **John DeLorean** (born with Jupiter–MC in the business sign of Capricorn, chart on right) created a business empire and promised hope and benefit to many, but his schemes ended in bankruptcy and massive layoffs.

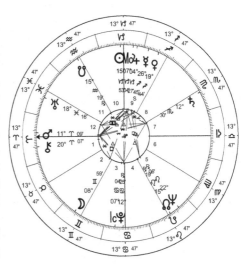

In spite of a series of business disasters, the

Don
King

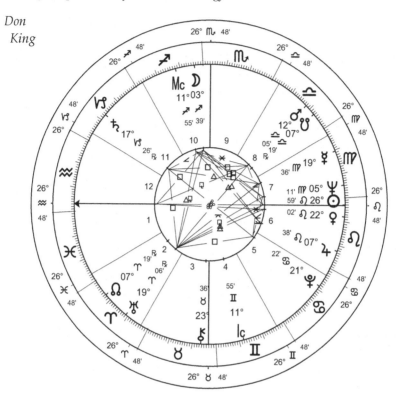

accusations of a major cocaine deal, and the loss of millions of dollars of investors' money, DeLorean is still thought of as an iconic entrepreneur, celebrity and 'dream maker'.

Another Jupiterian is **Don King**, the flamboyant boxing promoter known for his larger-than-life persona and stand-on-end hairstyle. His Jupiter is in a G-Zone in Leo and trine Moon–MC in Sagittarius. King had a colourful early life, working the Sagittarius–Jupiter overtone and scandalous Neptune square the Moon–MC to interesting effect: after quitting college, he ran an illegal bookmaking operation and was later implicated in two homicides. He was convicted of second-degree murder (reduced to non-negligent manslaughter) for the latter homicide and served almost four years in prison. Since his release, he has been dogged by various controversies, including alleged jury tampering, tax evasion, insurance fraud, lawsuits from boxers and links to organized crime.

As King has been a promoter of famous fighters, we would expect to see a dominant Descendant/7th-House complex and Jupiter synastry with his clients. Indeed, King made his name promoting Muhammad Ali[5] (Ali's Jupiter sits exactly opposite King's MC in Sagittarius) and, later, Mike Tyson (whose Mercury is conjunct King's Jupiter). The lunar link (near the MC in Sagittarius) shows King's grandiose patriotism and huge revenues from TV pay-per-view fights screened into homes across the world. King coined the phrase 'Only in America' and is known for his promotion of all things American – his MC is conjunct the US Sibly Ascendant, and his Ascendant is conjunct the Sibly Moon.

Believing the Hype
But who sold us this idea of Jupiter as the benevolent one who should be elevated? No doubt a Jupiterian! Yet, as Marlon Brando (Sagittarius Rising, Jupiter in Sagittarius in the 1st House) once said, 'I'm just another sonofabitch sitting in a motor home on a film set, and they come looking for Zeus.'[6]

Some Jupiterians are freeloaders, part of the entourage – influential by association (especially with Sun–Jupiter), always ready with a backstage pass. They feel born to a special destiny, appear greater and larger (often literally) than they truly are. Like social-climbing snob Hyacinth Bucket in the BBC TV series, *Keeping Up Appearances*, the aspiring Jupiterian complains: 'If there's one thing I can't stand, [it's] people who try to pretend they're superior. It makes it so much harder for those of us who really are.'

Still, when all is weighed and assessed, the wicked side of Jupiter isn't that wicked, because there's a certain élan – a flair, flamboyance and charm – to Jupiterian con artists, which means that being duped by them is often a lesson in seeing something, however immoral, done really well.

References and Notes
1. The author of various 'cosmic ordering' books, Bärbel Mohr, was born with the Moon in Taurus aptly conjunct Jupiter and opposite Neptune.

2. Keywords found by the Gauquelins are listed in *Psychology of the Planets* by Françoise Gauquelin (ACS, 1982).
3. Aside from the charts of actors, executives and politicians, the Gauquelins found Jupiter dominant in the charts of high-ranking Nazis.
4. From Elliot's biography in *The Future of Astrology*, ed. A.T. Mann, Unwin Hyman, 1987, p. 187.
5. When King pulled off Ali's much-publicized 'Thrilla in Manila' bout, King's secondary progressed chart had his Jupiter–MC line running through Manila.
6. http://news.bbc.co.uk/1/hi/entertainment/3863327.stm

Chapter 10

OUT OF THE SHADOWS – SCORPIO ELEVATED

Taking one placement in a horoscope and exploring it in depth can be a rewarding endeavour, particularly if that placement involves Scorpio. Scorpio is heavily maligned and misunderstood because it is – particularly when on the Ascendant – a sign that provokes many unconscious projections from others who refuse (or are unable) to deal with the issues and 'buttons' it often unwittingly pushes in them.

Scorpio on the Ascendant compels its owner to explore fundamental issues of trust, intimacy and closeness in relationship, and equips them with a penetrative insight. But the Scorpio Rising person discovers that the desire to unravel the mysteries of those around them is born out of a need to understand the greatest mystery of all: themselves. But for all their fortitude, reserve and potency, they can get stuck on an emotional treadmill and become unravelled by the need to control their immediate environment – a compulsion that can, ironically, control them.

If we consider Scorpio on the Midheaven (MC), though, the sign's power and intensity are heard as a compelling 'call' to be the master of one's destiny (and destination), to secure an influential position and to shape one's social environment (MC); in short, to be seen as powerful. It is one of the most intriguing of all MC placements because the sign of hidden depth, so often in the shadows, is now elevated, 'out there' culminating at the MC. Whereas a Scorpio Ascendant is adept at wearing many (dis)guises, at the MC this sign is called upon to expose itself and emerge with a public persona.

On the Midheaven, it has a wider spectrum, perhaps because in order to meet the world, Scorpio on the MC must work with the viewpoints and horizons of Sagittarius, Capricorn or Aquarius (the possible Ascendant signs in most habitable latitudes). But the image/public persona created (consciously or otherwise), the type of recognition coveted or sought, and one's particular impact on society (and that which one symbolizes for others) will be fundamentally Scorpionic in essence.

This MC can manifest in various ways: to seek depth from social or work experiences; to be called upon to undergo a personal metamorphosis; to assume a potent, transformative position in society. Those with Scorpio on the Midheaven need to assume an authentic role, one of gravitas to face – and shed light on – some of life's darker issues and taboos; to be aware of the political play at work; to recognize that Scorpio's natural dependency on others does not have to be a symbiotic sign of weakness, but is, in fact, indicative of a common bond and commitment. The journey is a challenging one: there are issues of crisis and life and death, creativity and destruction, major (no-) turning (back) points, and rebirths after teetering perilously on the edge of self-annihilation. The calling of a Scorpio MC is self-mastery and to emerge as a shrewd player of the game with an awareness of the power of interdependency.

One of the best ways to understand the various manifestations of a sign on the MC is to look at the charts and lives of people in the public eye – not only how they choose to be seen, but also how we experience them. The MC will, for example, show how the public perceive a famous person's lifestyle, as well as their carefully constructed social persona.

Actors have the best jobs in the world – and arguably the most therapeutic in terms of exploring their inner landscapes. When employed, they will find themselves drawn to roles that are 'written' in their horoscopes; roles that appear to have been scripted for them. The clients of mine who are actors never cease to be amazed by astrology's ability to describe the parts they've been chosen to play – and astrologers could certainly debate how much 'choice' there is in the matter. And on occasion I've been asked by casting directors to compare charts and suggest which actor from a number would be best suited to a role in a biopic or some other celebrity-based portrayal. Actually, it's one of the least demanding and most fun tasks in my line of work! Acting provides them with an opportunity to play out key themes and dynamics in their charts and, although there's usually a spectrum of possibilities inherent (the life stories and subsequent acting plots are 'found' in their hard aspects and T-squares), so often the reputation they gain is directly linked to the MC sign and any planets conjunct.

Studying the charts of actors, particularly those who are known for (or typecast in) a particular role, gives us a wide spectrum of possibilities of how the MC can manifest through the signs. Very often, the actor will play characters that are vivid personifications of the stereo- or archetypes of the sign on their Midheaven (and, to a lesser extent, the Sun's sign). In social and work situations, we all develop reputations and play roles described by our Midheaven, but actors tend to have tightly edited, less subtle scripts! Our own archetypal roles played out in real life are usually more difficult to discern.

I've looked through my data files and found the following examples of well-known actors, all of whom have Scorpio on the Midheaven, and considered whether their MC sign reflects the characters with which they're most associated.

Anthony Hopkins

This intense character actor has known Scorpio MC heights and depths, having fought his own self-destructive impulses and personal demons, but Anthony Hopkins is best known for playing the demonic, brilliant psychiatrist Hannibal Lecter – a cannibalistic serial killer incarcerated in a hospital for the criminally insane. Interestingly his 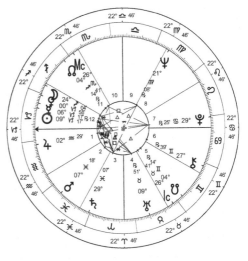 co-star in *The Silence of the Lambs*, Jodie Foster, has her Sun at 26° Scorpio, exactly conjunct Hopkins' MC. Foster played FBI trainee Clarice Starling, sent to interview Lecter on the behaviour of still-at-large killer 'Buffalo Bill', only to find herself probed and dissected by the terrifying master psychologist. (In one of the novels, the pair become lovers and elope to Argentina.)

Hopkins later played Pablo Picasso, whose Sun is in early Scorpio and whose Mercury is at 24° Scorpio.

Sean Connery

With his undeniable sexual charisma, Connery became an icon and the embodiment of James Bond. In his hands, Bond was a dark, potent, dangerous and ruggedly hands-on 007 (very different from the suave, Venusian Bond of Roger Moore, born with the Sun in Libra and an MC in Taurus). Connery's Secret Service agent was a

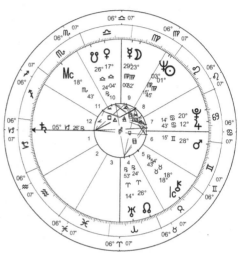

seductive womanizer but with a mark of cruelty (on occasion he struck his women); he was a 'man's man', unflinching in danger, fearless in combat – and who could forget his licence to kill? Many of his other films embody Scorpionic themes (*The Name of the Rose*, *The Untouchables*, *Marnie*, *Zardoz*, *The Hunt for Red October* and *Finding Forrester*). Those with Scorpio on the MC are naturally drawn to the political arena, and Connery is a high-profile and active member of the Scottish National Party. With Saturn dominant and the Scorpio MC (both of which place respect high on their list of priorities), Connery – never one to suffer fools – often took a moral stand and sued film companies to retrieve monies that were rightfully his.

Matt Damon

This intense young actor showed early signs of his Scorpio MC. For his role as an opiate-addicted soldier in *Courage Under Fire*, Damon lost 18 kilos in 100 days. And this was all for only two days of filming. According to reports, Damon was on medication for several years to correct the stress inflicted on his adrenal glands. He then embarked on a role that made his name. In *Good Will Hunting* he played a young, self-destructive genius who undergoes a personal transformation with the help of a washed-up psychologist. Damon continued to be drawn to Scorpionic roles, firstly as a confidence artist engaged in a cat-and-mouse game in *The Talented Mr. Ripley*, and later he reinvented himself as an action anti-hero in the box-office smash trilogy of Bourne films (*Identity, Supremacy, Ultimatum*), in

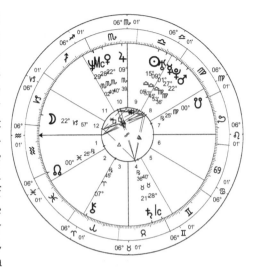

which he played an assassin tormented by amnesia (note Neptune conjunct natal MC; the project was filmed when Neptune crossed over Damon's Ascendant).

Catherine Deneuve
Famous for her elegant beauty, political activism and, on screen, for portraying mysterious, distant 'ice maidens', Deneuve has been an object of lust for international filmgoers for decades. A notable role was in Roman Polanski's psychological thriller *Repulsion*, in which she played a virgin attracted and repulsed by sex.

Larry Hagman
Hagman stuttered and bumbled his way through the light comedy *I Dream of Jeannie* before finding his niche as womanizing Texan oil baron J.R. Ewing in TV's *Dallas*. As big on revenge as he was on procuring women, Ewing was played as a Scorpio stereotype: a manipulative, utterly ruthless operator with a

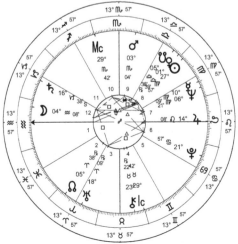

nose for a deal – and someone who only wanted what he couldn't have. J.R. Ewing was the ultimate villain 'viewers loved to hate', and never before has one character so dominated an on-going TV series. *Dallas* made Hagman, with the MC in Scorpio, the highest paid actor on TV.

Francis Ford Coppola

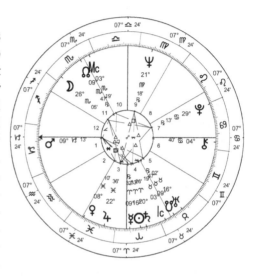

Producer-director Francis Ford Coppola's Scorpio MC is seen in his most famous work, *The Godfather* films. The trilogy examined the loyalties, betrayals and violent realities of a mobster clan of 'businessmen'. Issues of respect, loyalty, ruthlessness, fear, honour, corruption, criminality, hierarchy, revenge and the exchanging of favours are all high on the Mafia agenda.

Coppola has strong Mars–Pluto overtones in his chart:
- Sun at 16° Aries
- Mars at 9° Capricorn conjunct a Capricorn Ascendant at 7°
- MC at 3° Scorpio
- Moon at 26° Scorpio

Mario Puzo, the novelist and screenwriter of *The Godfather*, was born (time unknown) with the North Node at 6° Scorpio, Venus at 19° Scorpio and Pluto at 8° Cancer. Puzo later wrote *The Sicilian*, which was, in effect, a sequel to *The Godfather*, and based on the 'Robin Hood' bandit Salvatore Giuliano. Guiliano was born with Jupiter at 4° Scorpio, the Sun at 23° Scorpio, 17° Aries Rising, and the MC at 9° Capricorn in a one-degree opposition to Pluto (on the IC). The links between all three are quite remarkable.

Cinematic depictions of the Mafia appear to congregate in the final decan of Scorpio, the region of mid-Aries square to the end of the first decan of Capricorn ('It's business, not personal'). The

Martial-Plutonic themes are also seen in the charts of *Godfather* leads: Marlon Brando – Mars opposite Pluto, T-square Sun–Moon at 14° and 13° Aries; Al Pacino – Aries MC, Sun square Pluto on the Ascendant; James Caan – Sun in Aries, Jupiter at 18° Aries, Moon at 22° Scorpio conjunct the Ascendant at 27° Scorpio. Even Scorpio Rising Diane Keaton (Pacino's wife in all three films) has Venus in the mix at 8° Capricorn. Only Robert DeNiro's chart (with his questionable birth time) is lacking the requisite connections.

Kirk Douglas
Screen legend Douglas, the son of poor Russian immigrants, excelled in playing tough guys, flawed military men and hard-nosed intense types, all of which he famously called 'sons-of-bitches'. His best remembered roles were as the rebellious, charismatic slave who 'rises up from the dust' to challenge Rome in *Spartacus*, and as tortured genius Vincent Van Gogh in *Lust for Life*. (As an aside, Van Gogh's Moon–Jupiter conjunction in Sagittarius is straddled by Douglas' Sun–Mercury, and opposed by the Moon in Gemini.)

Jane Fonda
Few actresses have embarked on as many personal and professional metamorphoses as Jane Fonda. The daughter of actor Henry Fonda, from whom she was emotionally distant for many years, Jane's unstable mother committed suicide when the girl was twelve. As a teenager, she moved from fashion model to actress, and was soon cast in light glamorous roles that cemented her status as a 1960s sex symbol. During the 1970s, roles became more political and Scorpionic (as a prostitute in *Klute* and in the political films *Coming Home* and *The China Syndrome*), as

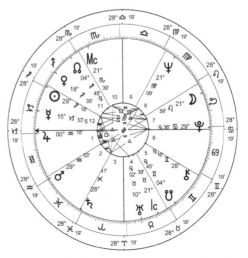

did her companions and co-stars (Vanessa Redgrave was one). An outspoken activist with Pluto on the Descendant in Cancer, Fonda's trip to Hanoi, where she was manipulated into being photographed straddling an anti-aircraft gun, made her one of the most hated, 'treasonous' figures in patriotic America. But she rebounded and revamped her image. Even her character in the 1980 film *Nine to Five* is relevant to her Scorpio MC – she played a woman returning to work and rebuilding her life after divorce and delivering payback to the company's boss, a 'sexist, egotistical, lying, hypocritical bigot'. Two years later, her next incarnation – as businesswoman and exercise workout guru – made her a force in the fitness industry, a household name again … and a fortune. She retired from film to marry Ted Turner (as TR Pluto conjunct her MC) and emerged fourteen years later, divorced 'from the world of patriarchy', and cast as the manipulative mother from hell in *Monster in Law*.

Dustin Hoffman

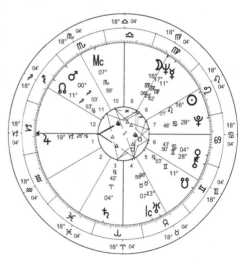

Famous for immersing himself in his roles, Method actor Hoffman once went without bathing and sleeping for two days to prepare for a scene in *Marathon Man*. Laurence Olivier spotted him and famously asked, 'My dear boy, why don't you try acting?'

Many of his roles personify his MC in Scorpio: the workaholic struggling with the crisis of divorce and custody in *Kramer vs. Kramer*, *The Graduate* seduced by Mrs Robinson, the reporter in search of the truth behind the Watergate break-ins in *All the President's Men*, and the struggling actor in *Tootsie* who poses as a woman to secure a role in a soap.

Robbie Coltrane

Best known for his role in the TV show *Cracker* as a foul-mouthed, anti-hero criminal psychologist (a 'cracker' of the motivations of psychotic, violent criminals), Coltrane is the son of a forensic police surgeon and has campaigned for various political and Socialist policies. He went on to play Hagrid, the loyal, giant guardian of Harry in the *Harry Potter* films.

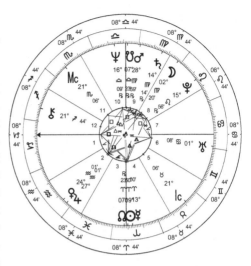

Val Kilmer

Val Kilmer has played his share of secret agents, risk-takers (including 'Iceman' – Scorpio – in *Top Gun*) and the dark knight in *Batman Forever*. Legend has it that Kilmer first learned that he had been offered the role while he was in a bat cave in Africa doing research for *The Ghost and the Darkness*.

Kilmer made an impact playing the sexy, leather-clad 'Lizard King'

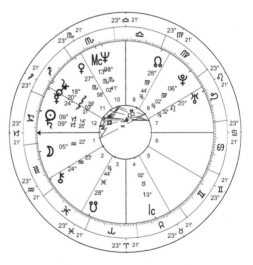

Jim Morrison in *The Doors*. The film focused on the frontman's personal and professional highs and lows, his addictions, as well as his growing obsession with death. Both actor and singer have the MC in Scorpio. With Kilmer's Venus conjunct Morrison's MC, he won the part by re-recording many of Morrison's vocals and challenging director Oliver Stone to tell them apart.

Maggie Kirkpatrick

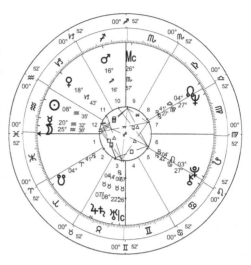

Anyone who has stayed up late and watched 1980s Australian soap repeats into the early hours could never forget this imposing actress who alarmed viewers as the sadistic, corrupt lesbian prison 'screw' Joan Ferguson in *Prisoner: Cell Block H*. Ferguson prowled the prison corridors, hair slicked back and clad in leather gloves to make her night-time body searches on unsuspecting female inmates. Nicknamed 'The Freak', she was one of soap's most memorable, complex, intimidating and terrifying characters. Another actress from the show, Val Lehman, was born with Scorpio on the MC. Lehman's character, a multiple killer, was 'Top Dog' in the prison, and Lehman herself was a vocal ringleader on set and Equity representative for the cast.

Brandon Lee

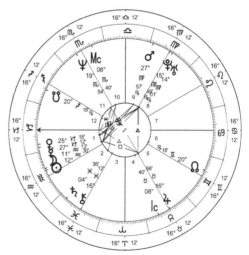

As the son of Bruce Lee, who died when Brandon was eight, this promising young actor looked set to conquer Hollywood in similar martial arts-themed films. True to his Scorpio MC, in *The Crow* he played a rock musician who comes back from the dead to avenge his own murder. While filming, Lee was killed in a freak gun accident, following in the footsteps of his famous father, who had died prematurely at the age of thirty-two.

Kiefer Sutherland

Another actor with a famous father, Kiefer was a child star in the 1986 film *Stand By Me*, a coming-of-age story of adventure and allegiance, in which he played a menacing bully. His adult roles have seen him negotiate the political manoeuvrings of the Marines in *A Few Good Men*, risk dangerous experiments to experience near-death thrills in

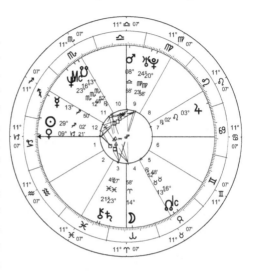

Flatliners, and haunt a couple of teens as a vampire gang leader in *The Lost Boys*. In his acclaimed role in the recent TV series *24* ('death on a deadline') he played a terrorist fighter ('a hero for dark times', say the ads). In late 2007, Sutherland began a seven-week stint in prison for DUI.

Sean Young

One of the most bizarre of the Scorpio MC examples surely must be supporting actress Sean Young, who has been tarnished with a wild, intense and 'difficult' label on and off set. One of the most damaging allegations was that she had hounded, stalked and threatened co-star James Woods, who had spurned her. Young's career and reputation never recovered fully from the negative publicity that ensued.

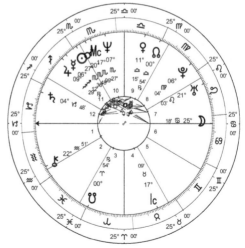

Rex Harrison

In Harrison's collection of charming but unsentimental 'English gentleman' roles, we meet his Capricorn Ascendant more than anything, but we cannot forget that Harrison's most famous role was as the misogynistic, volatile professor of phonetics, Henry Higgins, in *My Fair Lady*, in which he 'adopts' and bullies Eliza Doolittle into undergoing a metamorphosis from 'guttersnipe' flower girl to self-sufficient society lady.

Meg Ryan

Michael Parkinson certainly met the defensive side of this prickly actress in that infamous interview on the *Parkinson* show in October 2003. Often cast in perky romantic lead roles, Ryan's most famous scene is deliciously Scorpionic: in *When Harry Met Sally ...*, when her friend, played by Billy Crystal, argues that men can recognize when a woman is faking an orgasm, she goes right ahead in a packed Manhattan deli and vociferously proves him wrong! 'I'll have what she's having.'

Tom Selleck

Selleck was a major sex symbol in the 1980s, often cast in roles as playboys, firstly as a randy investigator in *Magnum, P.I.* and later in the *Three Men and a Baby* films. His support of the National Rifle Association in the US brought him much criticism from celebrity Liberals.

A look through my data files shows a number of other interesting entertainers with Scorpio on the MC who have followed various dimensions of the Scorpio archetype, from political animal to Svengali to serial killer to sex symbol. Even graceful Paul Newman – whose philanthropy and passion for auto racing are best seen by his Jupiter conjunct Ascendant and Mars in Aries – opposed the war in Vietnam and ended up on Nixon's enemies list. His fundraising efforts have included a camp for terminally ill children.

And there are a few Scorpio MC probables, including John Altman, who played nasty mum-tormentor Nick Cotton in *EastEnders*. Altman gave me a birth time that equates to 29°42' Libra, a minute or so of time off a Scorpio Midheaven.

Just as actors are naturally drawn to roles that can be 'seen' in their horoscopes, producers, writers and directors will be drawn to projects that 'act out' major themes in their birth charts. Maverick auteur film-maker and activist Derek Jarman depicted groundbreaking aspects of homosexuality on screen, and works by writers such as Irvine Welsh (*Trainspotting, Ecstasy, Filth* and *Glue*) demonstrate Scorpionic black humour, biting wit and a social commentary on the dark recesses of disaffected Edinburgh 'low-lifes'. With Neptune conjunct Welsh's MC, themes of addiction, self-destructiveness, boredom, nihilism – as well as attempts to escape the banalities of life by immersing oneself in a drug culture – are presented with stark realism.

Scorpio has the most fascinating range of expressions of all the signs, hence its enigmatic and fearsome reputation. And with Scorpio on the Midheaven, be aware that the bite may truly be worse than the bark, as this final snapshot of a powerful figure suggests.

Susan Sarandon

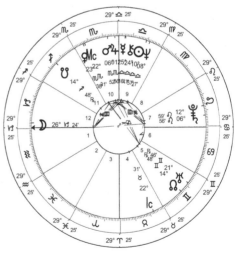

Few actresses have created such a political furore as Susan Sarandon who, with her former partner Tim Robbins, is an unapologetic, forthright political and social activist on the Hollywood scene. Together, their political agendas saw them dis-invited from awards ceremonies and considered 'too hot to handle'. Sarandon opposed the Bush Government and the Iraq War when it was potentially lethal in America to do so, and provoked a reaction similar to the nationalistic vitriol aimed at Jane Fonda and the Dixie Chicks. Her most memorable roles depict her Scorpio MC's attraction to characters of gravitas facing personal danger with unflinching courage and undergoing a personal metamorphosis in the process: *Thelma and Louise, The*

Client, and *Dead Man Walking,* a gut-wrenching portrait of Death Row. While in London some years ago, she was interviewed about the US gun lobby and one of its most famous supporters, Charlton Heston. She quipped, 'He and I share a birthday, so I don't know *what* that says about astrology.'

Chapter 11

BRIEF ENCOUNTERS: THE SYNASTRY OF INTERVIEWS

Nowadays when a public figure agrees to an interview, it's either for a confessional (making an apology for a sexual indiscretion or speaking 'frankly' about DUI or addiction, etc.), or it's traded for free airtime to promote a venture, like a book publication or film release. But the truly memorable meetings are those with another motive or those with unexpected consequences. These interviews can become turning points in a public figure's life and in how they are perceived. But *whom* they choose to talk to is even more intriguing, particularly if we consider natal synastry and how their charts interact at the *time* of the meeting. Using Solar Arc directions, we can see the *nature* of the interaction, the motivations behind the interview and its impact on both parties.

Natal inter-aspects (for instance, A's Sun conjunct B's Saturn) are necessary for a dynamic and a rapport between any two people. Using an orb of 5°, conjunctions and oppositions (and, to a lesser extent, squares) describe the main themes of the relationship and affinity. Few or no major inter-aspects show a lack of energy or interest in forming a relationship (be that one defined by empathy, cooperation, hostility or irritation). In these cases, there's little about the other that engages us; we are indifferent to the other person.

Frost Meets Nixon
Perhaps the most famous political interview of all time is the televised series of meetings starting in late March 1977 between disgraced former US president Richard Nixon and suave talk-show host David Frost. Nixon, reviled and branded a crook, wanted to restore his tarnished name. Frost, with a lightweight reputation as a playboy jetsetter who lived the high life (Jupiter conjunct Midheaven), was looking to create a more substantial name for himself. Knowing that many Americans felt cheated out of an apology when an unrepentant Nixon was officially pardoned

Richard Nixon (centre)
and David Frost
(outer wheel)

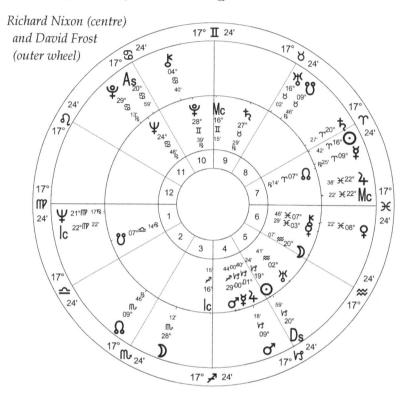

by his presidential successor, Gerald Ford, Frost sensed a TV coup if he could elicit a confession of wrongdoing from Nixon.

Although there are numerous inter-aspects between the two men's horoscopes, Saturn dominates the natal charts and synastry. **Richard Nixon** was Saturn personified: controlled, aloof, reserved, secretive, solitary. His all-important Saturn is at 27° Taurus. **David Frost**, with a natal Sun–Saturn conjunction, was looking for professional gravitas. At the time of the interview, Frost's Saturn had Solar Arc (SA) directed to 27° Taurus (Chart 2, outer wheel). Transiting Jupiter had also reached 27° Taurus, while Frost's natal Moon is at 28° Scorpio. (In August 2006, when the confrontation was first performed as a play, Frost's Jupiter–Midheaven (MC) had SA directed to 27° Taurus!)

Saturn and Taurus are the keys: the public felt that Nixon had *devalued* the presidency; he was keen to rebuild his reputation and needed the $600,000 offered to him for the interview. Frost had to put up his own money to pay Nixon a $200,000 advance. No network would finance Frost's project, fearing accusations of 'chequebook' journalism and the public's strong dislike of the former president. Appropriately for Jupiter, Saturn and Taurus, it was a huge financial risk for Frost (whose SA Uranus in Gemini squared his natal MC in Pisces, SA Mercury was conjunct natal Uranus in Taurus, and SA Mars in Aquarius was square to it). For David Frost, it may have seemed like the last chance to score a big win (Jupiter–MC had SA directed to 29° Aries).

At first, Nixon refused to budge, and he attempted to stonewall Frost (Saturn in Taurus). The turning point finally came when Nixon argued, 'When the President does it, that means that it is not illegal.' Eventually and reluctantly in the interview, he admitted to letting down his friends and country. The tension was palpable, the audience riveted. The first instalment (broadcast 4 May 1977) attracted 45 million viewers, which remains the largest TV audience for a political interview in history.

Transiting Neptune in Sagittarius was squaring Nixon's Ascendant, while his SA Neptune (at 29° Virgo) was squaring natal Mars and Mercury. For someone with an Earth- and Saturn-dominated chart and natal Neptune opposite the Sun (across Frost's natal Ascendant–Descendant axis), the loss of control as he unravelled must have been unbearable.

One Saturn Return later, the duel appeared on the London stage, followed by a film, *Frost/Nixon* (October 2008). The film's director, Ron Howard (whose Jupiter is on Nixon's MC in Gemini), said of the scandal, 'It had all been so murky and politicized and you wanted some sense of what the truth really was on the most elemental human level.' (He stated this in one of the extra features of the *Frost/Nixon* DVD.)

The X File

Alex Haley interviewed activist/minister Malcolm X in depth more than 50 times from 1963 to 1965, to co-author and collaborate in the writing of *The Autobiography of Malcolm X*, which was published shortly after the minister's assassination in 1965. The two men engaged in a power struggle as Haley (whose Sun was conjunct X's Neptune in Leo, with his Venus–Pluto conjunct X's Mars–Pluto in Cancer) fought to ensure that the book was a

Malcolm X (centre)
and Alex Haley
(outer wheel)

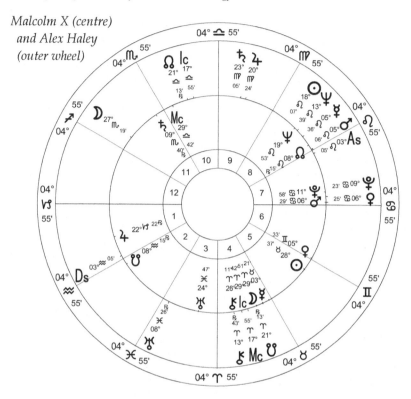

more *ideological* statement of X's journey, his *philosophy* of black pride and *nationalism*, and his *spiritual* conversion (and later disillusionment). Haley was also instrumental in censoring its anti-Semitic material.

When Haley's first article on Malcolm X was printed in the *Reader's Digest* in March 1960, his SA Saturn was at 0° Scorpio and the SA Moon at 4° Capricorn, each within a degree of Malcolm X's MC and Ascendant positions, respectively. When the famous *Playboy* interview was published in May 1963, Haley's SA Jupiter was at 0° Scorpio and his MC at 28° Taurus (on Malcolm X's Sun). Their names would be inextricably linked (MC–Sun) until Haley's novel *Roots* (1976) eclipsed these earlier literary efforts.

Houston Grounded

After years of aggressively defensive denials to the media, Whitney Houston came clean about her much-rumoured drug addictions and her tumultuous, mutually violent relationship with ex-husband Bobby Brown. The woman she trusted to unflinchingly share her secrets with was talk-show queen Oprah Winfrey: Whitney's SA Mars had reached 23° Scorpio, the degree of Oprah's Mars. The interview, which aired on 14 September 2009, would turn out to be a candid, no-subject-off-limits exchange that gave penetrating insights into the troubled diva's life behind closed doors (Scorpio). Interestingly, Houston had finally divorced Brown three years earlier, when her SA Mars was conjunct his natal Mars at 20° Scorpio.

Brando: The Truman Show
Japan, 1957. When Marlon Brando confided in Truman Capote, he spoke to a waspish, neurotic writer whose natal Mercury in Virgo was exactly conjunct Brando's MC. Fittingly for Virgo, Capote extracted from Brando the mess of his life and his hesitancy to go into analysis: 'I was afraid … it might destroy the impulses that made me creative, an artist.' The interview was published in *The New Yorker* on 9 November 1957, and Capote would later reveal the key to his Virgoan skills: 'The secret art of interviewing … is to let the other person think he's interviewing you. You tell him everything about yourself, and slowly you spin your web so that he tells you everything. That's how I trapped Marlon.' During the interview, Brando spoke of his vulnerability (Brando's Neptune is conjunct Capote's Venus–Neptune in Leo): 'The more sensitive you are, the more certain you are to be brutalized, develop scabs. Never evolve. Never allow yourself to feel anything, because you always feel too much.'

The Bashir Files
With Chart Ruler Mercury on the MC in Aquarius, Moon–Neptune in Scorpio, and Venus–Descendant square Jupiter in Pisces, it's not surprising that Martin Bashir made his name interviewing controversial media figures, getting under the skin of his subjects and 'persuading the most reclusive stars to part the curtain that protects their souls' (*The Guardian*, 22 January 2003). Princess Diana, Louise Woodward and Michael Jackson are among those interviewed by this devoutly Christian introvert.

Princess Diana (centre)
and Martin Bashir
(outer wheel)

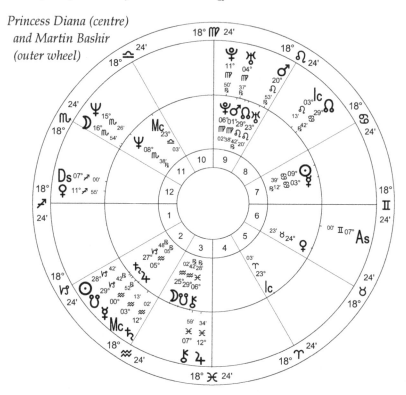

When transiting Uranus conjoined his Sun – and his SA Neptune directed to Diana's Ascendant degree of 18° Sagittarius – he became famous overnight for filming a series of clandestine interviews with the Princess in November 1995.

Diana's natal Jupiter conjoins **Bashir's** Aquarius MC (her direct-to-the-people promotional TV plea made his name), and her confessional Saturn sits on his Sun. The infamous 'revenge' interview, which aired on 20 November 1995 at 21:40 GMT, included Diana's comments on her husband's unsuitability for the throne, the 'system' (Saturn) being out to undermine her, her own infidelity, and the famous quote that 'there were three of us in this marriage, so it was a bit crowded'.

Although many people sided with the injured Princess (Bashir's SA MC had directed to her natal Chiron, which opposes her Pluto), the interview led to her royal title being removed and sped up her divorce (transiting Neptune in Capricorn was square her MC and transiting Uranus was conjunct natal Saturn, both suggestive of the dismantling of her royal status).

The interview was one of the final straws for her Private Secretary, Patrick Jephson, who resigned a while later. His Sun is conjunct Diana's Moon, and his Mars is close to her Ascendant.

Jupiter synastry can create maximum publicity, hyperbole and a promotional spectacle, but Neptune can produce sleaze or insinuation that never washes off. Bashir made headlines again when his heavily criticized interview with Michael Jackson (filmed over eight months, as Bashir's SA MC crossed his natal Jupiter) aired on 3 February 2003. *The New York Times* (6 February 2003) called Bashir's journalism style 'callous self-interest masked as sympathy.' Jackson had hoped to win public support and repair his tarnished reputation, but it proved to be a calamitous error of judgement. Bashir's natal Moon–Neptune squares his Mars, which is on Jackson's Venus in Leo: the programme ended with an uncomfortable confrontation where Bashir expressed concern over Jackson's inappropriate closeness to the boys who visited his Neverland ranch. Many commentators felt that this led directly to Jackson's second indictment for child molestation that November, his increasing dependency on medication and his self-imposed exile from the US. The backlash from Jackson fans ensured Bashir's notoriety and fall from grace.

Her True Story

Bashir's coup was, of course, the second time Princess Diana had sought to let the world in on her secret agony. For several months in mid to late 1991, she secretly tape-recorded her life story for journalist Andrew Morton. It was, in effect, the closest Diana could come to penning her autobiography *sotto voce*. Morton wrote an insider's account of her life behind palace walls, her eating disorder, suicide attempts and her husband's infidelity in *Diana: Her True Story*.

Morton's MC at 29° Leo is conjunct Diana's North Node – both at the degree of the royal star Regulus. His elevated Pluto at 24° Leo locks tightly into her Moon–Uranus opposition, suggesting the explosive nature of their secret tryst and the impact that her confessional would have on the myths surrounding the Royal Family.

Princess Diana (centre) and Andrew Morton (outer wheel)

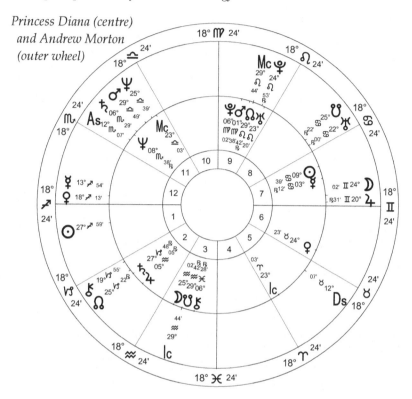

Morton's natal Neptune on Diana's MC and her Neptune near his Ascendant underscore the scandalous revelations that would undermine the monarchy. And the big Neptunian question was: How involved was Diana in the book's publication? Speculation was rife. When the book was released on 16 June 1992, Morton's SA Uranus was conjunct Diana's Mars, and his SA Venus was on her Saturn. Without the Princess's endorsement, he took the brunt of the public's scepticism and animosity, as well as the Establishment's vitriol. Only shortly after her death was her direct cooperation revealed.

Yet, Morton's natal Venus–Jupiter opposition (in Sagittarius–Gemini) straddles Diana's Ascendant, suggesting the enormous financial benefits Morton received, as well as how he provided the opportunity for her to speak her mind freely (Sagittarius) and express her profound sense of the injustice of having spent years shackled to an unsympathetic royal system.

Chapter 12

Talk-show Hosts and Interviewers

The soap opera, the local and national news, the weather forecasts, sporting events, dramas and films ... and then there's the talk show. For more than 60 years, millions of TV viewers have been glued to talk-show programming.

An inexpensive, powerful money-generating institution that's often been dismissed as synthetic or disposable, the talk show has taken many forms: a news show built around an expert panel; a magazine format with current-affairs topics; one-on-one host–guest interviews; and special-interest shows (such as those on economics, sports, psychology, cooking).

Talk shows range from topical (reflecting the social preoccupations of the times) to self-help, educational, or inspirational, to the tantalizingly titillating and exploitative confessionals first seen in the 1980s. Talk shows present cutting-edge social and cultural issues and encourage us to continue the debate at home. There's nothing quite like *talk* to get us interested, involved, reflecting and debating – it engages the Mercury principle in us all.

Some History
The TV talk-show format we know today was born on 29 May 1950 when *Broadway Open House* aired at 23:00 live from Manhattan, with theatre celebrities dropping in to chat after their performances on the Great White Way.

The first show's horoscope (see overleaf) has the Sun in the 5th House in talkative Gemini (two men shared host duties) square Jupiter, the Moon culminating at the Midheaven (MC) in Scorpio opposite Mercury in the 5th, and both T-squaring Pluto in the 8th. (Moon–Pluto and Mercury–Pluto aspects are common in the charts of those who influence the medium of entertainment.) The T-square is a key to the genre itself: viewers and the audience were, through informal conversation (Mercury), given the *impression of*

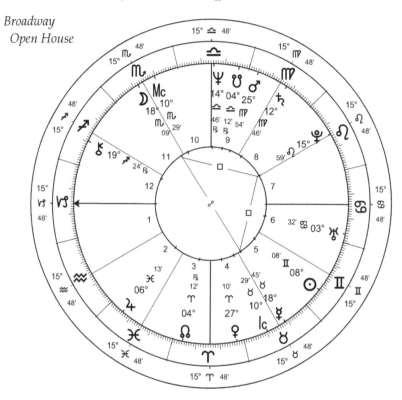

Broadway
Open House

intimacy with the celebrity (Moon in Scorpio square Pluto in Leo), even though they were unable to interact with that person directly. This remained the standard for many years.

Some Talk-show Hosts
Steve Allen set the format for late-night talk shows: a monologue to the audience, then sitting behind a desk conducting interviews with guests who were seated on a couch, the conversations being interspersed with musical or comedy performances. Unpredictable Allen (with Sun–Mercury Rising conjunct a late Sagittarius Ascendant, Jupiter conjunct the MC, and Mercury opposite Pluto) was deadly earnest and highly intellectual one moment, but bizarrely slapstick and spontaneous the next.

When Allen quit, his *Tonight Show* was taken over first by Jack Paar and then by Johnny Carson, who became the King of Late Night TV (Leo MC) for a complete Saturn cycle. With Mercury-

Saturn Rising in Scorpio and Moon–Jupiter in Capricorn, Carson turned a middle-American ironic eye on the absurdities and frustrations of society, poking fun at consumerism and pop culture. (His chart is shown on page 144.)

Later, Phil Donahue (Jupiter–MC in Sagittarius) would establish 'smart talk' and 'talk television', akin to the 'hot topic' live call-in shows on radio, and he'd invite members of the studio audience to express their opinions. Oprah Winfrey (Mercury opposite Pluto and trine Jupiter) would go on to eclipse Donahue in the mid 1980s and turn the medium into a part probe/confessional, part self-improvement exercise.

Geraldo Rivera (Mercury square Neptune; Moon–Jupiter–Pluto conjunction), Jerry Springer (Mercury opposite Pluto; Sun in the 5th opposite Jupiter in Leo which rules the 3rd), and Ricki Lake (Moon–Jupiter–Pluto) morphed the talk show into tabloid TV, targeting teenage viewers by offering trash talk and a Friday night frat-house party experience. And then there's radio's Howard Stern, a shock-jock who is as offensive to the establishment as a Sun–Mercury–Venus in Capricorn opposite Uranus (both squaring apex Neptune) could possibly be.

Astrological Signatures

What makes a successful talk-show host? Are we looking at the temperament of a journalist at heart, out to investigate, inform and educate? Is there a strong desire to be heard? An overpowering ego needing to be fed by being on TV?

The charts of talk-show hosts are, of course, as varied as the people themselves and their styles, interests and motivations. But in my research, a few stand-out features do appear regularly:

1. A strongly placed or aspected Jupiter or, to a lesser extent, Mercury.

Jupiter is linked to the ability to promote a vision and 'personality', to stay in charge and present, proselytize, b r o a dcast and sell something. Mercury is the go-between – a symbol of curiosity, inquisitiveness and analysis. It is linked to chat, opinions, conversational skills and coaxing information from others. The position of natal Mercury (along with the Ascendant complex) can describe the 'voice' and style of the talk-show host.

2. **A clear dialogue between the 3rd (talk format) and 5th (audience following) and/or 9th (promotion) Houses by rulership and aspect.**

3. A strong Pluto.

When prominently placed or aspected (to the inner planets, especially the Moon, Mercury, or Venus), Pluto suggests a powerful impact on one's generation and group, with the potential (and desire) to sway the masses.

Here are a few examples of 3rd-, 5th- and 9th-House interlinks (using Equal houses, my preference). In each example, Jupiter is also strongly placed.

Johnny Carson (chart below, left)
- Ruler of the 3rd (Saturn) is conjunct Mercury Rising in Scorpio, both trine Pluto in the 9th and sextile Moon–Jupiter in the 3rd.
- Ruler of the 9th (Moon) is conjunct the ruler of the 5th (Jupiter) in the 3rd – and both are opposite Pluto in the 9th.

Phil Donahue (chart below, right)
- Ruler of the 3rd (Venus) is conjunct the ruler of the 5th (Moon) in Scorpio in the 9th – both squaring Mars, ruler of the 9th.
- Modern ruler of the 9th (Pluto) is in the 5th.

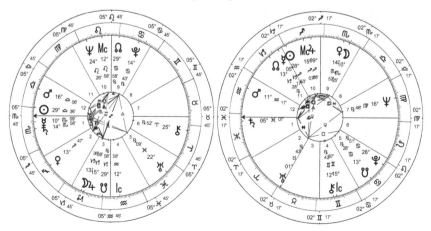

David Frost (for chart, see page 134)
- Rulers of the 3rd (Mercury) and the 9th (Jupiter) are in the 9th; modern ruler of the 9th (Neptune) is in the 3rd opposite Jupiter in the 9th.
- Ruler of the 3rd (Mercury) tightly squares the ruler of the 5th (Mars); Moon in the 5th trines the modern ruler of the 5th (Pluto), making a wide Grand Trine to Jupiter in the 9th.

Larry King (chart below, left)
- Ruler of the 3rd (Jupiter) in the 9th squares the ruler of the 5th (Venus on the Ascendant); modern ruler of the 3rd (Neptune) trines the ruler of the 5th (Venus).

Jack Paar (chart below, right)
- Ruler of the 3rd (Jupiter) is conjunct the ruler of the 5th (Venus).
- Ruler of the 9th (Mercury) is in the 5th.

Dr Phil (McGraw)
- Ruler of the 3rd (Venus) is conjunct modern ruler of the 9th (Pluto) in the 5th; ruler of the 3rd (Venus) squares the traditional ruler of the 9th (Mars).
- Ruler of the 5th (Moon) aspects both 9th-House rulers: Mars (opposition) and Pluto (square).

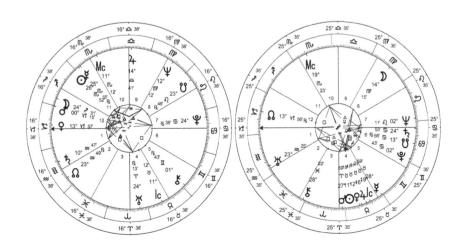

The Queen Bee

Barbara Walters (chart opposite) has worn many hats: reporter, news anchor, one-to-one interviewer of newsmakers and doyenne of an all-female TV discussion programme (*The View*). Poised, professional, coolly accomplished and as controlled as her Moon–Saturn opposition (see opposite page), Walters has always stood out as a pioneer for her gender in the competitive world of TV journalism. And since she has dodged sexist attacks along the way, it is not surprising to find the Sun Rising and Libra strongly tenanted.

Her chart has Mercury, Jupiter and Pluto strong, as well as the requisite house links:

- Ruler of the 3rd (Jupiter) is in the 9th.
- Ruler of the 5th (Saturn) is in the 3rd widely opposite the 3rd-House ruler (Jupiter) in the 9th.
- Ruler of the 9th (Mercury) closely sextiles Saturn in the 3rd.

Walters began as a publicity assistant writing press releases, then was promoted to reporter on the *Today* show in July 1961, when Solar Arc (SA) Neptune reached her Ascendant. Later, she became the first female co-anchor of the evening news on American TV in April 1974 – as SA Jupiter entered Leo, transiting (TR) Pluto retrograded back over her Ascendant, and TR Saturn inched towards her MC – before she moved to the news magazine show *20/20*. (On 26 January 2004, as SA Jupiter moved into Virgo and SA Pluto crossed her Ascendant, she finally left *20/20*.)

Other than reflecting Walters' self-confessed chronic indecision and a need to play family go-between and peacemaker, the Libra emphasis plus the Mercury–Mars conjunction suggest a journalist on the *charm offensive*, asking sugar-coated but frank questions and in pursuit of an exclusive one-to-one interview. Mercury–Mars is also a key to her success: Walters wrote personally to those she wished to interview, and that's how she usually got the exclusive. Over the years, she gained access to Richard Nixon (who proved to be one of her greatest champions), covered the peace process between Egypt and Israel in the mid 1970s, and interviewed almost every major celebrity, newsmaker and political figure (from Kissinger to Castro, Qaddafi to Sadat) of

Barbara
Walters

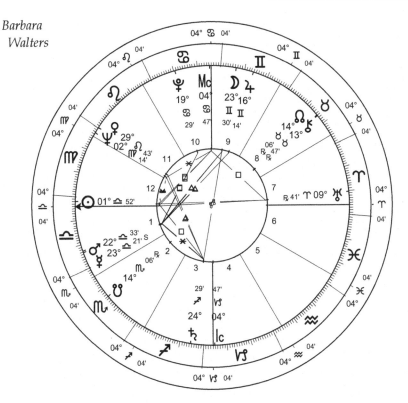

their day. Her biggest ratings sensation was her interview with Monica Lewinsky on 3 March 1999, when the SA Moon (the MC ruler) crossed over natal Neptune.

Mercury–Mars in Libra square to Pluto suggests the generational impact she had made, her number of female 'firsts' in journalism and her much-publicised million-dollar salary (in spring 1976, as SA Venus in Libra made a trine to natal Jupiter in the 9th).

With Chart Ruler/Sun dispositor Venus at the final degree of Leo (conjunct Regulus), Walters knew all about celebrity from an early age: she was surrounded by famous people because her father, Lou Walters, was a nightclub owner. Later, her TV *Specials* (celebrity confessionals, befitting her Venus–Neptune) were extremely popular and made her fortune.

Barbara and her family moved many times in childhood, due to her father's fluctuating fortunes (MC ruler Moon conjunct

Jupiter, Sun opposite Uranus, and 2nd-House rulers Mars and Pluto in square). She was born weeks before the stock market crash of 1929 and the financial rollercoaster of her dad's life contributed to her life-long fear and anxiety that her career could suddenly come crashing down around her.

But what else drove Barbara Walters to achieve? Her autobiography reveals how pivotal this Mercury–Mars square Pluto has been throughout her life. After years of guarding her sister's privacy (Mercury square Pluto), Barbara revealed in her 2008 memoir, *Audition,* the extent to which her sister (Mercury) Jacqueline had shaped her childhood and adult life. Branded mentally retarded from an early age, Jackie's condition put constraints on Barbara's life. Given Barbara's Moon in Gemini tightly opposite Saturn in the 3rd, Jackie became Barbara's responsibility and the reason Barbara became an over-achiever, feared failure and worked so hard. (The Gemini/3rd House/ Saturn emphasis here is apt when we discover that Jackie had an incapacitating stutter and we remember Barbara's own, much-teased speech impediment.)

Barbara carried around both resentment and sympathy towards Jackie: 'For so many years I was embarrassed by her, ashamed of her, guilty that I had so much and she had so little … My parents protected her. They never discussed her outside the family or explained her condition to anyone. People wouldn't understand, they felt, and Jackie would be shunned and humiliated.'[1] Here, we sense the pain and shame of the all-important square to Pluto. With Barbara's Saturn in the 3rd opposite the Moon, her sister Jackie was isolated and this contributed to Barbara's own feelings of isolation and insecurity when growing up.

Jackie was 'unwittingly the strongest influence'[2] on Barbara's life. Walters later named her adopted daughter after her, and this daughter would prove to be a challenging adolescent. As a final note, the asteroid *Jacqueline* was at 26° Sagittarius at Barbara's birth, close to her natal Saturn in the 3rd.

References and Notes
1. Barbara Walters, *Audition: A Memoir,* Vintage, 2008, p. 3.
2. Ibid.

Chapter 13

ICONIC VOCALISTS OF THE TWENTIETH CENTURY: THEIR MUSIC, THEIR LIVES, THEIR CHARTS

What follows is a collection of horoscopes and thumbnail biographies of some of the most memorable vocalists of the past few musical generations. Each is a one-of-a-kind song stylist — a distinctive interpreter of their genre. The profiles highlight some major chart themes and aspects, and I've added notes on the influence of certain planets in music and astrological signatures for some genres.

Mercury and the Moon

Where is the 'voice' in the chart? The first stop is Mercury (its sign position and aspects), which reveals how we compose and arrange both words and sounds. But really, the whole chart — in particular, its major aspects and the Sun, Moon and Ascendant signs — reveals the vocal style, interpretive qualities and 'personality' of a singer.

If Mercury links to a singer's physical, technical voice and left-brain analytic functions, the Moon (right brain) reveals how a singer interprets the lyrics and phrases a song. Both planets have specific 'connect and communicate' roles, but the Moon conveys a mood to the audience.

Venus has links to harmony, melody, popularity and the type of love song a vocalist sings, rather than being descriptive of the *type* of voice a singer possesses. Venus is not often a key player - by position or aspect - in the charts of well-known vocalists.

The Man, the Mood, 'The Voice'

The great interpreter of the 20th-century American Songbook, **Frank Sinatra,** was a vocal chameleon — an expert in nuance and phraseology — with an intuitive grasp of performing a song as if it were a story or poem (Moon in Pisces).

Frank
Sinatra

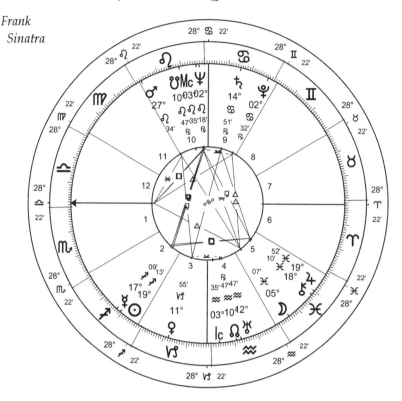

Sinatra augmented his elegant legato phrasing with a subtle use of portamento — sliding from note to note smoothly by bending the pitch of the notes.[1]

He was the first to record a whole album that created a mood and he wove a spell over his audience by choosing lush, intimate ballads and easy, swinging melodies.[2]

A charismatic Jupiter–Neptune overtone dominates Sinatra's chart. Both planets are linked to celebrity and fame. The Jupiter signature (including Sun–Mercury in Sagittarius square Jupiter in Pisces in the 5th) reflects his larger-than-life superstar status, the mass adulation and elevation (with Midheaven ruler, the Sun, conjunct Mercury, Sinatra was known simply as 'The Voice'). This also hints at his generosity and huge grudges, as well as the big mood swings of manic depression that scarred his life. (Jupiter's depression is one born of discontent — life not meeting one's expectations and search for meaning.)

The strong Neptune signature (Neptune on the Midheaven; Moon, Chiron and Jupiter in Neptune-ruled Pisces) suggests Sinatra's mass fandom, how he permeated every medium, outlived many fashions and launched an era of copycat performers. And who can forget the mythology surrounding the heart-throb crooner: the high-rolling Rat Pack bachelor lifestyle and the rumoured connections to the shady world of organized crime?

The self-importance and arrogance written in his chart and nature (his last wife revealed that he never apologized for anything) is perhaps best summed up in his signature tune 'My Way', a Sagittarian salute to self-aggrandizement and a few regrets — 'but then again, too few to mention.'[3]

Musical Notes on Neptune

Neptune has links to career longevity and the 'comeback kid'; timeless music; nostalgia, yearning for yesteryear; enigmatic performers who define a gentler era but are gone too soon (e.g., Buddy Holly: Sun–Neptune square Moon); fan mania, mass adulation; glamour; accessible, genre-crossing artists — that transcendent, indefinable 'something' that can be embraced by all; seduction, romance and 'swooners' (e.g., Julio Iglesias: Neptune conjunct Sun–Mercury; and Barry White: Neptune conjunct Venus–Mars in Libra); scandal, deception and bootlegging in the industry; chameleons and musical shape-shifters; androgyny in men (Virgo seems the key to androgyny in women); and gender ambiguity (e.g., Prince and 'drag addict' Boy George: both with Venus opposite Neptune; David Bowie: Sun–Mars and Mercury square Neptune; Marc Bolan: Sun–Venus–Neptune opposite the Moon).

Over the Rainbow

Just as **Judy Garland's** chart is dominated by two outer planets tightly conjoining and overpowering her 'public persona' angles — the Ascendant and Midheaven (MC) — so her legendary, short life was punctuated and eventually overwhelmed by crisis, exhaustion and addiction.

The perpetuated myth surrounding Garland is that of a fragile, needy, neurotic, unreliable figure (reflected in both Pluto–Ascendant in Cancer and Uranus–MC in Pisces). Yet, her children remember a devoted mother — a fun, positive spirit who was blessed with a marked sense of the ridiculous (Sun in Gemini,

Judy
Garland

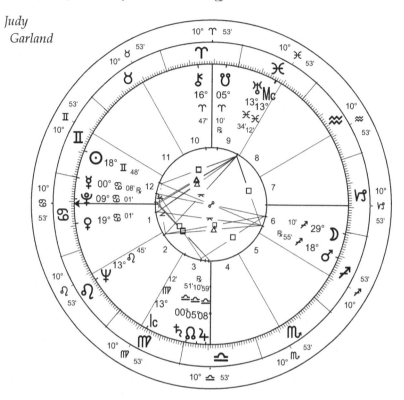

Moon in Sagittarius). We're left with an impression of a woman who, if tragic, was nevertheless forever hopeful.

What we do know is that, from childhood, Garland was the victim of a punishing, relentless work schedule and was treated as the property of MGM Studios. Lacking the foundation of a loving home, this icon without Earth and fixity in her chart was overworked, overdosed and underfed for the sake of stardom. She nevertheless possessed a remarkable work ethic and resilience.

Uranus on the MC in Pisces impacted Garland's whole life — even before birth and after her death. According to some sources, Judy's mother, while pregnant, uncovered her husband's secret gay lifestyle, and the family chose to relocate to avoid a scandal. And in 1969, Garland's death was the springboard for the Stonewall riots and the gay liberation movement — a Uranus/Pisces uprising of a repressed minority who could no longer tolerate victimization from the police. She remains the 'patron saint' of the gay community (many of whom are proud to declare themselves 'Friends of Dorothy'), and the rainbow flag of equality is said to have been inspired by her most famous song, 'Over the Rainbow',[4] which later became a lament for Garland's own life.

In addition to describing Garland's rollercoaster life, the symbolism of Pluto–Ascendant in Cancer and Uranus–MC in Pisces is depicted perfectly in her cinematic journey as Dorothy in *The Wizard of Oz* (1939): sensing paradise lost and yearning to be somewhere over the rainbow, young Dorothy runs away from home. Knocked unconscious during a tornado, she plunges into a dream state and is transported by the twister to the land of Oz. Lost, separated from family and far from home, she arrives with a crash into a magical kingdom, liberates a group of downtrodden small folk, makes friends with three outsiders, survives a field of deadly poppies, drowns the wicked witch — and then finds that all along she has had power to return to Kansas simply by clicking her heels (Pisces) together! 'There's no place like home,' Pluto Rising in Cancer chants in the final scene, while she wakes from her empowering, liberating dream.

Garland was never more endearing than when she appeared vulnerable. Germaine Greer summed up the public's continued devotion to the immortal Pisces MC icon: 'One of the ways in which her charisma worked is that you never knew when you pushed her out on stage whether she was going to collapse or perform triumphantly for hours.'[5]

Lady Day

Another instance of a public image engulfing the private personality can be found in the life and times of **Billie Holiday**. Like Garland, Holiday's inner tension and fragility characterized her singing and created a tragic myth for the public to hold on to. Both singers were sold as eternal victims whose private lives were in disarray — Holiday was seen as a weary woman, dependent on alcohol, shady men and narcotics.

Although Garland (Pluto Rising in Cancer, Sagittarius Moon) gave vibrant, even histrionic, performances to capture an audience's love, Holiday (Aquarius Rising, Moon in Capricorn)

Billie
Holiday

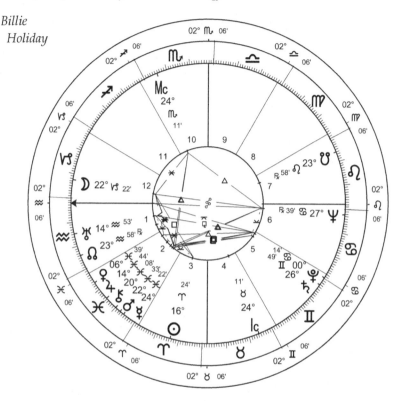

withdrew when she sang, detaching herself from her audience. With Scorpio on the MC and Mercury square Pluto, she performed with brooding, self-absorbed intensity. Holiday's distinctive, pinched voice of soulful despair suggested that she had more of a sound than a voice. The essence of 'cool' (Aquarius, Uranus in the 1st House), she influenced a generation of singers, including Sinatra, whose Pisces Moon stands one degree away from her Venus. Holiday's chart contains the conflicting energies of Neptune and Saturn themes:

- Four planets in Pisces ... but two are square Saturn;
- Aquarius Rising, Uranus in the 1st, Moon in Capricorn ... but the Moon is in the 12th and opposite Neptune.

May 1947 was a turning point in the life of Billie Holiday, with transiting Jupiter conjunct the MC, plus TR Saturn and Solar Arc

Nina
Simone

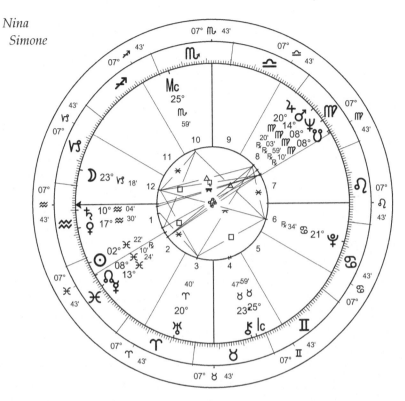

Pluto on the Descendant. At the peak of her popularity, she was arrested for possession of narcotics and served a prison term; the ensuing period, her addictions and the inevitable tabloid intrusion would leave her life and career in shambles. Her Pisces planets squaring the Saturn–Pluto conjunction might suggest how she was hounded and persecuted by the authorities.

The High Priestess of Soul

With a sign emphasis similar to Holiday's chart, **Nina Simone** had a 'fierce temperament born of the intense pain of being totally different, unique and special.'[6] She opposed the system by lending her political voice to the civil rights movement (Scorpio MC; the Moon in Capricorn in a T-square with Uranus and Pluto). Simone's T-square also describes her emotional volatility, the early rejection of her talent on racist grounds and the sudden, intense depression that would periodically descend over her.

Given her Aquarius and Scorpio angles, Nina Simone was mournfully regal, imperious and fiercely proud. Like Roberta Flack who followed her (and shared these angles), Simone was one of the first to adopt Afrocentric styles of dress. She felt everything intensely, and songs such as 'Mississippi Goddam' were her heartfelt, searing indictments of white prejudice in America.

Awarded two honorary doctorate degrees, Dr Simone could be hostile to audiences when she felt that she wasn't receiving the respect (Saturn Rising) she deserved. With the strong Pluto and Pisces–Neptune–8th House, she felt deeply betrayed by the music industry, suffering from years of theft due to bootlegged albums and unpaid royalties.

That Bad Eartha

Eartha Kitt: Siren. Sex kitten. Seductress. And, according to CIA files, a 'sadistic nymphomaniac'. These were labels that never fitted the true Eartha Mae, an intelligent, introverted woman who adopted a persona of Eurasian chic and a set of feline mannerisms, as she purred and snarled her rapid vibrato at audiences worldwide. With refined, Continental sophistication, this Capricorn chanteuse with 'Champagne Taste' mocked materialistic 1950s America by wanting 'such simple things' as 'an old-fashioned house, an old-fashioned fence ... and an old-fashioned millionaire'. And in her delivery was a Capricorn–Sagittarius dichotomy: deadly serious yet always poking fun at her femme fatale, man-eating image.

Kitt had a political sensibility and used her fame to erode racial barriers. But she found herself blacklisted and branded 'anti-American' for speaking out directly and honestly (Sagittarius Rising) about race issues at a White House luncheon on 18 January 1968. Later, she was condemned for performing in apartheid South Africa, even though she had insisted on singing to integrated audiences.

Her life was extraordinary. Eartha Kitt survived her mother's abandonment, a childhood of abuse and extreme hardship to become, according to Orson Welles, 'the most exciting woman in the world'. Yet, she summed up her life in six words that speak of Saturn Rising and Moon–Pluto buried in the 8th: 'Rejected, ejected, dejected. Used, accused, abused.'[7]

Eartha
Kitt

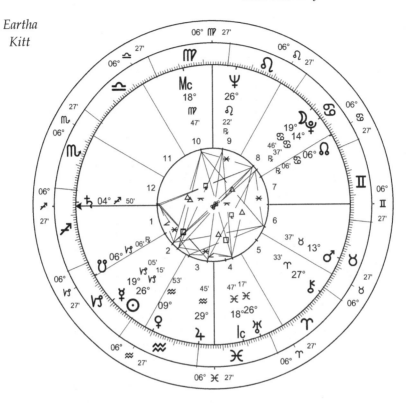

On Stage

Together, the Ascendant and the MC form the public persona. The Ascendant complex (its sign, hard aspects and ruler) comes to the fore when a singer is out in front, centre stage, whereas the MC is a collection of aspirations and attributes that forms the reputation. And the 5th and 7th Houses can provide clues about a singer's following, feelings about performing, their fan base and critics.

Sometimes a singer acts as a spokesperson for a new wave of music and embodies the outer planets which are personalized in their horoscopes: Kurt Cobain reluctantly carried the pressure and angst of the Uranus–Pluto in Virgo of Generation X on his Ascendant, while soulful iconoclast Erykah Badu has the Jupiter–Neptune conjunction of 1971 (which chanted in a new era of spiritual consciousness in music) on her Sagittarius Ascendant.

Tina
Turner

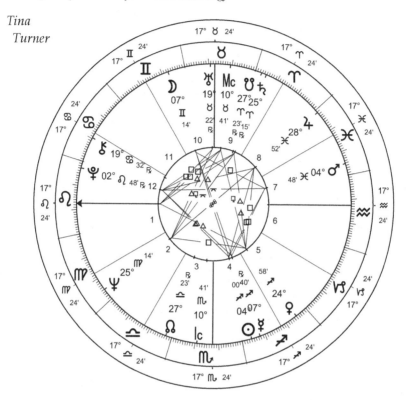

Proud Tina
Consider the Leo Ascendant of Martha Nell (later Anna Mae)
Bullock, who became **Tina Turner**, 'The Lioness of Rock'. Before
her retirement, Tina was brazen, sexual and powerful on stage,
her voice a gritty powerhouse of moans and cries. With an
audibly ferocious furnace-fire in her stomach, Tina was an all-
singing, all-dancing force of nature (note three planets – including
the Chart Ruler, the Sun – in Sagittarius). The T-square of Sun–
Mercury, the Moon and Mars (plus Uranus square the Ascendant)
suggests her high-voltage energy and electric stage presence.
She projected the persona of a wild jungle woman who would
strut across the stage in high heels, a leather miniskirt and a
punked-out wig (Leo is *all* about the hair). Yet, offstage Tina has
maintained a tasteful, quiet lifestyle, a Buddhist ritual (note the two
Jupiter–Neptune-themed T-squares) and a ladylike demeanour
of acquired European politesse.

Barbra
Streisand

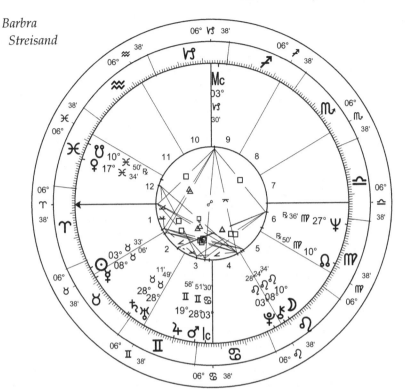

The Pursuit of Perfection

In **Barbra Streisand's** voice, we can note the sensuality of the
strong Venus (a singleton by hemisphere and the leading planet
of her Bowl-type chart) and the Sun–Mercury in Taurus square
the dramatic power and self-obsessed, theatrical instinct of
Moon–Pluto in imperious Leo. (The latter is on the cusp of the 5th
House, reminding us of her crippling stage fright and infamous
need for performance control.) And then there's the Aries
Ascendant, seen in the perfectionist with a forceful, dynamic song
delivery.

Addressing the paradoxes in her nature, Streisand has
described herself as 'simple, complex, generous, selfish,
unattractive, beautiful, lazy and driven.'[8] A combination of
instinct and individuality, Barbra is more personality than singer
or actress. This has been the key to — and the driving force of —
her bold, multifaceted career.

Roy Orbison

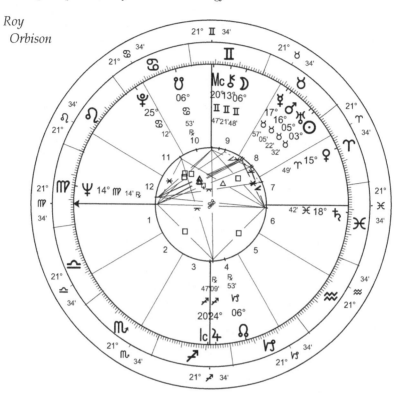

In Dreams: The Big O
Roy Orbison possessed a mysteriously soft and vulnerable yet soaring, symphonic three-octave voice. While the unaspected duet of Sun–Uranus in Taurus in the 8th suggests the shattering family losses that impacted Orbison's later life, quotes about the man and his voice bring to light his Neptune Rising in Virgo and his Mercury–Mars conjunction in Taurus. Musical collaborator k. d. lang (whose MC conjoins Roy's Gemini Moon and whose Ascendant conjoins his Neptune) said:

> I've always compared Roy Orbison to a tree: passive and beautiful yet extremely solid. He maintained a sense of humility and sensitivity and gentleness uncommon to his era … [Roy's sound] was a private place to go – a solace or a refuge.[9]

Patsy
Cline

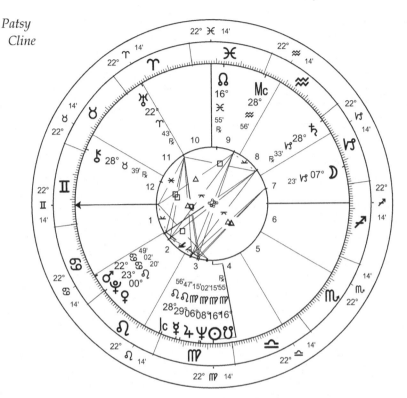

Singer Dion added, 'When he hit those high notes, it was quiet and heartfelt. But the emotion would go through you like a power drill.'[10]

'The Cline'

It took a woman with **Patsy Cline's** swagger, husky alto and an aching hiccup in her voice to break through the male-dominated world of country music and tread the boards of the Grand Ole Opry. The dignified beauty of her voice on 'Crazy', 'Sweet Dreams' and 'I Fall to Pieces' is matched only by her regal presence and confidence (Venus and Mercury bookend the sign of Leo).

After seven years of career delays due to a restrictive contract, money worries and the birth of her baby, Cline's career finally gathered momentum in 1961. But as she was hitting the big time, her potent T-square involving Mars–Pluto, Saturn and Uranus was triggered and two accidents befell her. The first was a car crash at 16:43 on 14 June 1961 in Madison, Tennessee (during her exact Saturn Return, as TR Mars–Uranus conjoined her SA Mars–Pluto at 21° Leo). This was followed by a fatal plane crash on 5 March 1963 (as SA Ascendant at 22° Cancer closed in on her tight natal Mars–Pluto conjunction and squared Uranus). Her early death resulted in a legacy of a few dozen timeless songs and an enduring mystique surrounding Cline herself.

Protest Singers

Where does the protest singer fit into the astrological pantheon? Taking an individual, sometimes risky stand is a principle of Mars and its signs. The countercultural impulse to shake up existing societal structures is Uranian, while the urge to speak out and shoot down hypocrisy – to have one's voice not simply heard (Gemini) but believed – is Sagittarian in nature. And Saturn or Capricorn (more so than Aquarius) features strongly in those who address society's ills and (with Uranus or Mars) rattle the Establishment's cage.

Grassroots activist Billy Bragg created waves in Margaret Thatcher's Britain during the 1980s. He has the Sun and Moon in Sagittarius, Venus opposite Uranus both squaring a Scorpio Ascendant, and Mars in Scorpio in the 1st House square Pluto–MC.

Odetta was a folk hero ahead of her time and instrumental in lending music's support to the civil rights movement. She had Mars on the Descendant square the Moon, Sagittarius on the MC, and Sun–Saturn in Capricorn square Uranus.

Odetta turned Bob Dylan on to folksinging (their Moons are conjunct, and his Sun is opposite her MC). Dylan's chart has Jupiter and Mercury signatures (plus a strongly aspected Uranus). Heralded as a musical prophet and revolutionary poet of his times, Dylan has Sagittarius Rising, the Sun square Mars, and the Moon conjunct Saturn–Uranus.

The Silver Flute

The pivotal aspect that ties together the chart of **Joan Baez** is the Moon at 3° Gemini (conjunct Bob Dylan's Sun) exactly opposite Chart Ruler Mars in Sagittarius in the 9th. This opposition (which tightly aspects her Ascendant, Sun–Mercury and Pluto) is the key to her story. Born of mixed Mexican and Scottish heritage, Joan met racism early on, but had a strong social conscience from her Quaker upbringing that helped to strengthen her resolve.

Devoted to civil rights and non-violent social change, Joan's first protest as a conscientious objector in high school made the

Joan
Baez

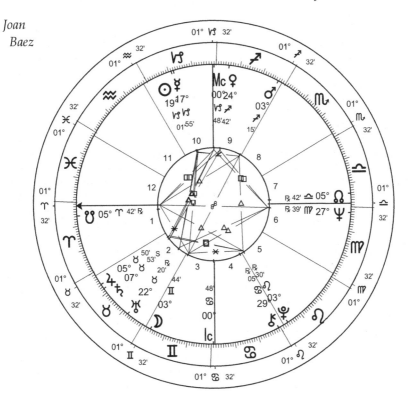

newspapers (6 February 1958, with TR Mars conjunct the MC/
10th-House cusp and SA MC conjunct Sun–Mercury). Soon after,
she began singing in public (and later sang in various languages
– Gemini).

Baez's voice and political awareness were the two pillars
(Gemini) that merged to form her music career. She became a
chronicler of social mores (Sun–Mercury in Capricorn), always
having the courage of her convictions (Mars/Sagittarius/9th).

For many years, she suffered from insomnia, panic attacks
and performance fears (note Pluto in the 5th and Neptune in the
6th conjunct the Descendant), and she eventually came to terms
with the multiple personalities formed as a result of childhood
trauma. She has spoken of how these personalities carry much
information and take on different voices, forms and names
(another expression of the Moon in Gemini).[11]

With her Neptune on the Descendant square Venus on the MC, some of Baez's greatest songs have been ones of suffering ('Sweeter for Me'), bittersweet laments and remembrances of passion lost ('Love Song to a Stranger' and the Aries/Capricorn-titled 'Diamonds and Rust') and prophetic poetry ('Lady Di and I').

Musical Notes on Pluto

Pluto is evident in the big business of music — the entrepreneurs/ men in suits/plutocrats who entered the scene in the late 1970s; those who shape their generation and 'push buttons'; era-defining artists who wrest control from the moguls and mass-market their product (e.g., Madonna: Pluto conjunct Sun, Ascendant and Chart Ruler Mercury; Michael Jackson: Pluto conjunct Sun and Mercury; and Prince: Pluto–MC opposite the Moon, square Mercury); those who reinvent themselves, manipulate their image, exploit sex and bring taboos into the musical mainstream; the obsessive side of fame and fandom.

Respect for the Queen

Other than her incomparable voice, what appears to separate **Aretha Franklin** from her contemporaries as an interpreter of song is a blend of honest emotion, sheer conviction, indefatigable confidence and raw passion. For an Aries Sun with a Leo MC (and Mercury square Mars–Jupiter), such blessings must seem a birthright for the reigning Queen of Soul. In 1967 (as TR Neptune squared her MC, and TR Saturn crossed back and forth over MC ruler Sun), Aretha became a chart-topping star and suddenly her music was the soundtrack to the emerging civil rights movement.

Sooner or later, all divas live their signature tunes in the storylines of their own lives. With hindsight, every key song in their repertoire becomes a chapter of their autobiography. Aretha's song 'Respect', an authoritative call for action, was delivered in an evangelical, fiery bawl of gospel and soul — reflective of the powerhouse Franklin truly was. Her legendary producer Jerry Wexler conceded: 'If she didn't live it, she couldn't give it.'

With Scorpio Rising, Franklin has always had an impenetrable reserve and need for privacy, and some have spoken of a sombreness and darkness about her. For years now, she has seemed most content in the comfort of her own home, watching

Aretha Franklin

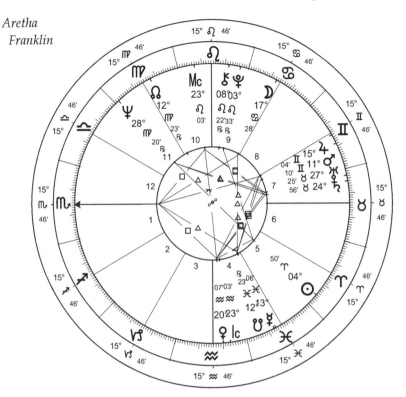

soaps — whether this is retreat (Moon in Cancer, Venus–IC) or her Martial chart languishing in Venusian indolence. But then, what more does she have to prove?

Signatures of Rock

Wild, raucous rock 'n' roll energy, Stadium Rock, raw sexuality and magnetism, groupies — this is the stuff of Scorpio, Mars and Pluto. Examining dozens of rock stars, the frontmen, we can throw in a few further ingredients:

- Neptune for stage presence and inspiring crowd euphoria;
- A helping of Jupiter (and its signs) for hedonism, excess and god-like adulation;
- A jolt of dynamic Uranus for shock value and explosive anarchy;
- A predominance of the sensual, pagan Earth signs (particularly rock-like Capricorn);[12]
- And finally, Leo or Sagittarius for charisma and performance exhibitionism.

> **Signatures of Rock – continued**
> Here are a few examples:
>
> • Black leather rock mystic Jim Morrison: Moon in Taurus square
>   Pluto setting (on the Descendant), Sun in Sagittarius opposite
>   Mars–Uranus, Jupiter in Leo square MC in Scorpio.
>
> • Wild woman and leather-clad Suzi Quatro: Mars Rising square
>   Uranus–MC, Moon in Capricorn plus four planets and Ascendant
>   in Earth signs.
>
> • INXS bad-boy Michael Hutchence: Moon–Neptune in Scorpio,
>   Venus–Jupiter in Sagittarius.
>
> • Oasis lead singer Liam Gallagher: Sun–Mercury–Mars in late Virgo
>   (and Pluto in early Libra) on the MC square Jupiter in Sagittarius,
>   Neptune Rising, Venus in Leo.
>
> • Ozzy Osbourne: Moon in Capricorn, Mars–Jupiter in Capricorn
>   (opposite Uranus), Moon square Neptune, Sun–Mercury in
>   Sagittarius, Venus in Scorpio square Pluto.

Bono Vox

'Bono's singing is 50% Guinness, 10% cigarettes — and the rest is
religion.'[13] U2's lead singer **Bono** — very much a 'normal bloke'
with integrity (Saturn Rising in Capricorn) — has used his rock
star status to help those who have suffered from the politics and
devastation of war (Moon–Neptune in Scorpio). He, too, has
the Scorpio, Neptune and Earth signatures of the rock star, and
articulated this blend:

> We write songs on so many different levels: politically,
> sexually, spiritually … [For a while] spiritual confusion
> knocked me off my feet. I felt very alone in that disorientation
> … But now I realize that rock and roll has always
> encompassed both spirituality and sexuality.[14]

A defining Saturn–Neptune moment in his life was the death of
his mother when he was 14 (half a Saturn cycle, and the number of
years spent by Neptune in one sign). This event 'pushed him into
two directions at once, towards the emotional exorcism offered by
punk rock and the meditative space to be found in Christianity.'[15]

Bono

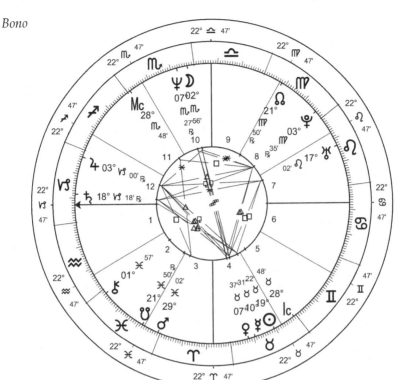

Neptune and Libra Causes

Alongside Uranus's instinct to wake people up to social causes, and Jupiter's flair for promotion and lobbying the influential, Neptune's function is to induce an emotional response to environmental issues and the plight of the needy. Bob Geldof (Sun–Neptune in Libra, and Mercury opposite Jupiter in Aries, the signature of the inspirational fundraiser) and Midge Ure (Sun–Neptune in Libra) gathered pop and rock royalty to record 'Do They Know It's Christmas?' four days after Neptune made its final ingress into business-minded Capricorn in November 1984. The song raised millions for famine relief in Ethiopia and was the start of numerous celebrity efforts to bring salvation to the forgotten and disenfranchised (Neptune), to tackle broader human rights issues (Libra) and to address the imbalances (Libra) of power and wealth. Another Libra Sun, Sting (with Moon conjunct Neptune in Libra, and Jupiter–MC in Aries), actively supported Amnesty International and launched a foundation in 1989 to preserve the rainforests.

> **The Disco Era**
> If Neptune relates to -isms that permeate popular culture, then new musical forms (such as jazz) or fads that revolutionize music and divide public opinion are undoubtedly Uranian in nature. None more so than disco, which gave Middle America three excuses to condemn it, emerging as it did from the gay, Hispanic and black subcultures. The notorious Studio 54 nightclub opened its doors during a T-square of Sun-Mercury opposite Uranus–Ascendant in Scorpio, both square Moon-MC in Leo. Astrologer and musician Jenni Dean Harte was there that night and described the club as a 'Mecca for the new music aristocracy … the spotlight was on youthful partying, psychoactive drugs and sexual abandon.'[16]

The First Lady of Lust

Thanks to her January 1975 recording of 'Love to Love You Baby' — disco's ode to the orgasm — **Donna Summer** became a star in America as transiting Pluto squared her Sun–Jupiter, and Solar Arc MC conjoined her Uranus. But feeling trapped by her

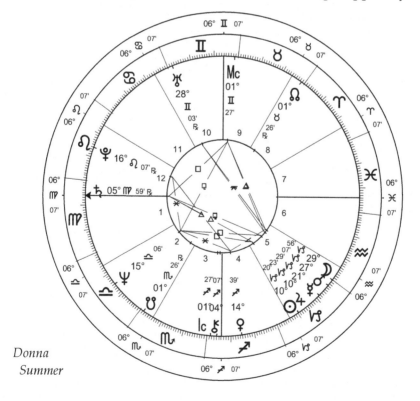

Donna Summer

erotic, prurient image and suffering from anxiety attacks and exhaustion, Summer struggled to reconcile her fame with her faith (natal Neptune square MC ruler Mercury and Sun–Jupiter). She swapped her siren image for a Born Again lifestyle in late 1979, the year she dominated the US pop charts. Not long afterwards, she sued to free herself from music mogul Neil Bogart (alleging undue influence and fraud). Both epiphanies coincided with TR Jupiter going over her Ascendant, and TR Pluto square Mercury, ruler of both the Ascendant and the MC.

Despite her scintillating diva persona, Summer maintained that she was an 'ordinary girl' (Saturn) — the title of her musical and autobiography — and later expanded her Capricorn/5th-House creative legacy to include dozens of abstract paintings.

Musical Notes on Venus

Venus is the planet directly linked to popular culture and manufactured, disposable bubblegum pop. Many who have been overnight (albeit brief) sensations — thanks to TV talent shows or the Internet — have hard aspects from the outer planets to Venus. But the ones who strike a more powerful, longer-held chord for their generation, such as Justin Bieber, tend to have Moon–Pluto or Mercury–Pluto contacts.

Neptune in Aquarius brought us a wash of talent shows where ordinary people (Aquarius) could have a shot at fulfilling their dreams of musical fame (Neptune). *American Idol* and *The X Factor* impresario Simon Cowell is a Libran with the 'pop mogul' signature: Venus conjunct Pluto. This is an aspect shared by reality judge and *American Idol* producer Nigel Lythgoe, who was born with Venus conjunct Pluto in Leo. Superstar entertainer Michael Jackson also had Venus in Leo and still is, of course, known as 'The King [Leo] of Pop [Venus]'. The other sovereign of the zodiac is stately, rock-like ruler Capricorn, and 'The King of Rock 'n' Roll' Elvis Presley was born with three planets in this sign — including Venus — all opposite Pluto (his chart is on page 50).

Stripped Bare

Christina Aguilera emerged on the scene just before the turn of the millennium. A few years into her recording career, she shed her teenybopper look for a more sexualized image — a move that was as controversial as that made recently by the current *enfant terrible* Miley Cyrus. Both share a Venus–Uranus conjunction, suggesting a rejection (Uranus) of female gender stereotypes, a refusal to

Christina
Aguilera

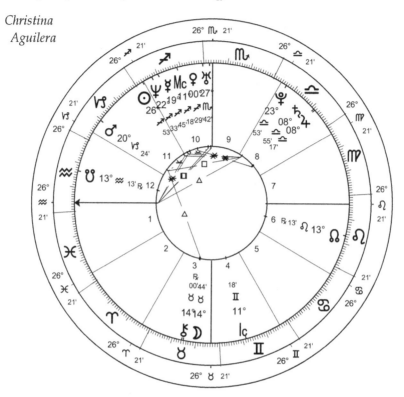

please others and the creation of a sassy, provocative form of 'femme-pop'. This conjunction is as empowering as Aguilera's song 'Beautiful', her coming-of-age ballad for the outsider (Aquarius Rising, Uranus square the Ascendant).

Her raw pop-rock-blues voice has enabled her to cross a number of genres — note the powerful Neptune straddled by the Sun and Mercury. In Sagittarius, these could suggest melisma as well as oversinging, a habit that's been a trademark of pop divas and wannabes since the 1990s. Aguilera's biggest vocal influence was Whitney Houston, whose MC is one degree away from Christina's Mercury.

Aguilera, Cyrus, Britney Spears and Justin Timberlake all emerged from adolescent fame courtesy of the Disney Studios and each has the Sun or Moon in Sagittarius. (Walt Disney himself had the Sun in Sagittarius, and his Disney vision is a manifestation of pure Sagittarian magic.)

*Janis
Joplin*

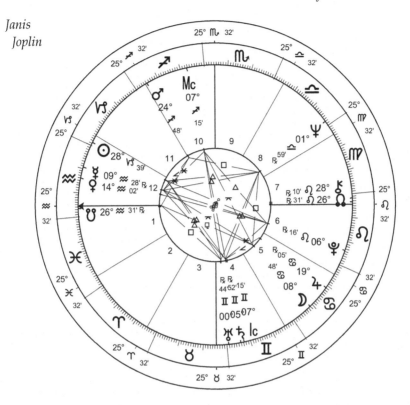

Pearl

Distinctive vocalist **Janis Joplin** was a fiercely burning meteor in
the musical firmament who vanished too soon. This sandpaper-
larynxed blues–rock singer had a chart of contradictions to match
her nature: the needy, do-right, status quo-conscious Cancer–
Capricorn and the wild, defiant gypsy (Aquarius, Sagittarius)
who sang with passionate abandon. She was a middle-class
white woman who cried her soulful, bluesy heart out on stage.
Describing Joplin's Mercury–Pluto opposition and the Sagittarius–
Aquarius combination, singer Roseanne Cash wrote:

> [Janis] had this focus that was relentless … She had an
> unshakeable commitment to her own truth, no matter how
> destructive, how weird or how bad … The beauty and the
> power of Janis Joplin as a singer is her complete lack of fear …
> She went to the edge every time she opened her mouth.[17]

References and Notes

(All URLs were accessed in December 2013 and January 2014.)

1. Roy Hemming and David Hajdu, *Discovering Great Singers of Classic Pop*, Newmarket, 1991, p. 119.
2. Sagittarius appears strong in charts of 'easy listening' artists. Consider, for instance, the lithe, sublime vocals of Johnny Mathis (Ascendant, Mars), Dionne Warwick (Sun, Mercury) and Andy Williams (Sun, Saturn).
3. Other memorable Sagittarian showstoppers include Edith Piaf's 'Je Ne Regrette Rien' and the half-condescending, half-grateful tearjerker 'Wind Beneath My Wings' by Bette Midler (both singers have the Sun in Sagittarius).
4. Eva Cassidy, whose own signature tune is a cover of 'Over the Rainbow', had her MC conjunct Garland's Ascendant–Pluto, and her Jupiter on Garland's MC; Cassidy's Sun–Saturn conjunction had Solar Arc directed to the degree of Garland's Pisces MC when she recorded the track in 1992.
5. As quoted in a Channel 4 TV documentary, *Viva La Diva*, 2001.
6. David Nathan, *The Soulful Divas*, Billboard, 1999, p. 46.
7. Both of these quotes come from Eartha Kitt's autobiography, *I'm Still Here: Confessions of a Sex Kitten*, Sidgwick & Jackson Ltd, 1989.
8. www.brainyquote.com/quotes/quotes/b/barbrastre114160.html
9. As quoted in *Rolling Stone: The 100 Greatest Artists of All Time*, 2011, p. 51.
10. As quoted in *Rolling Stone*, 27 November 2008, p. 86.
11. Baez in conversation with Jeremy Isaacs on BBC2's *Face to Face* (26 January 1998).
12. For details of rock music's link to the Earth signs, see Paul Wright, *Astrology in Action*, Anodyne, 1988.
13. Billie Jo Armstrong, *Rolling Stone*, 27 November 2008, p. 91.
14. As quoted in Timothy White, *Rock Lives*, Omnibus, 1990, pp. 731–732.
15. Interview with Bono by Chrissy Iley, in the *Evening Standard*, 17 August 2001.
16. As quoted in the astrology magazine *Data News Plus*, Issue 3, Flare, October 1998, p. 16.
17. As quoted in *Rolling Stone: The 100 Greatest Artists of All Time*, 2011, p. 60.

Your Stars: Plenty of 'Scope and Enough Rope

In 2012, my good friend Wendy Stacey called needing a comedy column for the Astrological Association of Great Britain's upcoming conference brochure. 'Something funny about the end of the world' was the instruction. I rang Wendy back with my ideas late that night. 'You can't write that!' came the reply. So we spent an hour on the phone constructing new, more politically correct offerings. When I put the phone down, I thought 'Screw that', dumped the ideas and wrote the following:

Well, we never did quite make it to the Age of Aquarius. Let's blame the void of *coarse* loons who predicted it – knowing full well that such a day would never come.

But it's too late now. Hope never arrived. Salvation stayed indoors. It's the end of the world and we all need to keep it real – even the starry navel-gazers among us.

So, as a final farewell, here are some home truths served up by sober Saturn (with an extra helping of Mercury–Pluto), to ensure that none of us leaves the table fully fed on self-satisfaction.

Aries ♈

Your two talents: looking out for number one and stepping in number two.

Taurus ♉

You're rock-like and granite-faced, but is your admirable firmness simply detestable stubbornness?

Gemini ♊

Never worry about the future – everyone knows you always land on someone else's feet.

Cancer ♋

Your life's menu consists of much food and even more whine.

Leo ♌

One philosophical question gives rise to your greatest fear: what's the sound of no hands clapping?

Virgo ♍

You're someone who knows the way but can't drive the car.

Libra ♎

There are two things people don't like about you: your face.

Scorpio ♏

As far as sex is concerned, most people need a reason. You need a location.

Sagittarius ♐

The truth may be hard to swallow, but you were born with a silver foot in your mouth.

Capricorn ♑

Experience is a comb that life gave you after you lost your hair. Now use it to brush up your skills.

Aquarius ♒

Yeah, you love humanity, but we all know the truth: it's people you can't stand.

Pisces ♓

Let's face it, you're so vague, you've got no idea this song is about you.

Chapter 14

THE LUNAR GESTATION CYCLE – AN INTRODUCTION

Whenever astrologers are on to something interesting – a technique that yields consistent results or an interpretative angle that sheds new light – I want 'in'! Oh, how Aries hates to miss out on a good thing! So, some time ago, when I heard that US astrologer Dietrech Pessin had arrived in the UK to lecture at the AA's Conference (Cirencester, 1997) with a couple of hundred copies of her spiral-bound book, *Lunar Shadows*, and returned to Massachusetts having sold the lot, I wanted to know *all* about her predictive method – The Lunar Gestation Cycle – that had aroused so much interest.

What follows, in a nutshell, is Dietrech Pessin's work on the Lunar Gestation Cycle, followed by an example of my own research.

As astrologers we know that every month there's a New Moon (where the Sun and Moon are at the exact same degree and same sign as each other), and this starts a 28-day cycle until the next New Moon. The First Quarter follows 7 days into the cycle, which culminates 7 days later at the Full Moon (14 days into the cycle), and 7 days on (21 days) there's the final stage, a Last Quarter Moon. But during each lunar month, these four Moon phases have no sign (or degree) in common with one another.

Yet, what Dietrech Pessin found was that *nine months* after every New Moon, there is a First Quarter Moon in the same sign and around the same degree.[1] And nine months after this First Quarter Moon, there's a Full Moon at around the same degree of both previous phases. And nine months after that, a Last Quarter Moon is around a similar degree of the same sign, completing a 'Moon Family' – four phases linked by time and the (near) degree of a sign.

Take a look at your ephemeris. Pick a recent New Moon and trace its very own Moon Family. The example I'll use is the first New Moon listed in the table below:

- On 29 September 2008, there's a New Moon at 6° Libra.
- Nine months later (29 June 2009), there's a First Quarter Moon at 7° Libra.
- Nine months later (30 March 2010), there's a Full Moon at 9° Libra.
- Nine months later (28 December 2010), there's a Last Quarter Moon at 6° Libra.

Most human cycles and life stories are not completed in a month. With the Lunar Gestation Cycle, though, there are four related lunar phases (each nine months apart) that speak of the development of a seed (New Moon) into a crisis/action phase (First Quarter), then to fruition (Full Moon) and finally into crisis/recap/recoup (Last Quarter Phase). It's a useful timing tool that shows events unfolding over two and a quarter years (0, 9, 18 and 27 months). No longer are we expecting a lunar cycle to hold all the answers or show a complete cycle of human affairs in a mere 28 days.

The Lunar Gestation Cycle is more akin to real life phases and timings. It is also, interestingly, the time it takes for Saturn to move through a sign.

What's on the agenda at each phase of the Moon?

New Moon (Moon conjuncts the Sun)
This is the 'seed' stage, the beginning of a cycle; it is a time of new ideas and fresh starts, but it is <u>never</u> a good time to take action because, as Dietrech says, there is not enough (Moon)light on the matter. *Wait until the First Quarter nine months later before taking action.*

At the New Moon, there's a feeling of something new to discover; we're clueless or too subjective. We are seeking direction and clarity. It is a perfect time to conceive ideas or plant seeds of an undertaking; to research, brainstorm or make a wish list.

First Quarter Moon (the waxing Moon now squares the Sun)
We're better (but not fully) informed at this stage. With the Sun squared by the Moon, it's a turning point, often crisis- or stress-driven with a need to move things up a gear. Something in our life (whatever is being triggered by this phase) that was in seed form nine months ago now springs into action, demands attention

or develops significantly. It's a time to make things happen, to pursue new endeavours, but commitments are premature until there's more 'light' available at the next phase.

Full Moon (the Moon opposes the Sun)
Here the Moon beams down a full spotlight upon us. Matters started 18 months ago (and triggered into productive action 9 months ago) are now in full bloom. Everything can be seen, particularly relationship concerns. (This is the Libra phase of the cycle and, as a general note, emotions run high at the Full Moon, as relationship issues invariably come to a head.)

At the Full Moon we're completely aware: ideas or circumstances are out in the open and cards are on the table. It's a great time for a launch or to achieve maximum exposure. There's a sense of fulfilment, whether it's the completion of a deadline or the fruits of one's labours.

Last Quarter Moon (the waning Moon squares the Sun)
This waning phase is busy and crisis-driven (the square), but it is time to close the matter, to review and evaluate what has taken place in the past 27 months and see what remains useful for the future. The final phase is an ideal time to get rid of deadweight and safeguard the seeds that can be replanted for the new phase in 9 months' time. It is a period for acknowledging aspects from the past, but leaving behind what no longer serves us (or a situation in our lives). It is also about preparing for the new cycle and preparing to re-invest what is still valuable.

So how do we know which phases we're in now? Well, we're probably in a few, as there are New Moons each month that may activate some aspect of our chart. One New Moon may conjunct our Mercury in March, and a month later the next New Moon squares our Saturn – both begin Moon Families of their own. So I advise students at the LSA to highlight New Moons and the aspects they make to their charts (usually with a 4–5° orb) and then follow the cycle through.

If a New Moon triggers our chart (e.g., by aspect to a planet or angle), it sets in motion a two-and-a-quarter year cycle. The events, emotions or circumstances that transpire will have in them the symbolism of the sign(s), house(s) and aspect(s) involved, and the stage of the development (New, First Quarter, etc.) will be significant, too.

So we have a clearly marked map. There's no need for predicting which of the three to five aspects from transiting Pluto, for example, will manifest in a 'meaningful event'. With this method, we have a ready-made timetable that links a storyline (a package of events), and we can watch it wax and wane through the months and years ahead. As Dietrech points out: dramas in our lives cluster around the dates of these phases usually within two weeks either side, but sometimes *to the day*. And when there's an Eclipse involved (whether it's a Solar or Lunar one), it becomes a power-packed Moon Family and the developments have more lasting consequences for us.

The cycle doesn't always end with the Last Quarter Moon. Sometimes the New Moon nine months later is still within orb of the original set of phases and this continues the storyline further (see the example that follows).

Although I had looked at this cycle in the late 1990s, it wasn't until I started using this in my own life and in the charts of clients that I saw how revealing it could be. When preparing for a seminar in Turkey a while ago, I started to research the Iraq invasion of 2003 to see if this had links to **George W. Bush's** chart (pictured below). I was surprised at the Moon Family involved (Uranus was triggered) and astounded at how accurately it pinpointed key dates in the developments that preceded and followed it.

Below, I've listed the dates, phases, degrees/ signs and corresponding events, but please take time to also consider the significance of the waxing and waning phases during both Moon Families.

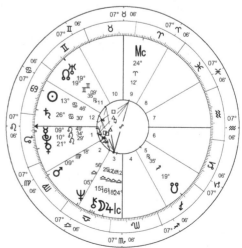

George W. Bush
- Natal Uranus conjunct North Node at 19° Gemini
- His father, George H.W. Bush, has the Sun at 21° Gemini
- The US has Mars at 21° Gemini in the 7th (Sibly)

Here's the Moon Family for George W. Bush that triggered his natal Uranus. It turns out to be a timeline of his Presidential journey and perhaps is the 'thread' revealing his true agenda.

Date	Phase	Pos.	Event
13/06/99	New Moon	22° ♊	Bush announces his candidacy on 13 June
13/03/00	First Quarter	23° ♊	Bush wins Republican nomination on 14 March
11/12/00	Full Moon	19° ♊	Election is decided by Supreme Court on 12 Dec
10/09/01	Last Quarter	18° ♊	Terrorist Attacks on 11 Sep, beg. of 'war on terror'

This Moon Family is re-triggered by being near same degree/conjunct the same planet, breathing new life into the story:

Date	Phase	Pos.	Event
10/06/02	New Moon Eclipse	19° ♊	Bush 'sells' the Iraq invasion to Congress
11/03/03	First Quarter	20° ♊	US invades Iraq on 20 March
08/12/03	Full Moon	16° ♊	Saddam Hussein is captured on 13 December
06/09/04	Last Quarter*	14° ♊	Bush accepts Republican nomination for 2nd term
	* now out of orb		

This is an extraordinary timetable and remarkably exact. But why was Bush's Uranus in Gemini in the 11th the planet triggered? It doesn't immediately reveal Bush's impact as President of the USA: he was *not* a visionary or a reformer nor did he speak for social change, although he *did* divide opinion throughout his presidency like no other before him (Uranus in Gemini in the 11th). Yet Uranus, *the* planet provocateur, co-rules his Descendant (the critical angle for politicians), it is his most elevated planet, the first to rise (his 'leading' planet) and is exactly conjunct his North Node. Even more telling is that it's two degrees away from his father's Sun at 21° Gemini (after all, he *was* completing George Senior's oil mission in the Middle East) and two degrees from the US's (4 July 1776) Mars at 21° Gemini. These links and the triggering lunar phase suggest the making of a President of War and one who would declare a 'war on terror'. The Solar Arc directions to and from his Uranus reveal key times in Bush's life and, arguably, reveal his true motives/mission. Developments with his own oil company, his announcement to run for President, and the capture of Saddam Hussein all occurred under significant Solar Arcs involving Uranus.

We can use the Lunar Gestation Cycle to plan projects, observe relationship patterns, identify life cycles and predict/watch these stages unfold. In fact, most events or developments are connected to a nine-month period, regardless of the Moon phase. A job we start today may have had the seeds planted some nine months ago, or some action was taken back then that directly relates to the happenings today.

Dietrech had discovered the Lunar Gestation Cycle while working as a 900-Line astrologer in the US – the type of telephone consultancy job that requires you keep your head while others around you are losing theirs (Dietrech herself called it an 'emergency room internship of astrology'). Being aware of the four phases of the Cycle opens up a treasure trove of interlinked information. It is also the first Moon cycle noted to roughly parallel the nine-month human gestation cycle (hence its name). It's an area I now teach every year at the LSA.

Despite an influx of new significators said to improve or broaden chart delineation, computer programs offering countless additional features, and the quest to 'prove' astrology (or rather, prove *something* to universities and scientists), some of the most important advances in recent years (in my opinion) have been linked to the age-old cycles of the Earth, Sun and Moon – work that Dietrech has explored and researched. With her Lunar Gestation Cycle, we're challenged to delve deeper and explore further the profound, eternal dance between the Sun, Moon and Earth.

Further reading: *Lunar Shadows: The Lost Key to the Timing of Eclipses* and *Lunar Shadows III* (updated, expanded version) by Dietrech Pessin. www.lunar-shadows.com

References and Notes
1. Occasionally it's a different sign but only a few degrees (at most) away from the previous phase nine months earlier.

Chapter 15

REVISITING THE FIRST SATURN RETURN

It happens often in the twenty-ninth year of life that all the forces that have been engaged through the years of childhood, adolescence and youth in confused and ferocious combat range themselves in ordered ranks ... The straight and narrow gateway of maturity and life which was all uproar and confusion narrows down to form and purpose, and we exchange a great dim possibility for a small hard reality ... [At thirty] we find at last that vocation for which we feel ourselves fit and to which we willingly devote continued labour.
                          – Gertrude Stein, *Fernhurst*, pp. 29–30

I've collated over 30 published observations on the first Saturn Return from two dozen astrologers. What follows is a range of opinions on, and insights into, this significant, often monumental life-time transit, which occurs around the age of 29.

The maturation process; a time of commitment; an invitation into adulthood

Grant Lewi
   [The Saturn Return is] the most important period of introspection and self-analysis, which may rise directly from yourself or may be forced on you by circumstances ... You are reviewing the past, taking stock of your aims ... revising deeply your notions of many things ... You will stand freed, when this transit is past, of many erstwhile inner restrictions. You will have swept your nature clean of dead wood.
   Astrology for the Millions, Llewellyn, 1990 edition, p. 337

Alexander Ruperti
   This is often a year of choice which determines the direction of the life, the type of associates one values, and the profession or

business activity [one] adopts ... The individual is obliged to
act according to principle, fulfilling a definite function or role
in society as significantly as possible.

Cycles of Becoming, CRCS, 1978, p. 139

Noel Tyl

For the year or year and one-half preceding Saturn's return
to its natal position, the identity finally grows up on its own,
having learned from many false starts and mistakes: the life
changes direction and/or level conspicuously. This change
calls for full resourcefulness of the whole identity, the whole
horoscope.

*The Principles and Practice of Astrology, Volume VII:
Integrated Transits*, Llewellyn, 1974, p. 34

Steven Forrest

We are in the process of delineating our personal identity,
seeking a Vision for our lives. Throughout this phase, our
roadsigns are insights into our own personality and destiny.
Their purpose is to lead us eventually into maturity.

The Changing Sky, ACS, 1998, p. 100

Charles and Suzi Harvey

We have to face the real challenges of adulthood with a more
realistic attitude ... we have a sense of knowing ourselves well
for the first time.

Principles of Astrology, Thorsons, 1999, p. 213

Erin Sullivan

There is an increasing willingness to explore alternatives to
what one has been doing with one's life. Initially, this urge is
instinctive, infantile and undeveloped ... The first year of the
Saturn Return is filled with the ambivalence of whether one
really wants to grow up or not ... [After the Saturn Return] we
are less likely to resent or blame parents ... and more inclined
to absolve them for their flaws, taking personal responsibility
for our own lives and direction.

Saturn in Transit, Arkana, 1991, pp. 73, 75

Sherene Schostak and Stefanie Iris Weiss

The precipice of adulthood. Now childhood is finally and irrevocably over ... We have a choice at this moment, and if we make the right decision and live out the will of our hearts, the next twenty-nine and a half years will be richer, happier, and smoother.

Surviving Saturn's Return, Contemporary Books, 2004, p. 6

Linda Reid

One feels an inner urge to make a bid for authority and maturity, while at the same time there is a growing awareness that such matters may constitute a trap.

Astrology Step by Step, Canopus, 2001, p. 185

Crisis; the Lord of Karma; the principle of cause and effect

Robert Hand

If you have built your life up to now around activities that are inappropriate for you, it will be a time of crisis.

Planets in Transit, Whitford Press, 1976, p. 348

Martin Freeman

There is likely to be a testing relating to whatever Saturn refers natally ... The tests may come through other people or in external events; in dark moods or in inner striving. It depends on either the individual's ability to contain the tension within and allow growth and transformation to take place, or his need to externalize the experience, projecting difficulties onto other people so that they are the apparent cause of the problems and personal responsibility is supposedly excused.

Forecasting by Astrology, Faculty of Astrological Studies, 1982, p. 27

Nicholas Campion

This frequently coincides with an individual's profound dissatisfaction at what has been achieved in life so far, and can thus be a time of crisis. People who made young and inappropriate marriages sometimes split up, while those who have resisted commitment suddenly settle down. The end result is usually a greater sense of stability and maturity.

The Ultimate Astrologer, Rider, 2002, p. 133

Stephen Arroyo

It depends entirely on how one has lived during the previous 29 years ... to what extent the individual has expressed or suppressed his or her 'fundamental nature' ... The first cycle of Saturn ... is primarily based upon *reaction* to past conditioning, karma, parental influences, and social pressures.

Astrology, Karma and Transformation, CRCS, 1978, pp. 82–3

Lyn Birkbeck

[Saturn] checks out whether or not you are realizing your potential and living up to your responsibilities. Depending on how you are doing, it will impose tests and/or promote or consolidate your position in life ... If after several good attempts to realize an ambition there is, under Saturn's influence, still no success, then you can be sure that your dream is only that, or that the efforts you have made will come in useful at some later date.

Do It Yourself Life Plan Astrology, Element, 2000, p. 115

James R. Lewis

[It] forces us to examine our lives truthfully: if we have been striving with integrity and growing the best we know how, a Saturn Return can bring the fulfilment of many years of hard work ... If, however, we have been drifting along with the strongest wind, having built our lives on foundations of sane, Saturn tends to pull the rug out from under us ... Even at their best, however, Saturn Returns are rarely pleasant.

The Astrology Encyclopedia, Visible Ink Press, 1994, p. 455

Jamie Binder

The point in time when people enter full-fledged adulthood ... Realistically grounded individuals, who have laid a proper foundation, strengthen and solidify their careers, or start on a fresh, new, more stimulating path ... [But] the pipe dreamer

often runs into a real problem during a Saturn Return.
Planets in Work: A Complete Guide to Vocational Astrology,
ACS, 1988, p. 24

Reality bites; reconciliation

Adam Smith

Dreams of all sorts may come up against reality with an uncomfortable bump at this time and it is only the practical and viable options that survive ... Saturn is convention personified, of course, so it is somewhat in the nature of the Saturn Return to reconcile our own fundamental truth with the pressures and formal expectations of our environment.
Saturn: Fatal Attraction, O Books, 2007, pp. 71–4

Rose Elliot

We begin to feel uncomfortable with, constrained by, the life structures that we've spent our first thirty years working so hard to build up ... Somehow it no longer seems to be a true expression of us as we really are.
Life Cycles, Polair, 2008, p. 74

Steven Forrest

Dreams must make a deal with reality – and reality is a notoriously hard bargainer ... The time has come to strike a bargain. Maybe that aspiring young 'rock star' decides to become a music teacher. He has compromised; but the heart of his youthful vision remains intact.
The Changing Sky, ACS, 1998, p. 101

Bernadette Brady

The Saturn Return is the realization that ... if we really want to live happily ever after then we have to take control and set up our life in a more realistic manner. The unrealistic expectations we carry from childhood of our right to a hassle-free marriage, children, career and so on, crumble and hit the cold light of day.
Predictive Astrology: The Eagle and the Lark, Weiser, 1999 ed, p. 20

Jamie Binder

The chance to make a change and get on a more realistic course is disguised as a menacing obstacle which forces a re-evaluation of the career path … Individuals who unconsciously choose to run away are childishly attempting to play dodge ball with life.

Planets in Work: A Complete Guide to Vocational Astrology, ACS, 1988, p. 24

Pruner of the false self

Robert Hand

Consciously or unconsciously, you are pruning your life of everything that is not relevant to what you really are as a human being.

Planets in Transit, Whitford Press, 1976, p. 348

Liz Greene

It is possible for the individual to face and free himself from painful feelings of inadequacy, spheres of overcompensation, parental ties, and values borrowed from the past … [There is a] disintegration, disillusionment, as well as the recognition of all that is false, one-sided, and unrealistic within the personality … [There is] ultimately a process of death and rebirth, the sloughing of the old mask and the discovery of the real – and often less 'perfect' – individual.

Relating, Samuel Weiser, 1977, pp. 241–4

Eve Jackson

We cannot escape the reality of any disjunction between our chosen direction and our true needs and abilities … The age of thirty is a milestone after which society finds it less easy to accept those 'follies' associated with youth. Now middle life approaches and one is an adult in earnest.

Astrology: A Psychological Approach, Dryad, 1987, p. 112

Stephen Arroyo

At the first Saturn Return, it often seems like an old debt
is being discharged and many old karmic patterns and
obligations are rather suddenly removed ... There is
simultaneously a feeling of unalterable *limitation* in one's life
structure and a feeling of inner *freedom* that in some cases
is accompanied by exhilaration and inspiring joy ... This
feeling of unlimited inner freedom is also based on a clearer
understanding of your real needs, capabilities, and creative
potentialities.

Astrology, Karma and Transformation, CRCS, 1978, p. 83

Rose Elliot

We may feel a good deal of inner conflict ... Yet in spite of
the disruption, something within us is urging us to go on; we
simply cannot accept the limitations any longer.

Life Cycles, Polair, 2008, pp. 74–5

Rewards; personal development; an adult role

Adam Smith

The Saturn Return highlights the balance between having
some solid measure of achievement, against relying
excessively on superficial success badges ... It becomes
a reward in itself to become successful at something we
are good at ... Choices become finite and seemingly more
irrevocable – making life-defining decisions with further-
reaching consequences represents another of the main
differences in being past thirty.

Saturn: Fatal Attraction, O Books, 2007, pp. 71–4

Lois Rodden

There is a condition in your life that is a payoff for prior
character commitments; either in achievement and results,
or in a hard lesson to learn. With patience, perseverance,
discipline, and steadfast effort you can pay off old obligations
and establish long-range goals for the future.

Modern Transits, AFA, 1978, p. 88

Basil Fearrington

It marks deep, conspicuous, important change. There is almost always a complete revision of one's awareness of surrounding conditions ... [By the end of the Return], one can be living a new life with a deeper purpose ... All of this change potential frequently indicates a dramatic shift in human relations ... [It] can be the most profoundly important period of conspicuous developmental change in one's life.

The New Way to Learn Astrology, Llewellyn, 1999, p. 205

Sherene Schostak and Stefanie Iris Weiss

[Saturn] is an ally in that his vision for us is nothing less than that of a great father ... He wants us to manifest our potential, accomplish our dreams, be indebted to no one, and be true to ourselves ... If we don't address those lessons that our cosmic daddy has been patiently yet consistently trying to alert us to, he can show up in our life as a seemingly externally imposed crisis.

Surviving Saturn's Return, Contemporary Books, 2004, p. 12

Steven Forrest

People who successfully navigate the Saturn Return are able to maintain intensity and a quality of mission or inspiration in their lives. Why? Because the adult identity they have created reflects the Visions of youth, modified and partly compromised, but still recognizable ... The horror of a failed Saturn Return is that it is so often hidden behind veils of 'maturity' and 'practicality' ... A curious blend of nostalgia and cynicism about our own youth begins to enter our awareness, and our picture of midlife becomes one of noble futility in the face of failing systems.

The Changing Sky, ACS, 1998, p. 102

Wendell C. Perry

You can expect the call to grow up, take on the work or the role that will occupy your adult life, and face the limitations and problems that will define you as a person. It is a transit that is generally characterized by hard work, hard choices, and fateful decisions ... Opportunities always come with heavy responsibilities and far-reaching implications ... Missteps here almost always have major ramifications later on in life.

Saturn Cycles, Llewellyn, 2009, p. 284

Grant Lewi

[It is] the most important point at which free will operates in the life, untrammelled and as free of circumstances as it ever will be. Accept the obligations of this privilege: assume here and now the mastery over life and over yourself that is yours for the taking ... Your free will in a very real sense forges your fate for a long time to come.

Astrology for the Millions, Llewellyn, 1990 edition, p. 337

The Shadow Saturn Return at 31–32

We astrologers often see clients at the time they are going through their first Saturn Return. But I was a bit flummoxed when clients returned two to three years later, at age 31–32, saying they were experiencing similar situations and themes to those at 28–29. I soon realized that the process of the Saturn Return isn't really over until the *Shadow Saturn Return* occurs some two to three years later. This is when transiting Saturn meets up with Solar Arc directed Saturn, some 31–32 degrees further along in the zodiac. This would take around 2.5 years to catch up and, by then, it would occur in a new sign and often a new house.

The Shadow Saturn Return repeats themes, events and feelings that transpired during the original Saturn Return at 29. As astrologers, we can help clients draw parallels and gain insight into what is re-emerging. The transit at 31–32 provides another chance to tidy up unfinished business, another stab at an opportunity, or a further possibility to recognize a pattern from the past – and to make different choices, if necessary.

For example, a client came to see me when transiting Neptune was conjunct her Solar Arc (SA) Descendant at 0° Pisces. She was attempting to be in relationship with a man who was uncertain about his sexual orientation; he was more interested in pursuing his first opportunity with a man. He was, simply put, unavailable. My client 'felt' that they had a very important link and was attempting to forge a greater bond by wanting to start a committed relationship. As we spoke about this, I mentioned several dates in 1992–3 when TR Neptune was conjunct her natal Descendant. At this time, my client was immersed in a one-sided, devotional relationship trying to 'save' a man who was non-committal and troubled in many emotional ways. During our consultation, my client was able to see the link and its importance on a number of levels, and realize that this was a 'second chance' to revisit and examine her own compulsion to rescue or pursue the unavailable. In her words, she didn't want to 'drown again' in a less-than-ideal situation. (With a heavy emphasis on the Water signs in her chart, there is a strong natal theme of possible dependency in relationship.)

Knowing what happened during the transit-to-natal period enables us to understand themes that might be revisited when that transiting planet finally catches up with the Solar Arc position. Of course, the length of time it will take to do so depends on the transiting planet, so it may not happen in our lifetime. As already stated, the Shadow Transit will bring up the same issues (planet/angle) but with a different emphasis (sign) and usually in another arena (house).

My client files are packed with fascinating examples of these links. Often the same person reappears or a similar situation arises that forces a client to confront an area of their life/horoscope once again. When trying to anticipate how a transit to a Solar Arc directed planet is working in a client's life, I now track the date of the original transit to the natal chart and ask, 'What happened back then?' Usually the client recalls an event that has a direct link to current circumstances. It may be a repeat, 'here we go again' experience but in a different setting with different players. With the benefit of hindsight, we can make useful, meaningful links between past and present conditions that can empower our clients to make informed choices about their lives.

Chapter 16

CRITICAL POINTS:
THE FIRST AND FINAL DEGREES OF A SIGN

In this essay, I'll be looking at the first degree and, in particular, the last degree of a sign and their significance.

The Ingress

When a planet is at the very beginning of a sign, it has moved into new territory (a new element and mode) and is in dialogue with that sign's planetary ruler.

In the natal chart, planets or points at 0° of a sign take a stance that either indulges in or embraces the very pure, undiluted nature of the sign. There's a fresh, unstudied quality to a planet at this degree. Some of the most familiar, prima facie traits linked to that sign will be obvious in the person's nature, but the sign's true essence and the challenges the planet must face and embrace on its journey are just being discovered and are yet to be mastered. Simply put, there's a new language to learn and much work to be done. Embarking on this voyage, the planet at 0° appears and 'acts' highly eager to encounter that which it will become.

When a planet Solar Arc directs to a new sign, this indicates a 'year of getting to know and beginning to experience the essence of that sign ... In some ways it's a portent – a signpost indicating much of what we can expect for the next thirty years condensed (and intensely heightened) into the first twelve months.'[1] Astrologer Fernando Guimaraes suggested to me that the first degree is like an 'operatic overture', an introduction that sets the mood for what will follow.

The Middle Degrees

Planets or points at the middle degrees, from 14° to 16°, appear to be truly entrenched in that sign's *raison d'être*. When in a cardinal sign, the planet/point is fully engaged in the process of moving forward and encountering challenge and conflict. In mid fixed degrees, the planet is at its most permanent, solid, and durable but sometimes becomes stagnant or stuck. In mutable, it is at its most versatile and diverse but precarious, scattered and prone to fluctuation and instability.

The Final Degree: Poised for Change

Known as the anaretic degree or 'degree of fate', the final degree (29°) is often given a negative spin. Astrologer Richard Swatton reminded me that, according to traditional bounds and dignities by term, the malefics rule the final degrees of all the signs. Some horary practitioners observe that the querent can do nothing to affect the outcome; it's simply too late to have control over a situation.

Natally Whereas the 0° planet is taking initial steps on the road ahead to envision, discover and create its journey, the 29° planet senses inevitability, irrevocability and finality – the end of a familiar path. But a planet at the final degree has a 'knowingness' about it; it's a seasoned player, very skilled in that sign, having earned its stripes. Those of us with a natal planet at 29° – though we're equipped to deal with issues linked to the sign – will likely encounter some of the most challenging facets of that planet-in-sign's meaning in our lifetime. There may also be a desire to understand what has already happened that cannot be undone – a lifelong mission to resolve and come to terms with these issues which we seem to have been saddled with at birth.

In Forecasting When a planet reaches the final degree by Solar Arc direction (where it stays for a year), we are poised for change but must attend to pertinent, sometimes crisis situations (relevant to that sign) and resolve these before we move on to a new scenario. As the closing of a chapter, there's the anticipation of transition, of stepping into the unknown and a sense of urgency to wrap things up (or a last chance to get it right) 'before it's too late.'

By Solar Arc, it's the end of a 30-year era and often coincides with an intense 12 months (the final degree) that 'packs a punch' – a time when exaggerated manifestations of that sign appear as life events. For instance, **Whitney Houston's** SA Neptune was at 29° Sagittarius in her 10th House on 11 February

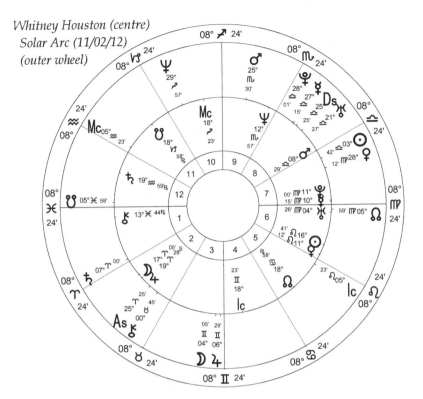

Whitney Houston (centre)
Solar Arc (11/02/12)
(outer wheel)

2012, when she drowned. I certainly wouldn't link the final degree to death, but it *was* the end of Houston's 30 years in the limelight (Sagittarius is the sign on her Midheaven and 10th House), which ran the Neptunian gamut from elegant, glamorous performances to seedy, drug-induced stupors.

Her public life had begun so promisingly in November 1981, when SA Neptune moved to 0° Sagittarius. Whitney – 18, beautiful and charismatic but already doing drugs – had started her modelling career and had just become one of the first African-American models to grace the cover of a national magazine (*Seventeen*).

Positively, that which has been mastered – skills that have been acquired – can be put to good use in these twelve months. This is where the last degree can truly come into its own. It can be a year of distinction and wrapping up a long period of endeavour.

In 1997, intrepid British politician Mo Mowlam worked to restore an IRA ceasefire in Northern Ireland and persuaded various sides to participate in the peace process – all during a time when she was fighting a brain tumour. Mowlam was instrumental in the signing of the Good Friday Peace Agreement on 10 April 1998, when her SA Saturn had reached 29° Libra. She retired from Parliament two years later. Although her career was cut short, in hindsight, it's clear that her historic work had been completed.

By Solar Return, a year with 29° on the Ascendant can have the same sense of finality, or an understanding of the difficulties inherent in that sign. A few years ago, when my own Solar Return Ascendant was at 29° Libra, it coincided with the end of my marriage. During those twelve months, I met three people who would be influential in my life, all of whom had the Moon or Ascendant at this degree. Through these people, I learned much about the chronic indecision and second-guessing inherent in the final degree of Libra, as well as the importance attributed to making the right decision.

To illustrate the power of the final degree, I've chosen three examples where the Sun is at 29° of that most enigmatic sign, Scorpio.

Queen of the Court, Master of the Game

The horoscope of tennis legend **Billie Jean King** has the Sun at the final degree of Scorpio, plus the Moon at the first degree of Libra. How have both manifested in her life?

Firstly, with the Moon at 0° Libra, Billie Jean King was an early advocate for equal prize money for women athletes and in the 1970s she became an American figurehead of the struggle for female equality. Yet, King is someone who hates confrontation and, with her Moon–Neptune conjunction, was never quite comfortable with the feminist ideology of the time, which she felt could be intolerant and doctrinaire. In a chapter of her autobiography, 'Always on the Cusp', she wrote, 'I don't believe you can legislate people's minds. I believe that it is persuasion you need, not force.'[2]

With King's Sun at the final degree, the buck stops with her. She was born (Sun) to take control (Scorpio) and complete (29°) some Scorpio theme. And which facets of Scorpio has she

Billie Jean
King

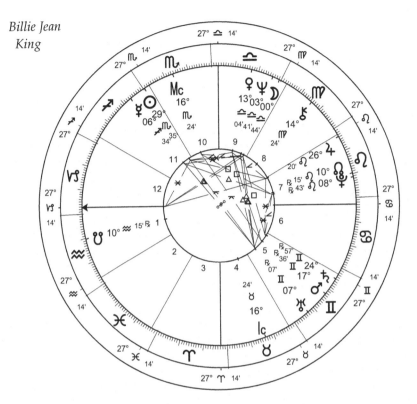

instinctively known how to harness? What in her Scorpio nature is exaggerated? Scorpio is a politically savvy sign that experiences (and is adept at handling) crises and extremes. At the final degree, in Scorpio, the following may be greatly in evidence: lifelong compulsions; a steely will, tunnel vision and total intensity one-on-one; an unflinching focus on the final, ultimate goal (be that victory or an obsession with death and endings); an ability to execute under pressure; an all-or-nothing, winner-take-all philosophy; authenticity and integrity; emotional inscrutability; and an innate understanding of the relationship between power, money and gender. King is known to demand total attention from others and to pour all of herself into whatever she does (Scorpio).

For King, the Sun at 29° Scorpio reveals her involvement with, and impact on, gender politics, as well as the influence she has had on sponsorship and prize money in the women's game. (The eighth sign, like its corresponding house, has links to 'other people's money'.) This Sun placement was not without heavy personal consequences: she had to keep her (homo)sexuality hidden because the newly founded women's tennis tour and her own livelihood depended on secrecy. When news of her abortion and homosexual affair was made public, many of her endorsements evaporated, but she kept on fighting (Scorpio).

The final degree of Scorpio knows how to play the game – to suss out the competition and devise a strategy. When King agreed to participate in a **Battle of the Sexes tennis match** (for the chart, see opposite page), she needed nerves of steel to beat hustler Bobby Riggs, who had defeated the women's #1 player in the world, Margaret Court. The match was heavy with political significance (Scorpio). King knew what victory truly meant and had what it took! Riggs, with Sagittarius Rising and Jupiter on the Descendant in Gemini, was a born promoter and gambler looking to be a major player of a Big Event (chart not shown). Given King's Sun in Scorpio square Jupiter in Leo, it could be argued that it was her 'destiny' to accept a heroic challenge and 'kill off' patriarchal chauvinism. So, where were you when Billie Jean beat Bobby Riggs?

The Houston Astrodome, 20 September 1973, just weeks after King had successfully lobbied for equal prize money for women at the US Open; 30,000 spectators; 40 million in front of their televisions. Uranus and Pluto were traversing the sign of Libra – a simple divide: women vs. men. The cameras started rolling at 20:00 and Billie Jean King, current Wimbledon champ of 1973 and in her prime, took on Bobby Riggs – Wimbledon winner of 1939, a 55-year-old self-styled male chauvinist and an out-of-shape clown. The scene was set for a match between the sublime and the slightly ridiculous.

On that night, Venus and Mars were in opposition and mutual reception. What a perfect planetary set-up for a 'battle of the sexes'! Venus in powerful, premeditated and poker-faced Scorpio stood less than one degree opposite Mars in solid but slow Taurus, which had turned retrograde the day before. King stayed focused and made Riggs look old and slow. It was a tactical (Scorpio) win for majestic King, while chauvinist pig Riggs squealed and spread rumours that the outcome may have been, er, rigged.

Not surprisingly, at the time of this sports circus extravaganza, King's Sun had directed/progressed to 29° Sagittarius.[3] It was an over-the-top, surreal spectacle befitting Sagittarius: one night of raucous high drama, hyperbole and publicity on the world stage, which would overshadow the lifelong sporting achievements of both athletes. The win over

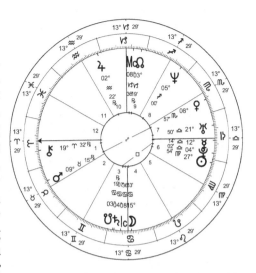

Riggs would give King and her cause professional credibility (the Sun directed from Sagittarius to Capricorn soon after).

With transiting Saturn in Cancer in an exact square to Pluto in Libra, the larger question in the air was: Should women attain equal power (Pluto in Libra), or stay at home and feel bound to a life of domesticity (Saturn in Cancer)? At the time of the Equal Rights Amendment, the Education Act and Roe v. Wade, Billie Jean gave Women's Lib a mainstream face and legitimized women's tennis.

In victory, King slew myths about women and weakness. She hit the first sporting strike for gender equality and freedom of choice (natal Moon at 0° Libra); her win sounded a death knell to male chauvinists who had perpetuated the myth of sexual inequality (her Sun at 29° Scorpio).

Provocative in the Extreme
Another example of 29° Scorpio (this time, natal Sun and Mercury at this degree) is **Pat Condell**, a former stand-up comedian who has, over the past five years, outraged many corners of the Muslim world.

In a series of more than 150 articulate but hard-hitting, provocative monologues on YouTube, he has challenged religion and the beliefs of religious zealots (particularly those who follow Islam). To many people, he is an intolerant, ignorant bigot and

Pat
Condell

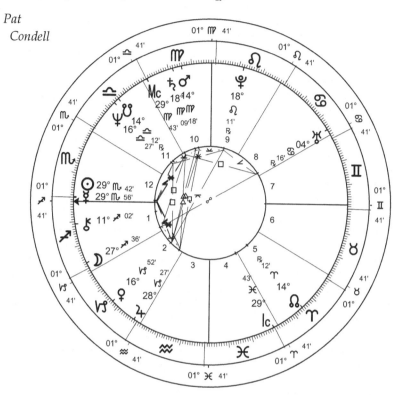

xenophobe who incites racial hatred (and his website chronicles the numerous death threats he's received). To others, he is the daring voice of rational atheism in a society fearful of reprisals and crippled by Saturnian political correctness.

Condell's issue is not with God, he says, but with religious dogma and the people who 'take it upon themselves to police the rest of us on His behalf.' An early awareness of (and frustration with) hypocrisy and excess is common when evangelical Sagittarius is dominant (his Moon and Ascendant are in that sign). The son of a compulsive gambler who was controlled by his obsessions (Sun in Scorpio) and worked in a betting shop, Condell soon became aware of 'the gulf between what people profess to believe and how they actually behave.'[4] The political edge, provocative bluntness and satirical 'bite' of Condell's message, as well as extreme reactions from others which have brought him immense notoriety, are reflected in his Sun–

Mercury conjunction at 29° Scorpio. And broadcasting to camera on YouTube, he also gets the last word.

The End of Power

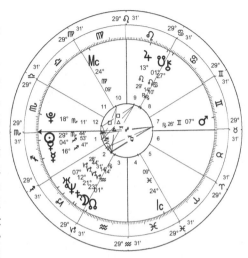

To get a final feel for the last degree of Scorpio as a 'hotly political' degree, consider the horoscope for **Margaret Thatcher's resignation** (chart on right). Facing the humiliation of defeat in a leadership contest and a lack of support from colleagues, the three-time Prime Minister signed her resignation statement at 07:35 on 22 November 1990.[5] The Sun and Ascendant were at 29° Scorpio. Thatcher never recovered from the betrayal, branding it 'treachery with a smile on its face'. It was the end of her 'acid reign' – eleven ruthless, controversial years in power.

Here's a summary of the information in this essay:

• **0° Natally** Initial steps; a new territory/language yet to be mastered; an eagerness to explore the pure, undiluted nature of the sign; a tendency to exhibit its most familiar, obvious traits.

• **0° in Forecasting** A major shift and new script; an augury, setting the mood of the period to come; an 'operatic overture' – an intense period in which we are swamped by images of this new sign and experience issues around it. (A directed planet or angle's ingress into a sign 'speaks to' and begins to activate every planet/angle natally in that sign, regardless of the actual degree. In addition, the ingress can be more challenging when it moves into a sign that is empty or is 'foreign' to natal chart placements.)

• 29° natally: the end of an era – inevitable, irrevocable, 'fated'; a knowingness about the dynamics of the sign; displaying some of the sign's most challenging facets and possibilities.

• 29° in forecasting: the end of a familiar path/chapter; poised for change; what has passed cannot be undone; a period of crisis – experiencing exaggerated or intense manifestations of the sign; mastery; wrapping up long-term endeavours.

References and Notes
All URLs were accessed in September 2012.
1. Frank C. Clifford, *Solar Arc Directions*, Flare, 2011, p. 11.
2. Billie Jean King with Frank Deford, *Billie Jean*, The Viking Press, 1982; additional information from Selena Roberts, *A Necessary Spectacle*, Crown, 2005.
3. Also, the Astro*Carto*Graphy line for King's Jupiter (natally in Leo) sets through Houston, and her Local Space Jupiter line runs nearby.
4. www.timeout.com/london/comedy/features/2217/Pat_Condell-interview.html
5. www.margaretthatcher.org/speeches/displaydocument. asp?docid=108254

Chapter 17

PIVOTAL YEARS:
PLANETS DIRECTED TO 0° AND 29° BY SOLAR ARC

In this essay, following on from Chapter 16, I'd like to present the charts of three famous entertainers and document how their marriages ended in dramatic fashion when planets either entered a new sign or reached the final degree by Solar Arc (SA) direction.

Doris Day
SA Jupiter at 29° Scorpio, Sun–Chiron at 29° Taurus

There's no reliable formula I know of that can predict death in an individual's chart. Perhaps that's just as well, since ethically it's not an area I would feel comfortable exploring with a client. Death does, however, tend to be 'seen' in the horoscopes of a deceased's loved ones. But any planet could be implicated, depending on the actions and subsequent reactions of those left behind.

Actress and animal rights campaigner Doris Day suffered a great shock when her husband–manager, Marty Melcher, died suddenly on 20 April 1968. Appropriately, by Solar Arc, she was receiving a Venus–Uranus double whammy: SA Venus had moved to 11° Gemini (square natal Uranus), and SA Uranus had reached 26° Aries, conjunct natal Venus in the 8th House. By transit, Uranus was on her Ascendant.

But this was just the start of a series of shocks and crises that left her nearly catatonic (Uranus). Both Solar Arcs are linked to Venus and to the 8th House. Soon after her bereavement, in July 1968, Day discovered enormous debts of some $450,000, as SA Jupiter reached 29° Scorpio. Day's husband had left her penniless and her attorney, Jerry Rosenthal, had ripped her off. Both men had squandered current holdings and borrowed against future earnings (Jupiter), including an album she had yet to record and a TV show and specials she had no idea she'd been committed to filming.

Doris Day (centre)
Solar Arc (20/04/68)
(outer wheel)

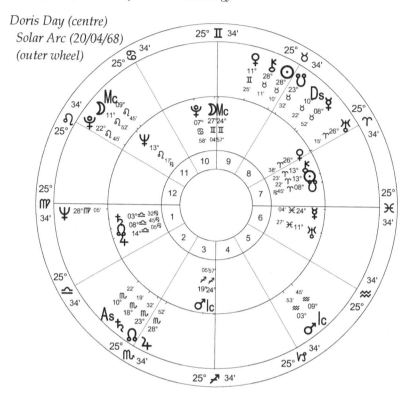

After firing Rosenthal, she filed suit against him in February 1969, as SA Sun–Chiron entered the final degree of Taurus in her 9th House. It was a long, slow battle that would include a complex, 99-day trial in March 1974 and culminate on 18 September in a judgment of $22.8 million in her favour (then, the largest civil award in California history). Rosenthal declared bankruptcy and Day eventually settled with his insurers for $6 million, although he continued to counter-sue into the late 1980s.

Natally, Jupiter opposes the Sun from the 1st/Libra to the 7th/Aries, indicating the influence that both men had on her life and how she had elevated them and allowed them to (mis) manage the bulk of her fortune and her professional decisions (Jupiter in Libra). Transiting Jupiter was conjunct her Descendant in Pisces on her 3 April 1951 wedding to Melcher, and Jupiter suggests their shared devotion to Christian Science, a faith she left soon after his death. (Interestingly, Melcher died from complications linked to an enlarged heart: Sun–Jupiter.)

As always, the main themes and life scripts are underscored and reiterated in numerous ways. Day's victimization and exploitation by her husband and her advisor are also reflected by Mercury in Pisces on the Descendant, the Sun in the 7th House ruling the 12th, the all-important Jupiter ruling the IC/4th and the Descendant, plus Sun–Chiron in naïve Aries squaring Pluto.

Carol Channing
SA Neptune at 29° Libra
Born with exactly the same angle degrees as Doris Day, fellow Christian Scientist Carol Channing had a similar, sudden departure from her controlling husband–manager, Charles Lowe. But it was one that Channing instigated herself on 19 May 1998. Her filing for divorce baffled many, as it came 42 years into their marriage and some months after Lowe's debilitating stroke.

They had married in 1956 (Channing's third trip down the aisle) when her SA Saturn had reached 29° Libra. Theirs was a show-must-go-on partnership of Saturnian dedication, discipline and workaholic drive – the two were seemingly inseparable and secure.

Fast forward to 1998, and transiting Uranus was conjunct her Sun in Aquarius (natally in the 5th House opposite Neptune), coinciding with Lowe's sudden stroke and her break (Uranus) from her husband (Sun) – a man she claimed had controlled and victimized her (Neptune). SA Pluto had reached 24° Virgo in Channing's chart, conjunct controlling Saturn and square her Midheaven (MC), and SA Chiron was minutes from her MC.

Interestingly, Neptune had moved to the final degree of Libra in her 2nd House (where SA Saturn had been when they married 42 years earlier). It was a messy, bewildering dissolution to a long-term personal and professional partnership. After years of quiet obedience, newly independent Channing soon went on a rampage (as SA Sun travelled through the final degree of Aries). There were ugly claims that Lowe was impotent, gay and had only had sex with her twice (both occasions on their

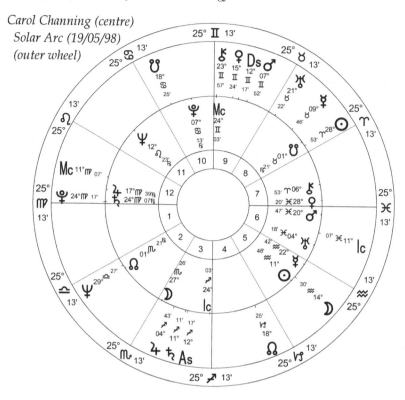

Carol Channing (centre)
Solar Arc (19/05/98)
(outer wheel)

honeymoon). He had allegedly left her close to bankruptcy. In her petition, she asserted that he was 'spending [my] money like a drunken sailor'. This sounds like SA Neptune at 29° Libra in the 2nd House!

Lowe died in September 1999 before the divorce was finalized and Channing did an about-face, never again discussing their marriage or their split in public.

Again, let's consider if and where the natal chart shows the potential for a controlling husband. Lowe was certainly Channing's 'rock' for many years: supporting her, handling her business and engineering her greatest stage triumphs. In her chart, we find natal Saturn in Virgo opposite Venus–Mars in Pisces straddling the Ascendant/Descendant axis, and the Sun opposite Neptune. The Moon in Scorpio is in square both to Mercury in Aquarius (a sign pairing linked to issues of freedom versus control) and to Uranus.

In early 2003, Channing reconnected with old flame Harry Kullijian, after 70 years apart. They married on 10 May 2003, but he died on 26 December 2011, when Channing's SA Sun in Taurus had reached a square to natal Neptune, SA MC was on Saturn, and SA Saturn was conjunct the IC.

Diana Ross
SA Sun at 0° Gemini, MC at 29° Libra
It was 24 April 1999, a day that pop diva Diana Ross later described as the worst of her life: live on Norwegian TV, her husband of 14 years, Arne Naess, announces the end of their marriage – and shortly afterwards takes up with another woman.

Just two weeks prior to the announcement, Ross's SA (and progressed) Sun had left the safety of Taurus (the sign of her Moon and Descendant) and entered Gemini for a 30-year stretch.[1] In Ross's chart, the mutable sign of Gemini is occupied by

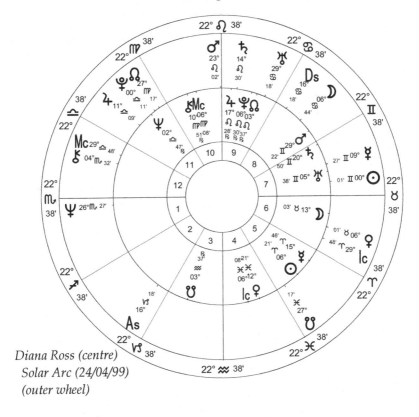

Diana Ross (centre)
Solar Arc (24/04/99)
(outer wheel)

unpredictable, unstable Uranus (in the 7th) as well as Mars and Saturn. This suggests somewhat uncomfortable ground for the singer, who has a fixed Moon and Ascendant.

At the time of her husband's announcement, her SA Venus was square natal Pluto, and SA Pluto had entered the first degree of Libra. In addition, Ross's SA MC had reached the final degree of Libra – the last attempt at (and end of) relationship mediation and the end of the public's perception of a fairytale marriage (natally, Neptune is the only planet in Libra). Deeply affected by Naess's betrayal and his refusal to discuss their problems (natal Mars in Gemini in the 8th, Saturn in Gemini in the 7th), Ross had what she characterized as 'almost an emotional breakdown'. She was also going through a devastating menopause. Fittingly, SA Uranus was at 29° Cancer in her 9th House, which also suggests the shattering end to their bi-continental marriage.

Later that year, on 21 September 1999, she was arrested for manhandling a security officer at Heathrow Airport; SA Sun remained at 0° Gemini, but the MC had plunged into Scorpio. The woman with the legendary work ethic and drive was unravelling – losing control of her carefully crafted reputation and direction (natal MC in Virgo). The next few years were to see Ross enter rehab (21 May 2002), find herself under arrest for drunk driving (30 December 2002, serving time in February 2004) and be forced to deal with the accidental death of Naess, father to her two teenage sons, while he was mountain-climbing (13 January 2004).

The year 1999 was not without some successes, however: Ross had a new album in the stores, there were optimistic plans to reunite with the Supremes and go on tour, and she was heralded as the most successful female singer of all time. It was during this year that SA Mars was conjunct the 10th Equal House cusp in Leo.

References and Notes

1. Thirty years before, when Diana's SA Sun moved into Taurus, her Svengali, Berry Gordy, was grooming her for solo superstardom and career longevity.

Chapter 18

PLUTO – A HISTORY AND BIOGRAPHY OF AMERICA

If history repeats itself, and the unexpected always happens,
how incapable must Man be of learning from experience.
                                                    – George Bernard Shaw

In this final essay (written in July 2013), I shall be looking at
the US's Pluto placement, and the impact of the Pluto cycle on
America's history. In an attempt to identify and understand
how Pluto manifests in the US's chart, I'll be investigating the
types of events that have occurred in the past when Pluto has
been activated. These should give us clues as to the effects of the
upcoming Pluto transits to the US's Sun–Saturn square in
2014-16, and its Pluto Return in 2022-3. I'll be looking at some
past transits and Solar Arc directions but, in particular, I'll be
introducing and drawing from the Huber Life Clock.

There are many 'birth moments' for Independence Day of the
United States of America, as well as significant dates around 4
July. The Uranus Rising in Gemini Chart was a former favourite
of many, and some astrologers favour the late morning (Virgo
Rising) chart, while others feel Libra or Scorpio Rising is more
fitting.[1] Whichever chart you prefer to work with – and there
seem to be valid reasons for using one of many times that day
or week – it will ultimately reflect and influence how you see
the US: your vision of America. For this article, I'll be using the
Sibly Chart (4 July 1776, 17:10, Philadelphia), which works
remarkably well with the Huber Clock. And because the Hubers
used the Koch system of house division, the charts will be cast
using this method (it doesn't change the position of Pluto).

The Astrological Pluto
Pluto's role is to excavate, purge and recycle. During this process,
long-standing issues, themes or circumstances – areas that have
been buried which perhaps secretly control us – are brought to

the surface for truthful examination in the harsh light of day. Our compulsions and emotional crutches are exposed, giving us the opportunity to restructure or eliminate them. All Pluto change is painful and this process may leave us (or our situation) stripped, undermined or downsized. As with all outer planet transit processes, chapters of our lives come to an end and that which has outlived its usefulness is brought into question.[2]

If Saturn represents old age and the final boundary of physical death, Pluto is concerned with the living process of death followed by rebirth. While both planets are linked to karma, with Pluto we are faced with wipe-out or extinction. Pluto's theme is to trigger our survival instinct and test our ability to rise from the ashes. In doing so, we emerge with some loss of innocence about the people and world around us. In its non-negotiable elimination of what was once considered powerfully pervasive, a seed is planted which allows for something new to evolve. Ultimately, Pluto is concerned with irrevocable change which forces the process of metamorphosis. Here are some keywords describing Pluto's functions:

- Compels, obsesses, shames, victimizes/empowers;
- Buries, suppresses, erupts, uncovers, exposes;
- Undermines, violates, humbles, strips, downsizes, makes redundant;
- Transforms, evolves, rebirths, regenerates, purges, cleanses.

Natal Pluto in the Sibly Chart's 2nd House

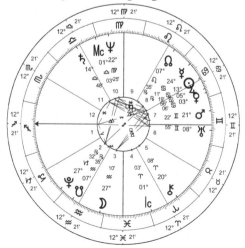

With Pluto in Capricorn in the 2nd House, the following four phrases and ideas come to mind:

1. **Money is power** Pluto in the 2nd can be seen in the strength of the 'Almighty Dollar' and the US being seen as a hyperpower that exerts strong economic

influence/coercion. With Pluto in the 2nd, power lies in ownership (particularly gold, oil/'black gold' and water). Here, wealth (especially extremes in wealth) becomes a measure of the country's self-worth (2nd).

2. **Underlying obsessions about values and ownership** Not only is Pluto in the 2nd fixated on its own worth, values and economy, it is also obsessed with the financial situation and values (2nd) of other people and countries. But with Pluto, there's an inability to see the extent of the preoccupation or fanaticism. Jessica Murray suggests that Pluto's placement shows a 'stunted awareness … The truth is hidden in plain sight.'[3]

On a mundane level, Pluto relates to powerful, transformational belief systems, such as Islam and Scientology (to name just two). Pluto in the 2nd House could suggest America's strong territorial stance and its paranoia about seemingly extreme values that others possess. This could generate anxiety about how these values might have an impact on its own security. Howard Sasportas wrote of Pluto in the 2nd: 'It is necessary to discover the underlying motivations which propel such strong and passionate feelings about money and security.'[4]

3. **Black power** The African–American struggle in America has also been viewed as Plutonic, and America's karma – from the dawn of its history – is inextricably bound to the concept of ownership of slaves: a disenfranchised, subjugated people (Pluto) seen as commodities (2nd House).

4. **The pen is mightier …** Pluto's main natal aspect is an opposition from Mercury in Cancer, suggestive of America's powerful media, propaganda, surveillance systems (CIA, FBI), cover-ups and witch-hunts, along with the mass influence and use of psychoanalysis. (It also suggests a pre-emptive strike is an emotional response when national security – Cancer – is considered to be at risk – i.e. attack as the best form of defence.)

It's interesting to note that when former CIA/NSA employee **Ed Snowden** blew the whistle on the excessive government surveillance of the American people, his directed/progressed Sun had reached the exact degree opposite the US's Pluto (and

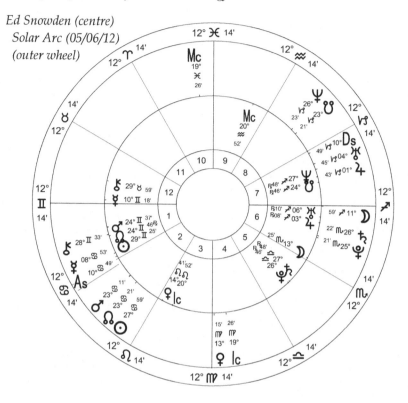

Ed Snowden (centre)
Solar Arc (05/06/12)
(outer wheel)

his SA Moon was within a degree of the Sibly Ascendant degree). Snowden was also born with the Sibly Ascendant degree on his own Descendant, and his and the US's Mars placements (in information-savvy Gemini) are a few degrees apart.

America's Recurring Pluto Themes

Before I look at the transits, directions and Huber Life Clock examples involving Pluto in Capricorn in the 2nd, here's a glimpse of the themes that emerge when the planet is activated:

- Boundaries – redefining colonies, the frontier; key changes to the Constitution; new laws and structures put in place;
- Industry and innovation – new power bases formed;
- Gender and race issues – slavery, race riots; the formation of organizational structures to protect or restrict;
- Religious extremism – massacres; threats to security

- Censorship and morality – a crackdown on obscenity; bans/ vetoes; deep conservatism;
- Coinage – changes in the Dollar and to the Gold Standard;
- Depression – financial crashes, money panic; power failures.

A Few Transits to Natal Pluto

Looking at historical events when natal Pluto was triggered can provide clues to the upcoming events of the next ten years when TR Pluto opposes the Sun and Mercury in Cancer and returns to its natal position. The world is, of course, a very different place now so, rather than exact repeats, what should be obvious are patterns and themes (as listed above) that reveal the nature and manifestations of Pluto in the US chart. Here are a few:

September 1873: Neptune in Aries square natal Pluto in the 2nd
The Wall Street panic undermines (Neptune) the power structure.

May 1848–Feb 1851: The US's first Pluto square Pluto (from Aries to Capricorn)
During this time, the Gold Rush sees a mass movement (Pluto) to California – a scramble to pioneer (Aries) and mine for wealth (Pluto). The women's movement is born, too, when Lucretia Mott presents a declaration suggesting that women should be free to speak in public and have the right to vote (July 1848).

Sept 1935 to May 1938: Pluto opposite Pluto (from Cancer to Capricorn)
The Social Security Act and Revenue Acts had recently been signed; the FBI is given its name; Alcoholics Anonymous is formed; and Jesse Owens travels to the 'Nazi Olympics' in Berlin and challenges Hitler's notion of Aryan superiority. During this opposition, *How to Win Friends and Influence People* is published (October 1936) and strongly influences the American psyche (showing how to win others over to your way of thinking, increase prestige, influence and earning power). (Interestingly, just before this transit, when TR Pluto made a conjunction to Mercury, the book of the century, *Gone with the Wind*, set in the Civil War, was published.)

In a longer essay, it would be tempting to examine a series of Pluto's transits to America's chart, but consider two events around Pluto's discovery in February 1930 that are very Pluto/ Capricorn/2nd: despite the Great Depression, two titanic, powerful constructions – symbols of wealth and prestige – were built: The Chrysler Building and The Empire State Building.

Solar Arc Directions to Natal Pluto

Looking at some Solar Arcs (conjunction, square and opposition only; orb: 30'/6 months either side) to the US's natal Pluto, we can see the Pluto/Capricorn/2nd House themes emerge again:

Aspect Exact hit	Event (using a 6 month/30' orb either side)
Sun to Pluto	
opp. 06/1791	First Bank of the United States founded; US Bill of Rights.
sq. 12/1883	Doctrine of racial segregation is legalized.
conj. 10/1972	Watergate scandal; Roe vs. Wade (Jan 1973); Dow Jones plummets to an all-time low.
Moon to Pluto	
sq. 05/1839	Women win (limited) rights to own property.
opp. 10/1929	Wall Street Crash.
Mercury to Pluto	
sq. 01/1873	Coinage Act of 1873 passed; Susan B Anthony defies the law and votes; Comstock Law enacted, making it illegal to send 'obscene, lewd, or lascivious' books through the mail.
conj. 02/1962	John Glenn orbits the Earth; Cuban Missile Crisis; Trade Expansion Act of 1962; start of Vietnam War.
Mars to Pluto	
sq. 11/1905	San Francisco earthquake/fire follows in April 1906 (3000 killed, 80% of San Francisco is destroyed).

conj. 06/1994 — NAFTA signed; the double murder of Nicole Simpson/Ron Goldman leads to the 'Trial of the Century' (Mars is natally in dual Gemini).

Jupiter to Pluto
opp. 02/1799 — NY passes a law aiming to abolish slavery.

Saturn to Pluto
sq. 11/1789 — Supreme Court convenes for the first time (Feb 1790); first census; US Depts of Foreign Affairs, War, State and the Treasury are all established.

conj. 06/1882 — Chinese Exclusion Act; 1882 Immigration Act passed.

sq. 05/1971 — Nixon ends US gold standard; US ends trade embargo against China.

Uranus to Pluto
opp. 04/1827 — Freedom's Journal (first African-American owned/published newspaper) is founded.

conj. 10/2006 — Iraq War troop surge; iPhone announced; Saddam Hussein is tried/hanged.

Neptune to Pluto
sq. 05/1993 — The World Trade Center is bombed; David Koresh/Waco siege; the Rodney King civil trial follows the LA Riots; 'Don't Ask, Don't Tell' policy of gays in the military.

Pluto to Pluto
sq. 08/1869 — The National Woman Suffrage Association is formed; Wyoming territorial legislature gives women the right to vote (the first to do so in the world).

opp. 11/1958 — The National Defence Education Act is signed into law; NASA is formed; the US begins secret nuclear tests over the South Atlantic.

Pluto and the Huber Clock

There are many ways to consider Pluto's meaning in (and track its impact on) the US chart, but only a few predictive methods allow us to view a complete cycle of Pluto for our study. One is the Life Clock, a simple but ingenious 72-year 'Age Progression' timing device developed by leading Swiss astrologers Bruno and Louise Huber.

This fascinating tool, introduced to me by Faye Cossar, turns the chart into a 72-year clock where every house starting from the Ascendant (using the Koch method of division) represents 6 years of life (regardless of house size). The 'hand' of the clock (the 'Age Point') ticks through the degrees in those houses/signs. Applying this to the 4 July 1776 Chart, the 1st House starts on this date, the 2nd House begins exactly 6 years later, the 3rd House on the US's twelfth birthday, the 4th House on its eighteenth birthday, and so on. It returns to the 1st House at 72 and continues through the houses again (i.e. hitting the 2nd House cusp at age 78). In Diagram 1 (opposite page), we can see how the Age Point moves through each of the houses of the US Chart from its 'birth' at the Ascendant.[5]

When the Age Point reaches a planet, its astrological principles come to the fore. Although the Hubers didn't use this with country or business charts, the Life Clock works repeatedly well with the Sibly chart. In Diagram 2 (opposite page), we can see some fascinating 20th century examples of Age Points registering (using a 3–4 month orb either side of an exact hit).

The Age Point moved into Pisces weeks before Hurricane Katrina devastated New Orleans, showing up governmental incompetence, chaos and disarray. At the time of writing (August 2013), it is in Aries, approaching the same opposition to Saturn (exact on 22 December 2013) that took the US into World War II.

Looking at the Koch houses chart of the US (Diagram 2, opposite), we can see that Pluto is roughly midway through the 2nd House, corresponding to the age of 9 (and at 72-year intervals: age 81, 153 and 225). Put another way, the Age Point first hit Pluto at 9 (1785) and again 72 years later (1857), and so on.

Each time the Age Point conjuncts Pluto, we should expect to see a manifestation of Pluto in Capricorn in the 2nd House. (Also consider the opposition to Pluto 36 years into the cycle, and the

Diagram 1

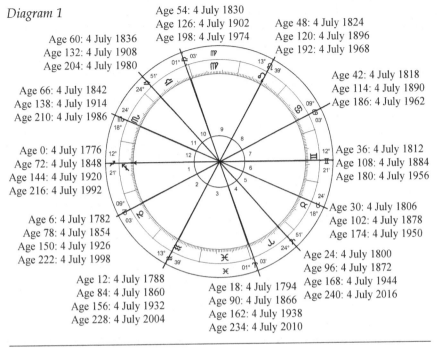

Age 54: 4 July 1830
Age 126: 4 July 1902
Age 198: 4 July 1974

Age 48: 4 July 1824
Age 120: 4 July 1896
Age 192: 4 July 1968

Age 60: 4 July 1836
Age 132: 4 July 1908
Age 204: 4 July 1980

Age 42: 4 July 1818
Age 114: 4 July 1890
Age 186: 4 July 1962

Age 66: 4 July 1842
Age 138: 4 July 1914
Age 210: 4 July 1986

Age 0: 4 July 1776
Age 72: 4 July 1848
Age 144: 4 July 1920
Age 216: 4 July 1992

Age 36: 4 July 1812
Age 108: 4 July 1884
Age 180: 4 July 1956

Age 6: 4 July 1782
Age 78: 4 July 1854
Age 150: 4 July 1926
Age 222: 4 July 1998

Age 30: 4 July 1806
Age 102: 4 July 1878
Age 174: 4 July 1950

Age 24: 4 July 1800
Age 96: 4 July 1872
Age 168: 4 July 1944
Age 240: 4 July 2016

Age 12: 4 July 1788
Age 84: 4 July 1860
Age 156: 4 July 1932
Age 228: 4 July 2004

Age 18: 4 July 1794
Age 90: 4 July 1866
Age 162: 4 July 1938
Age 234: 4 July 2010

Diagram 2

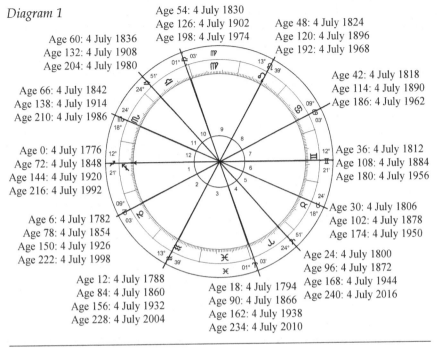

• (In Libra) On the MC/10th House cusp (exact 6 July 1974): Nixon resigns a month later.

• (In Virgo) Conjunct Neptune (exact 1 June 1973): Nixon orders the Watergate break-in that month.

• (In Leo) In the 9th opposite the Moon in Aquarius (exact 22 March 1969): Stonewall Riots (the start of the Gay Liberation movement in June) and Apollo 11 lands on the Moon in July.

• (In Gemini) Conjunct Uranus in Gemini (exact 26 August 1955): Rosa Parks is arrested for defiantly refusing to budge (1 December).

• (In Aries) Opposite natal Saturn in Libra (exact 22 December 1941): America enters World War II.

square – the timing of which can vary depending on the house size.) Using an orb representing 3-4 months either side of the exact hit, the Clock doesn't disappoint.

Huber Clock <u>conjunctions</u> to the Pluto Age Point (exact 18 September):

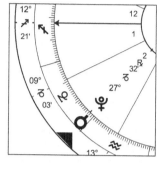

Exact date hit *Events around the time*

18 Sep 1785 The Treaty of Hopewell with Cherokee natives creates a western boundary for white settlement.

18 Sep 1857 Following a court decision declaring blacks are not US citizens, the constitutional protection of slavery is affirmed but leads to Panic of 1857 and civil war; 120 emigrants are killed in Mountain Meadows massacre.

18 Sep 1929 Eugene O'Neill's play *Strange Interlude* is banned for obscenity; the Great Depression begins on 'Black Tuesday'; Richard Byrd flies over the South Pole; the Immigration Act favours nationalities already established in the US.

18 Sep 2001 Planes crash into the World Trade Center, triggering a 'war on terror' and the Patriot Act, which allows indefinite detentions; anthrax attacks.

Huber Clock <u>opening squares</u> in Aries to the Pluto Age Point (exact 13 March):

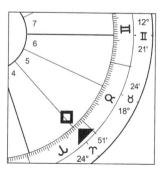

Exact date hit *Events around the time*

13 Mar 1801 John Marshall, who would go on to shape the legal system and Constitution, is made Chief Justice; Jefferson is elected after a

dirty campaign – his win ushers in the Democrat–Republican two-party rule.

13 Mar 1873 The start of major censorship laws as the Comstock Act prohibits obscene materials being sent by mail; the Coinage Act embraces the gold standard and prompts the Panic of 1873.

13 Mar 1945 The Yalta Conference creates conditions that will divide control of Europe between Communist USSR and Western countries; Iwo Jima falls to the US, providing a strategic base for air operations against Japan; FDR dies; V-E Day.

Next hit: 13 March 2017

Huber Clock <u>oppositions</u> in Cancer to the Pluto Age Point (exact 18 Sep):

Exact date hit   Events around the time

18 Sep 1821 Stephen Austin (the 'Father of Texas' in charge of recruiting new settlers) founds the first American colony in Texas (he dies before the first closing square of 1837).

18 Sep 1893 Stocks plummet on the New York Stock Exchange, starting a nationwide financial panic as foreign investors withdraw investments, railroads go bankrupt and 500 banks go into receivership – 20% are unemployed and riots sweep the country, beginning a four-year depression; Professor Frederick Jackson Turner delivers his 'Frontier Thesis' and many see this as a sign of the US entering a new age of imperialism.

18 Sep 1965 The Medicare Act becomes law; the long hot summer of 1965 of race riots, Malcolm X's assassination and 'Bloody Sunday' in Alabama; the Voting Rights Act outlaws literacy tests that had restricted the rights of African-Americans to vote.

Next hit: 18 September 2037

Huber Clock closing squares in Libra to
the Pluto Age Point (exact 12 March):

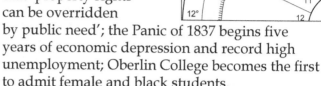

Exact date hit   *Events around the time*

12 Mar 1837   Charles River Bridge vs.
Warren Bridge declares
that 'property rights
can be overridden
by public need'; the Panic of 1837 begins five
years of economic depression and record high
unemployment; Oberlin College becomes the first
to admit female and black students.

12 Mar 1909   Jack Johnson becomes the US's first black sports
hero; NAACP is formed; 'Dollar Diplomacy' –
President Taft attempts to establish control over
Honduras by buying up its debt to British bankers;
the first men (including an African-American)
reach the North Pole.

12 Mar 1981   President Reagan introduces 'Reaganomics' to
jump-start the stagnant economy, causing cutbacks
in social services; Reagan announces a $5 billion
increase in defence spending; an uncommon
skin cancer appears in young gay men in New
York City – it is soon identified as AIDS; the first
Mexican–American mayor of a major American
city is elected; the first space shuttle Columbia flies
a successful three-day mission.

Next hit: 12 March 2053

Uranus Square Pluto

Certainly Pluto thrives on – and embodies – emotional crisis and
seismic turbulence. And with an upcoming transit from Pluto,
we must expect some crisis to emerge for change, demolition,
rebirth and rebuilding to take place. As TR Pluto opposes the
Sun – an 'identity crisis' – from February 2014 to November 2015,
and then Mercury, will the Dollar be on its knees as the US teeters
on bankruptcy? As China overtakes the US, the 2020s may be
somewhat of a renaissance as the US regroups and restructures.

The Uranus–Pluto squares (from June 2012 to March 2015) are inauspicious omens: the last set of squares in 1933 coincided with FDR closing the banks. The current squares see the individual at war with the government, while the conjunction in the mid 1960s brought civil disobedience that led to the free speech movement and greater civil rights.

Uranus is a violent earthquake: splitting up and shattering the existing order. It is more devastating than the volcanic eruptions of Pluto because, with Uranus, there are no emotions attached – it's the principle and ideal at all costs. Brutal and swift, anything that doesn't reflect the zeitgeist gets the chop. We mustn't forget the Uranus–Pluto opposition of 1792-3 in Leo/Aquarius when, during the French Revolution, the aristocracy literally lost their heads by guillotine.

The current Uranus–Pluto (from Aries to Capricorn) suggests the sudden removal of institutional and governmental heads, too, the decapitation and castration of people in power. (Saturn in Scorpio also describes the deaths of long-established statespeople.) Yet the irony is that, during Uranian times, dictatorships are broken up only to be reformed into new ones, just with different names …

Recalling the last time Pluto was in Capricorn, America – fearful of the tyranny of the British – was searching for a government and a constitution. The Pluto Return to 27° Capricorn begins in February 2022 and makes its last stop at that degree in October 2023. The American people may speak up against a tyrannical system and demolish it and/or be subjected to a new, harsh set of measures seeking to imprison them. As always with Pluto, if we don't take individual power and play a role in empowering the collective, then imperial force is imposed upon the people.

The Broader Picture
We are at the start of some very conservative times. The more things change, the more (we need) them to stay the same. Some of us are just 'going for it', knowing that we can't wait for retirement to follow our hearts. Others are deeply fearful and looking for someone to blame or persecute. But the planets suggest the need to live for (and in) the moment (Uranus in Aries) because the long-term perspective (Capricorn) has changed forever (Pluto).

The wave of anti-materialism (Neptune in Pisces) means people will either be obsessed with playing the victim and expecting to be rescued, or looking for alternative ways out of the rat race.

The true cold, hard winter of Pluto in Capricorn is now being felt as Saturn wades through Scorpio. It will reach a climax in the lead-up to early 2020, when Saturn conjuncts Pluto in the sky at 22° Capricorn – a period of economic frostbite, pruning, demolition and survival.

Many astrologers have written of Saturn–Pluto being about aftermath – the need to pick up the pieces and rebuild. This occurs just before the hope-filled Jupiter–Saturn conjunction at 0° Aquarius (December 2020) and the US's Pluto Return between February 2022 and October 2023. Both aspects augur much that is positive in bringing facets of the American spirit back to the fore. America has the chance to divorce itself from its imperial, conquering past and embrace the true Aquarian (Moon) spirit of the times ahead, to invest in its domestic talent, build fair alliances with its neighbours and create a vision for its future with its own people and for its own people.

References and Notes

1. For evidence supporting various US charts, I direct readers to Nicholas Campion's *The Book of World Horoscopes*, Ronald Howland's *A Chronology of American Charts* and Robert Currey's investigation at http://www.astrology.co.uk/news/USA.htm
2. For an in-depth study of outer planet transits, see Howard Sasportas's *The Gods of Change*, Arkana 1989, Wessex, 2007.
3. From pages 30 and 47 of *Soul–Sick Nation*, MotherSky Press, 2008, an excellent book on the astrology of America by Jessica Murray.
4. *The Twelve Houses*, Flare, 2007, p. 243.
5. Age Progression (the Life Clock) offers additional considerations (such as Low Points and house meanings), which I am not looking at here. For more details, see the work of the Hubers, Joyce Hopewell, Richard Llewellyn and others. www.astrologicalpsychology.org

Astrological Data and Sources – compiled with Sy Scholfield

In 1980, data collector Lois Rodden created a simple system to rate the integrity of birth data. The Rodden Rating (RR) letters below are now widely used to indicate a 'shorthand' of data accuracy, as well as a writer's awareness of data etiquette.

AA   Data from birth certificate, hospital, church or governmental birth record; notes from the Vital Statistic Registry Offices; notations in a family Bible, baby book or family written record.

A   Data from the person, family member, friend or associate; newspaper birth announcements; times given within a 'window of time' of thirty minutes (e.g. 'between 15:00 and 16:00') from any of these sources.

B   Data from biographies, autobiographies and personal websites, where no other source is given.

C   Caution, data not validated. No source; vague, rectified/speculative data, 'personal' ambiguous sources, approximate birth times (e.g. 'early morning', 'around lunchtime').

DD   Dirty Data. Two or more unsubstantiated quotes of time, place or date. Any unverified data that are contradicted by another source.

Abbreviations used in the following section:
BC – birth certificate
CAH – Contemporary American Horoscopes (Astrolabe, 1990) by Janice Mackey and Jessica Saunders
GBAC – The Gauquelin Book of American Charts (ACS, 1982) by Michel and Françoise Gauquelin
FCC – Frank C. Clifford

'Copy on file' indicates the author has direct access to the record.

Aguilera, Christina: 18 December 1980, 10:46 EST, Staten Island, NY, USA (40N35, 74W09). From her mother to Kevin Bold by e-mail. RR: A.
Aherne, Caroline: 24 December 1963. From various online resources. RR: X.
Ali, Muhammad: 17 January 1942, 18:35 CST, Louisville, KY, USA (38N15, 85W46). From BC obtained by Ed Steinbrecher; copy on file. RR: AA.
Allen, Steve: 26 December 1921, 07:00 EST, New York, NY, USA (40N43, 74W00). From him to astrologers at the Church of Light. RR: A.
Altman, John: 2 March 1952, 03:15 GMT, Reading, England (51N28, 00W59). From him to FCC. RR: A.
Badu, Erykah: Confidential data from Badu to a trusted source. RR: A.
Baez, Joan: 9 January 1941, 10:45 EST, Staten Island, NY, USA (40N35, 74W09). From BC obtained by Ed Steinbrecher; copy on file. RR: AA.
Bakker, Jim: 2 January 1940, 11:00 EST, Muskegon Heights, MI, USA (43N12, 86W15). From BC obtained by Genevieve Edwards; copy on file. RR: AA.
Bakker, Tammy Faye: 7 March 1942, 03:27 CWT, International Falls, MN, USA (48N36, 93W25). Note from birth registry obtained by Edwin Steinbrecher; copy on file. RR: AA.
Ballard, Florence: 30 June 1943, 05:45 EWT, Detroit, MI, USA (42N20, 83W03). From BC obtained by FCC. RR: AA.
Bankhead, Tallulah: 31 January 1902, 21:00 CST, Huntsville, AL, USA (34N44,

86W35). Doris Chase Doane quotes her, but the day is in question. RR: A?

Bardot, Brigitte: 28 September 1934, 13:15 GDT, Paris, France (48N52, 02E20). From BC obtained by Michel and Françoise Gauquelin. RR: AA.

Bashir, Martin: 19 January 1963, 12:30 GMT, London, England (51N30, 00W10). From him to FCC via a private source. RR: A.

Bieber, Justin: 1 March 1994, 00:56 EST, London, Ontario, Canada (42N59, 81W14). FCC quotes *Justin Bieber: The Unauthorized Biography* by Chas Newkey-Burden (Michael O'Mara, 2010), p. 15. RR: B.

Bolan, Marc: 30 September 1947, 12:30 GDT, Hackney, London, England (51N33, 00W03). Adam Fronteras quotes Bolan on Wax Records Company literature, information from his parents. Same data in the biography *Marc Bolan: A Tribute*, edited by Ted Dicks (Omnibus, 1978). Copies on file. RR: A.

Bono: 10 May 1960, 02:00 GDT, Dublin, Ireland (53N20, 06W15). Edwin Steinbrecher quotes a mutual friend, from Bono, 'two on the dot'. RR: A.

Bowie, David: 8 January 1947, 09:00 GMT, Brixton, London, England (51N28, 00W06). From his parents, as quoted in *Alias David Bowie* by Peter and Leni Gillman (Hodder & Stoughton, 1986), p. 41; same time in *Backstage Passes* by his wife, Angela Bowie, and Patrick Carr (Orion, 1993), p. 31. Bowie gave Gary Lorig a time of 09:30 (Asc: 15° A). 'Just before midnight' was given in the biography *Presenting David Bowie!* (Pinnacle, 1975) by David Douglas, p. 3, with a Libra Ascendant but no source, and is likely to be literary licence. RR: A.

Boy George: 14 June 1961, 02:30 GDT, Bexley, Kent, England (51N26, 00E10). From him to Laura Boomer, checking with his mother a couple of times to clear up confusion surrounding various conflicting birth times (including 00:45 given to Russell Grant in the 1980s by George's mother). RR: A?

Boyle, Susan: 1 April 1961, 09:50 GDT, Blackburn, West Lothian, Scotland (55N52, 03W37). From BC quoted by Caroline Gerard. RR: AA.

Bragg, Billy: 20 December 1957, 04:00 GMT, Barking, London, England (51N33, 00E06). From Bragg to Neil Spencer. RR: A.

Brando, Marlon: 3 April 1924, 23:00 CST, Omaha, NE, USA (41N15, 95W56). BC quoted in *GBAC*. RR: AA.

Broadway Open House: 29 May 1950, 23:00 EDT, Manhattan, NY, USA (40N46, 73W59). Sy Scholfield quotes 'Radio and Television', *New York Times*, 29 May 1950, p. 19. RR: A.

Brown, Bobby: 5 February 1969, 05:21 EST, Boston, Massachusetts, USA (42N22, 71W04). From BC obtained by FCC. RR: AA.

Brown, Chubby: 3 February 1945, Grangetown, North Riding of Yorkshire, England (54N35, 01W09). From various online resources. RR: X.

Brown, Janet: 14 December 1923, 07:45 GMT, Rutherglen, Scotland (55N50, 04W12). From BC quoted by Caroline Gerard. RR: AA.

Bush, George H. W.: 12 June 1924, 10:00–11:00 EDT, Milton, MA, USA (42N15, 71W04). Wayne Turner quotes an email from the George Bush Presidential Library, 'between 10:00 and 11:00 a.m.' from his mother's *Reminiscences*. RR: A.

Bush, George W.: 6 July 1946, 07:26 EDT, New Haven, CT, USA (41N18, 72W55). Karen Castilla quotes hospital records; same on BC. RR: AA.

Caan, James: 26 March 1940, 22:31 EST, Bronx, NY, USA (40N51, 73W54). From BC obtained by Thelma and Tom Wilson; copy on file. RR: AA.

Callas, Maria: 2, 3 or 4 December 1923, 'dawn', New York, NY, USA (40N43, 74W00). BC gives 2 December 1923 and New York; Callas gave 06:00 and 3 December; her mother gave 'dawn' and 4 December. RR: DD.

Capote, Truman: 30 September 1924, 03:00 CST, New Orleans, LA, USA (29N57, 90W05). From the biography *Capote* (Simon and Schuster, 1988) by Gerald Clarke. RR: B.

Carpenter, Karen: 2 March 1950, 11:45 EST, New Haven, CT, USA (41N18, 72W56). Note from birth registry obtained by Edwin Steinbrecher; copy on file. RR: AA.

Carpenter, Richard: 15 October 1946, 00:53 EST, New Haven, CT, USA (41N18, 72W56). Note from birth registry obtained by Edwin Steinbrecher; copy on file. RR: AA.

Carson, Johnny: 23 October 1925, 7:15 CST, Corning, IA, USA (40N59, 94W44). From BC quoted in *Contemporary Sidereal Horoscopes* by Janice Mackey et al (Sidereal Research Publications, 1976). RR: AA.

Carter, Jimmy: 1 October 1924, 07:00 CST, Plains, GA, USA (32N02, 84W24). From BC quoted by Marion March. RR: AA.

Cassidy, Eva: 2 February 1963, 22:00 EST, Washington, DC, USA (38N54, 77W02). From her mother, as quoted by Laura Claire Bligh (Cassidy's cousin) on her website: http://evacassidy.org/eva/q&a.shtml. RR: A.

Channing, Carol: 31 January 1921, 21:00 PST, Seattle, WA, USA (47N36, 122W2). From BC quoted in *CAH* and *GBAC*; copy on file. RR: AA.

Cline, Patsy: 8 September 1932, 23:05 EST, Winchester, VA, USA (39N11, 78W10). BC posted online, as quoted by Stephen Przybylowski. (FCC had been given 23:15 when he called Winchester Memorial Hospital in 1995.) RR: AA.

Clinton, Bill: 19 August 1946, 08:51 CST, Hope, AR, USA (33N40, 93W35). Note from his mother to Shelley Ackerman; copy on file. RR: AA.

Cobain, Kurt: 20 February 1967, 19:20 PST, Aberdeen, WA, USA (46N59, 123W49). Date and place from BC obtained by Thomas Germine; time from Cobain's mother to Muriel Foltz. RR: A.

Coltrane, Robbie: 31 March 1950, 03:00 GMT, Strathbungo, Glasgow, Scotland (55N53, 04W16). From BC quoted by Caroline Gerard. RR: AA.

Condell, Pat: Confidential data from Condell to FCC, from memory. RR: A.

Connery, Sean: 25 August 1930, 18:05 GDT, Edinburgh, Scotland (55N57, 03W13). From BC; copy on file. RR: AA.

Cooper, Alice: 4 February 1948, 22:33 EST, Detroit, MI, USA (42N20, 83W03). BC quoted in *CAH*. RR: AA.

Coppola, Francis Ford: 7 April 1939, 01:38 EST, Detroit, MI, USA (42N19, 83W02). BC quoted in *GBAC*. RR: AA.

Cowell, Simon: 7 October 1959, Lambeth, London, England (51N25, 00W08). Date from various official online sites, including www.justsimoncowell.com. RR: X.

Cyrus, Miley: 23 November 1992, 16:19 CST, Nashville, TN, USA (36N10, 86W47). Note from the Tennessee Vital Registry Office obtained by FCC; copy on file. RR: AA.

Damon, Matt: 8 October 1970, 15:22 EDT, Boston, MA, USA (42N21, 71W03). From his BC quoted by Frances McEvoy. RR: AA.

Day, Doris: 3 April 1922, 16:30 CST, Cincinnati, OH, USA (39N10, 84W27). From BC obtained by FCC; copy on file. RR: AA.

DeLorean, John: 6 January 1925, 12:00 EST, Detroit, MI, USA (42N20, 83W03). From BC quoted in *GBAC*. RR: AA.

Deneuve, Catherine: 22 October 1943, 13:35 GDT, Paris, France (48N52, 2E20). From BC quoted in *Cahiers Astrology*. RR: AA.

DeNiro, Robert: 17 August 1943, 03:00 EWT, Brooklyn, NY, USA (40N38, 73W56). Neil Marbell quotes DeNiro via a colleague. RR: A.

Diana, Princess: 1 July 1961, 19:45 GDT, Sandringham, England (52N50, 00E30). From a letter to Charles Harvey from the Queen's assistant press secretary quoting Diana's mother; same from Diana to her astrologer Debbie Frank and in letters from Buckingham Palace (copies on file). RR: A.

Disney, Walt: 5 December 1901, 00:35 CST, Hermosa, Chicago, IL, USA (41N55, 87W43). Marion March quotes the Disney Studio office. Sy Scholfield quotes *The Animated Man* by Michael Barrier (University of California Press, 2008), p. 332, for verification of birth date and place of Hermosa from Saint Paul Congregational Church (Chicago) records. RR: A.

Donahue, Phil: 21 December 1935, 11:25 EST, Cleveland, OH, USA (41N30,

81W42). From BC obtained by FCC. RR: AA.

Douglas, Kirk: 9 December 1916, 10:15 EST, Amsterdam, NY, USA (42N56, 74W11). Note from birth registry obtained by Ed Steinbrecher; copy on file. RR: AA.

Dylan, Bob: 24 May 1941, 21:05 CST, Duluth, Minnesota, USA (46N47, 92W06). From BC obtained by Bob Garner; copy on file. RR: AA.

Elliot, Roger: 25 June 1937, 03:15 GDT, Torquay, England (50N28, 03W30). David Fisher quotes him via Elliot's mother. RR: A.

Elton, Ben: 3 May 1959, 23:30 GDT, Catford, London, England (51N26, 00W00). From Elton to FCC. RR: A.

Evert, Chris: 21 December 1954, 04:30 EST, Fort Lauderdale, FL, USA (26N07, 80W09). BC quoted by Robert Jansky; Evert's office gave FCC 04:00. RR: AA.

Federer, Roger: 8 August 1981, 08:40 MEDT, Basel, Switzerland (47N33, 07E35). From his website: www.rogerfederer.com/en/rogers/profile/index.cfm – the birth time was later removed. RR: B.

Flack, Roberta: 10 February 1937, 06:30 EST, Black Mountain, NC, USA (35N37, 82W19). Note from birth registry obtained by Edwin Steinbrecher; copy on file. RR: AA.

Fonda, Jane: 21 December 1937, 09:14 EST, Manhattan, New York, USA (40N46, 73W59). BC obtained by Lois Rodden; copy on file. RR: AA.

Foster, Jodie: 19 November 1962, 08:14 PST, Los Angeles, CA, USA (34N04, 118W15). From BC obtained by Thelma and Tom Wilson; copy on file. RR: AA.

Franklin, Aretha: 25 March 1942, 22:30 CWT, Memphis, TN, USA (35N09, 90W03). From BC obtained by Edwin Steinbrecher; copy on file. RR: AA.

Fricke, Janie: 19 December 1947, 06:03 CST, South Whitley, IN, USA (41N05, 85W38). Time from Fricke to FCC; date and place from online sources. RR: A.

Frost, David: 7 April 1939, 10:30 GMT, Tenterden, England (51N05, 00E42). Paul Rosner quotes Diahann Carroll, who asked (former fiancé) Frost. RR: A.

Gallagher, Liam: Confidential data from him. RR: A.

Garland, Judy: 10 June 1922, 06:00 CST, Grand Rapids, MN, USA (47N14, 93W31). Note from birth registry obtained by Ed Steinbrecher; copy on file. Same on BC quoted in *CAH*. Scott Schechter's thorough biography *Judy Garland* (Cooper Square Press, 2002) gives '5:30 a.m'. RR: AA.

Gauquelin, Michel: 13 November 1928, 22:15 GMT, Paris, France (48N52, 02E20). From BC quoted by Jany Bessiere. RR: AA.

Geldof, Bob: 5 October 1951, 14:20 GDT, Dublin, Ireland (53N20, 06W15). David Fisher quotes Jo Logan's letter, who obtained the data from Geldof. RR: A.

Giuliano, Salvatore: 16 November 1922, 15:10 MET, Montelpre, Sicily (38N05, 13E10). Grazia Bordoni quotes him in an interview (June 1958) saying his birth was recorded four days late (his BC gives 20 November). RR: A.

Gordy, Berry: 28 November 1929, time unknown, Detroit, Michigan, USA (42N20, 83W03). Date and place from his autobiography, *To Be Loved* (Warner, 1994), p. 15. RR: X.

Graf, Steffi: 14 June 1969, 04:40 MET, Mannheim, Germany (49N29, 08E29). Hans Taeger quotes birth record from a German data collector. RR: AA.

Graham, Billy: 7 November 1918, 15:30 EST, Charlotte, NC, USA (35N13, 80W51). From BC quoted in *GBAC*. RR: AA.

Hagman, Larry: 21 September 1931, 16:20 CST, Fort Worth, TX, USA (32N43, 97W19). From BC obtained by Stephen Przybylowski; copy on file. RR: AA.

Haley, Alex: 11 August 1921, 04:55 EDT, Ithaca, NY, USA (42N26, 76W30). From BC quoted in *CAH*. RR: AA.

Hamilton, Neil: 9 March 1949, 08:45 GMT, Fleur de Lis, Wales (51N39, 03W13). From Hamilton to Caroline Gerard, 'around breakfast'. RR: A.

Harrison, Rex: 5 March 1908, 05:00 GMT, Huyton, England (53N25, 02W52). Blanca Holmes, in *American Astrology* (January 1957), quotes Lili Palmer, Harrison's former wife. RR: A.

Hendrix, Jimi: 27 November 1942, 10:15 PWT, Seattle, WA, USA (47N36, 122W20). From BC obatined by Janice Mackay; copy on file. RR: AA.
Hoffman, Dustin: 8 August 1937, 17:07 PST, Los Angeles, CA, USA (34N04, 118W15). From BC quoted in *GBAC*. RR: AA.
Holiday, Billie: 7 April 1915, 02:30 EST, Philadelphia, PA, USA (39N57, 75W10). From BC quoted in the biography *Billie Holiday* by Stuart Nicholson (Victor Gollancz, 1995), p. 18.
Holly, Buddy: 7 September 1936, 15:30 CST, Lubbock, TX, USA (33N35, 101W51). Mary Keeley quotes Holly's mother in an interview printed in *Reminiscing*. Nick Dagan Best found a news clipping at www.buddyhollyarchives.com/1936/08/buddy-hollys-birth-announcement/ which gives the birth time as 18:10. Pat Taglilatelo spoke with Buddy Holly historian Bill Griggs of Lubbock, TX in December 2005, who claimed that Buddy's mother insisted that she remembered that Buddy was born at home just as the older children were coming home from school. RR: A?
Hopkins, Anthony: 31 December 1937, 09:15 GMT, Margham, Wales (51N34, 03W44). His astrologer David Hayward quotes him in 1991 (Hopkins gave 10:30 to Joan Abel in 1978). RR: DD.
Houston, Whitney: 9 August 1963, 20:55 EDT, Newark, NJ, USA (40N44, 74W10). From BC obtained by Kathryn Farmer; copy on file. RR: AA.
Howard, Ron: 1 March 1954, 09:03 CST, Duncan, OK, USA (34N30, 97W57). From BC quoted in *CAH*. RR: AA.
Hubbard, L. Ron: 13 March 1911, 02:01 CST, Tilden, NE, USA (42N03, 97W50). From him to Doris Chase Doane, published in *Progressions in Action*. RR: A.
Hutchence, Michael: 22 January 1960, 05:00 AEST, Sydney, Australia (33S52, 151E13). Scott Whitters quotes an article, 'A Life Lived INXS', by Toby Cresswell featured in *Juice Magazine*. RR: A.
Iglesias, Julio: 23 September 1943, 11:30 BDST, Madrid, Spain (40N24, 03W41). From BC obtained by FCC; copy on file. (Iglesias gives '3 p.m.' in his autobiography, and his mother has stated '11 a.m.') RR: AA.
Jackson, Michael: 29 August 1958, 19:33 CDT, Gary, Indiana, USA (41N36, 87W21). There are various, conflicting birth times from Jackson, but 19:33 was given by Jackson to his astrologer Chakrapani Ullal and the same time from Jackson's mother Katherine to grandson Taj Jackson. RR: A?
Jarman, Derek: 31 January 1942, 07:30 GDT, Northwood, England (51N37, 00W25). From his autobiography, *At Your Own Risk* (Vintage, 1993), p. 4. RR: B.
Jephson, Patrick: 14 February 1956, Londonderry, Northern Ireland (55N00, 07W19). From Jephson to FCC. Jephson has no idea of his birth time. RR: X.
Joplin, Janis: 19 January 1943, 09:45 CWT, Port Arthur, TX, USA (29N54, 93W56). From BC obtained by FCC; copy on file. RR: AA.
Keaton, Diane: 5 January 1946, 02:49 PST, Los Angeles, CA, USA (34N04, 118W15). From BC obtained by Thelma and Tom Wilson; copy on file (the minutes on the certificate are hard to read). RR: AA.
Keller, Helen: 27 June 1880, 16:00 LMT (+5:50:49), Tuscumbia, AL, USA (34N44, 87W42). From her secretary, quoted in *Fowler's Compendium of Nativities* (Fowler, 1980), p. 331.
Kennedy, John F.: 29 May 1917, 15:00 EST, Brookline, MA, USA (42N20, 71W07). From his mother to Garth Allen. RR: A.
Kilmer, Val: 31 December 1959, 07:58 PST, Los Angeles, CA, USA (34N04, 118W15). From BC obtained by FCC; copy on file. RR: AA.
King, Billie Jean: 22 November 1943, 11:45 PWT, Long Beach, CA, USA (33N46, 118W11). From BC obtained by Doris Chase Doane. RR: AA.
King, Don: 20 August 1931, 19:15 EST, Cleveland, OH, USA (41N30, 81W42). From BC obtained by FCC; copy on file. RR: AA.
King, Larry: 19 November 1933, 10:38 EST, Brooklyn, NY, USA (40N38, 73W56). From King live on air. RR: A.

Kirkpatrick, Maggie: 29 January 1941, 07:20 AEST, Albury, Australia (36S05, 146E55). From Kirkpatrick to Frank Clifford. RR: A.

Kitt, Eartha: 17 January 1927, 04:00 EST, St. Matthews, SC, USA (33N40, 80W47). According to various newspaper interviews, Kitt was shown her BC (traced by students of Benedict College) and discovered her birth date to be 17 January 1927. She confirmed this to FCC in person, in 2007, also stating she had no idea of her birth time. The Gauquelins' book, *GBAC*, gives 26 January 1928 in North, a town in South Carolina (the date and place Kitt used arbitrarily for many years) and 04:00. The Gauquelins, however, wrote to US Vital Registry offices with birth names, places and dates, requesting birth times and usually only received the birth time in reply. It is *possible* that the BC for a different date was found, the 1928 date left uncorrected, and the 4:00 a.m. time sent to the Gauquelins. RR: AA?

Lake, Ricki: 21 September 1968, 08:00 EDT, Bronx, NY, USA (40N51, 73W54). Lois Rodden quotes Lake's associate producer, Rachel Miskowiec, in October 1996. RR: A.

lang, k. d.: 2 November 1961, 02:03 MST, Edmonton, Alberta, Canada (53N33, 113W28). From lang, quoting her birth record, to three students of Marion March. RR: AA.

Lee, Brandon: 1 February 1965, 05:48 PST, Oakland, CA, USA (37N48, 122W16). From BC obtained by FCC; copy on file. RR: AA.

Lehman, Val: 15 March 1943, 05:00 AWDT, Cottesloe, Perth, Australia (31S59, 115E45). From Lehman's mother, Kathleen Malta, to FCC, quoting a time of 'between 4am and 6am … probably towards the latter'. RR: C.

Lucas, Matt: 5 March 1974, Paddington, London, England (51N31, 00W10). From online biography. RR: X.

Luciano, Lucky (Salvatore Lucania): 24 November 1897, 12:00 MET, Lercara Friddi, Italy (37N45, 13E36). From BC obtained by Grazia Bordoni. RR: AA.

Lythgoe, Nigel: 9 July 1949, time unknown, Wirral, England (53N24, 3W04). From various online sites. RR: X.

Madonna: 16 August 1958, 07:05 EST, Bay City, MI, USA (43N36, 83W53). Tashi Grady quotes Madonna's father, who originally gave 7:00 a.m. and then telephoned the hospital of Madonna's birth. (Madonna has been quoted as saying she is Aquarius Rising and, more recently, has said she does not know her Ascendant or birth time.) RR: AA.

Malcolm X: 19 May 1925, 22:25 CST, Omaha, NE, USA (41N16, 95W56). From BC published online, as quoted by Sy Scholfield. RR: AA.

Manning, Bernard: 13 August 1930, 04:30 GDT, Manchester, England (53N30, 02W15). From the well-researched biography *Bernard Manning* by Jonathan Margolis (Orion, 1997). (N.B. Manning had given Marjorie Orr the time of 06:00). RR: B.

Margaret, Princess: 21 August 1930, 21:22 GDT, Glamis Castle, Scotland, (56N36, 03W00). From BC obtained by Joanne Clancy. RR: AA.

Mathis, Johnny: 30 September 1935, 12:00 CST, Gilmer, TX, USA (32N44, 94W57). From BC obtained by Sy Scholfield (correcting the handwritten note sent to Ed Steinbrecher that states 12:00 a.m.); copy on file. RR: AA.

McEnroe, John: 16 February 1959, 22:30 MET, Wiesbaden, Germany (50N05, 08E14). From the biography *McEnroe: A Rage for Perfection* by Richard Evans (Simon and Schuster, 1982); Marc Penfield quotes a letter from McEnroe's mother for 22:20 (not confirmed). RR: B.

McGraw, Phil: 1 September 1950, 19:15 CST, Vinita, OK, USA (36N38, 95W09). Sy Scholfield quotes *The Making of Dr Phil* by Sophia Dembling and Lisa Gutierrez (Wiley, 2004), pp. 1–2. RR: B.

Midler, Bette: 1 December 1945, 14:19 HST, Honolulu, HI, USA (21N18, 157W51). From BC quoted in *GBAC*. RR: AA.

Mohr, Bärbel: 5 July 1964, between 01:45 and 03:30 MET, Bonn, Germany

(50N44, 07E05). Rolf Liefeld quotes 'Gemini Rising' given by her on her website. RR: C.

Moore, Demi: 11 November 1962, 14:16 MST, Roswell, NM, USA (33N24, 104W31). From Moore to Basil Fearrington. RR: A.

Moore, Roger: 14 October 1927, 00:45 GMT, London, England (51N30, 0W10). Ed Steinbrecher quotes Moore to Talia Shire in August 1989. Sy Scholfield quotes Moore's autobiography, *My Word Is My Bond* (Michael O'Mara, 2008), p. 11, for 'just after midnight'. RR: A.

Morrison, Jim: 8 December 1943, 11:55 EWT, Melbourne, FL, USA (28N04, 80W36). From birth registration card obtained by Bob Garner; copy on file. RR: AA.

Morton, Andrew: 20 December 1953, 04:20 GMT, Dewsbury, England (53N42, 01W37). FCC quotes Morton via Penny Thornton. RR: A.

Mowlam, Mo: 18 September 1949, Watford, England (51N40, 0W25). From various online sources. RR: X.

Nadal, Rafael: 3 June 1986, 18:20 MEDT, Manacor, Spain (39N34, 03E12). From BC quoted in the Spanish newsletter *Cyklos* (December 2010). Previously Patrick de Jabrun quoted an unspecified biography for a time of 19:15. RR: AA.

Nallon, Steve: 8 December 1960, 14:00 GMT, Leeds, England (53N50, 01W35). FCC quotes him, from his aunt. RR: A.

Navratilova, Martina: 18 October 1956, 16:40 MET, Prague, Czechoslovakia (50N05, 14E26). From Navratilova to Frank Clifford, 1995 ('16:40 give or take a few minutes'). RR: A.

Newman, Paul: 26 January 1925, 06:30 EST, Cleveland, OH, USA (41N30, 81W42). From BC obtained by FCC; copy on file. RR: AA.

Nixon, Richard: 9 January 1913, 21:35 PST, Yorba Linda, CA, USA (33N53 117W49). From his birth record obtained by T. Pat Davis. Sy Scholfield quotes same data from a card handwritten by his nurse reproduced in *The Real Nixon* by Bela Kornitzer (Rand McNally, 1960). RR: AA.

Obama, Barack: 4 August 1961, 19:24 AHST, Honolulu, HI, USA (21N18, 157W52). From BC; copy on file. Birth place confirmed by two birth announcements published in local newspapers in August 1961. RR: AA.

Odetta: 31 December 1930, 09:20 CST, Birmingham, AL, USA (33N31, 86W48. From BC quoted in *CAH*. Same from her to Ed Steinbrecher. RR: AA.

Orbison, Roy: 23 April 1936, 15:50 CST, Vernon, TX, USA (34N09, 99W16). Note from birth registry obtained by Ed Steinbrecher; copy on file. RR: AA.

Osbourne, Ozzy: 3 December 1948, 'morning' GMT, Birmingham, England (52N30, 01W50). Shelley Ackerman quotes *Officially Osbourne: Opening the Doors to the Land of Oz* by Todd Gold (Pocket, 2002) for 'in the morning'. RR: C.

Paar, Jack: 1 May 1917, 23:55 CST, Canton, OH, USA (40N48, 81W23). From BC obtained by FCC; copy on file. RR: AA.

Pacino, Al: 25 April 1940, 11:02 EST, Manhattan, NY, USA (40N46, 73W59). From BC obtained by Lois Rodden; copy on file. RR: AA.

Parton, Dolly: 19 January 1946, 20:25 CST, Sevierville, TN, USA (35N52, 83W34). Note from birth registry obtained by FCC; copy on file. RR: AA.

Picasso, Pablo: 25 October 1881, 23:15 LMT, Malaga, Spain (36N43, 04W25). From BC obtained by Filipe Ferreira. RR: AA.

Piaf, Edith: 19 December 1915, 05:00 GMT, Paris, France (48N52, 02E20). From BC obtained by Françoise Gauquelin. RR: AA.

Presley, Elvis: 8 January 1935, 04:35 CST, Tupelo, MS, USA (34N15, 88W42). From BC obtained by Eugene Moore; FCC has copies of two BCs filed in 1935 (one with no birth time and 'Elvis Aron Presley', the other stamped in 1953 with the birth time and Elvis Aaron Presley). RR: AA.

Prince: 7 June 1958, 18:17 CDT, Minneapolis, MN, USA (44N59, 93W16). From BC obtained by FCC; copy on file. RR: AA.

Puzo, Mario: 15 October 1920, Manhattan, NY, USA (40N46, 73W59). From online sources. RR: X.

Quatro, Suzi: 3 June 1950, 13:40 CDT, Detroit, MI, USA (42N20, 83W03). From Quatro to Andrea Miles, via Quatro's fan club assistant Lynn Chapman. RR: A.

Riggs, Bobby: 25 February 1918, 01:00 PST, Los Angeles, CA, USA (34N03, 118W14). From BC quoted in *GBAC*. RR: AA.

Rivera, Geraldo: 4 July 1943, 00:01 EWT, New York, NY, USA (40N46, 73W59). Marc Penfield quotes an article in *Dell Horoscope*, November 1990, 'from him'; author unnamed and no other reference. Sy Scholfield quotes *Contemporary American Success Stories: Famous People of Hispanic Heritage* by Barbara J. Marvis (Mitchell Lane, 1995), p. 12, 'Born on the stroke of midnight that hailed in the Fourth of July in 1943.' RR: A.

Roberts, Oral: 24 January 1918, 11:30 CST, Ada, OK, USA (34N46, 96W41). From Roberts' publication *Abundant Life*, quoted by Howard Hammitt. RR: A.

Ross, Diana: 26 March 1944, 23:46 EWT, Detroit, MI, USA (42N20, 83W03). From BC as quoted in *CAH*; same in *GBAC*. RR: AA.

Rushdie, Salman: 19 June 1947, 02:30 IST, Bombay (now Mumbai), India (18N58, 72E50). From Rushdie to Penny Allen (former wife of novelist Ian McEwan), who told astrologer Catriona Mundle; copy of Mundle's letter to Sally Davis on file. RR: A.

Ryan, Meg: 19 November 1961, 10:36 EST, Fairfield, CT, USA (41N08, 73W15). From Ryan to Ed Steinbrecher via Matthew Shields, April 1998. RR: A.

Sarandon, Susan: 4 October 1946, 14:25 EST, New York, NY, USA (40N42, 74W00). From Sarandon to Fredrick Davies as a client. RR: A.

Selleck, Tom: 29 January 1945, 08:22 EWT, Detroit, MI, USA (42N20, 83W03). Barbara Ludwig quotes Selleck, from his BC. RR: AA.

Simone, Nina (Eunice Kathleen Waymon): 21 February 1933, 06:00 EST, Tryon, NC, USA (35N12, 82W14). From BC as quoted in *GBAC*. RR: AA.

Simpson, O. J.: 9 July 1947, 08:08 PST, San Francisco, CA, USA (37N47, 122W25). From BC quoted in *CAH*. RR: AA.

Sinatra, Frank: 12 December 1915, 03:00 EST, Hoboken, NJ, USA (40N45, 74W02). Lynne Palmer quotes Sinatra's father. RR: A.

Snowden, Edward: 21 June 1983, 04:42 EDT, Elizabeth City, NC, USA (36N18, 76W13). From BC obtained by Eric Francis Coppolino; copy on file. RR: AA.

Spears, Britney: 2 December 1981, 01:30 CST, McComb, MS, USA (31N15, 90W27). From her and her mother to Barry Street of The Astrology Shop, London, in November 2000. RR: A.

Springer, Jerry: 13 February 1944, 23:45 GDT, Highgate, London, England (51N34, 00W09). From Springer to FCC; same in a *CNN* interview. Date and place from his autobiography *Ringmaster* (St Martin's Press, 2000). RR: A.

Spurlock, Morgan: 7 November 1970, Parkersburg, WV, USA (39N16, 81W32). From various online resources. RR: X.

Stallone, Jacqueline: 30 November 1921, 02:52 EST, Washington, DC, USA (38N54, 77W02). From Stallone to a colleague of Ed Dearborn. RR: A.

Stern, Howard: 12 January 1954, 13:15 EST, Jackson Heights, NY, USA (40N45, 73W53). Basil Fearrington quotes an unnamed astrologer; time allegedly from Stern's BC. RR: C.

Stevens, Cat: 21 July 1948, 12:00 GDT, London, England (51N30, 00W10). Ruth Dewey quotes Richard West, 'from him'. RR: A.

Sting: 2 October 1951, 01:30 GDT, Wallsend, England (55N00, 01W31). From Sting to Arthyr Chadbourne in October 1996. RR: A.

Streisand, Barbra: 24 April 1942, 05:04 EWT, Brooklyn, New York, USA (40N38, 73W56). From birth announcement printed at http://barbra-archives.com/bjs_library/60s/barbra_beginnings.html (Ed Steinbrecher quotes Streisand to a mutual friend for 05:08, quoting her BC). RR: AA.

Summer, Donna: 31 December 1948, 21:00 EST, Boston, MA, USA (42N21, 71W03). From BC obtained by FCC; copy on file. RR: AA.

Sutherland, Keifer: 21 December 1966, 09:00 GMT, St. Marylebone, London, England (51N31, 00W09). From BC (the time is on the BC because Sutherland is a twin) obtained by FCC; copy on file. RR: AA.

Swaggart, Jimmy: 15 March 1935, 01:35 CST, Ferriday, LA, USA (31N37, 91W33). From BC quoted by Jeannine Pace. RR: AA.

Tate, Catherine: 12 May 1968, between 5:45 and 7:30 GDT, London, England (51N30, 00W10). Sy Scholfield quotes her in *Sunday Times*, 17 July 2005, p. 51, 'Gemini Rising'. RR: C.

Taylor, Elizabeth: 27 February 1932, 02:30 GMT, London, England (51N30, 00W10). From American Consulate birth report published on www.ancestry.com; copy on file. (Taylor gave 02:00 to Bob Prince.) RR: AA.

Thatcher, Margaret: 13 October 1925, 09:00 GMT, Grantham, England (52N55, 00W39). From Thatcher's private secretary to Charles Harvey. RR: A.

Timberlake, Justin: 31 January 1981, 18:30 CST, Memphis, TN, USA (35N09, 90W03). From BC obtained by FCC; copy on file. RR: AA.

Trump, Donald: 14 June 1946, 10:54 EDT, Jamaica, New York, USA (40N41, 73W48). From BC released by Trump to the media in 2011; copy on file. RR: AA.

Turner, Tina: 26 November 1939, 22:10 CST, Nutbush, TN, USA (35N42, 89W24). Note from birth registry obtained by FCC; copy on file. RR: AA.

Tyson, Mike: 30 June 1966, Brooklyn, New York, USA (40N38, 73W56). From various online resources. RR: X.

Ure, Midge: 10 October 1953, 08:30 GMT, Cambuslang, Scotland (55N59, 04W09). From BC quoted by Caroline Gerard. RR: AA.

Van Gogh, Vincent: 30 March 1853, 11:00 LMT, Zundert, Netherlands (51N28, 4E40). From birth record quoted by Ed Steinbrecher. RR: AA.

Walters, Barbara: 25 September 1929, 06:50 EDT, Boston, MA, USA, (42N22, 71W04). Frances McEvoy quotes the date and place from Walters' BC and the birth time from her, given in an interview. RR: AA.

Warwick, Dionne: 12 December 1940, 15:08 EST, Orange, NJ, USA (40N46, 74W13). From BC quoted in *GBAC*. RR: AA.

Welsh, Irvine: 27 September 1957, 15:20 GDT, Edinburgh, Scotland (55N57, 03W13). From BC quoted by Caroline Gerard. RR: AA.

West, Mae: 17 August 1892, 22:30 EST, Brooklyn, NY, USA (40N38, 73W56). Marianne Dunn quotes Paul Novak, West's companion for 20 years, in 1980; Sy Scholfield quotes *Becoming Mae West* by Emily Wortis Leider (Thorndike Press, 2001), p. 20: 'I was born on August 17 at 10:30 p.m.' 1893 is also suggested by some biographers and researchers. RR: A.

White, Barry: 12 September 1944, 16:42 CWT, Galveston, TX, USA (29N18, 94W48). From BC obtained by FCC; copy on file. RR: AA.

Williams, Andy: 3 December 1927, 06:00 CST, Wall Lake, IA, USA (42N16, 95W06). From BC obtained by Stephen Przybylowski. RR: AA.

Williams, Kenneth: 22 February 1926, 14:30 GMT, Islington, London, England (51N32, 00W07). From his autobiography, *Just Williams* (J. M. Dent, 1985), p. 2, from his mother's recollection. RR: A.

Wilson, Mary: 6 March 1944, 10:11 CWT, Greenville, MS, USA (33N25, 91W04). From BC quoted by Wilson to her astrologer, Lois Rodden, in 1971 (confirmed in 1991). RR: AA.

Winehouse, Amy: 14 September 1983, 22:25 GDT, Enfield, London, England (51N40, 00W05). From Winehouse's mother to a mutual friend of astrologer Margaret Zelinski. RR: A.

Winfrey, Oprah: 29 January 1954, 04:30 CST, Kosciusko, MS, USA (33N03, 89W35). Robert Marks quotes producer Diane Hudson and Winfrey herself while on the *Oprah* show in May 1988. RR: A.

Young, Sean: 20 November 1959, 10:46 CST, Louisville, KY, USA (38N15, 85W46). From BC obtained by Kathryn Farmer. RR: AA.

CPSIA information can be obtained
at www.ICGtesting.com
Printed in the USA
FSOW03n2331120515
7094FS

9 781903 353226